Creating
Philanthropic
Capital
Markets

The Deliberate Evolution

LUCY BERNHOLZ

WILEY

John Wiley & Sons, Inc.

Library of Congress Cataloging-in-Publication Data:

Bernholz, Lucy.
   Creating philanthropic capital markets : the deliberate evolution / Lucy Bernholz.
      p. cm.
   Includes bibliographical references and index.
   ISBN 0-471-44852-4 (CLOTH)
   1. Endowments. 2. Charities. 3. Charitable uses, trusts, and foundations. I. Title.
HV16.B47 2004
361.7'632—dc22
                                        2003017975

Contents

List of Exhibits

Acknowledgments

This book draws on experiences and insights gained from more than 12 years of work in philanthropy. I am indebted to all of my colleagues, clients, advisors, and peers for the questions they ask, the innovations they have developed, and the work they do every day.

My job consists of working directly with clients—foundations, individuals, philanthropic associations, and other grant makers—and then stepping back from those practical engagements to ask big questions about the philanthropic industry. I have learned from each and every client, and their collective wisdom infuses this book, although any faults in interpretation are solely mine.

I wish to thank several people for their good-natured professional and intellectual guidance and critique. Jack Chin, Lindy Flynn, Lori Jones, Gabriel Kasper, Stephanie Fuerstner Gillis, Susan Grand, Kendall Guthrie, Amy Luckey, Kaitlin McGaw, Adelaide Nalley, and Alan Preston inform and challenge my thinking on a daily basis. Deborah Alvarez Rodriguez, Rachel Newton Bellow, Daniel Ben-Horin, Laura Breeden, Paul Brest, Diana Campoamor, Jim Canales, Emmett Carson, Winnie Chu, Cristina Cuevas, Alexa Culwell, Katherine Fulton, Diane Frankel, David Kennedy, Elan Garonzik, Nancy Glaze, Crystal Hayling, Peter Hero, Barbara Kibbe, Joe Lumarda, Robin Larson, Rochelle Lefkowitz, Lance Linares, Milbrey McGlaughlin, Julie Rogers, Peggy Saika, Bruce Sievers, Ralph Smith, Sterling Spiern, Kirke Wilson, Tim Wilmot, Jim Watson, Sylvia Yee, and board members of the David L. Klein Jr. Foundation have all pushed me in some important way over the years, and I am a better thinker because of it. Thank you.

I intend this book to start many conversations. It proposes a new way of thinking about philanthropy that I believe can add tremendous strength to this vital component of American, and global, society. The book is focused on American philanthropy not because that is what matters most, but because that is what I know best. I hope it will inform established and emerging philanthropic entities; spark innovation and excellence in philanthropic products, services, and organizations; contribute to more diverse philanthropic networks and stronger communities; and mark the beginning of my thinking on these issues on a global scale.

This book would not have been written if not for the loving support of Paula Fleisher. I extend to her my deepest thanks.

Lucy Bernholz

San Francisco, California
June 2003

This book is dedicated to my niece Morgan, my nephews Max and Sam, my sister Jane, and to the memory of her husband and their father—
Christian Hartwell Maltby
February 20, 1964—September 11, 2001

Introduction

[The result can] be explained in the same basic mode as most . . . phenomena—that is, as a contingent circumstance that did not have to unfold as it did, but that makes perfectly good sense as a reasonable outcome among a set of possibilities . . . purely as a contingent circumstance of numerous, albeit not entirely capricious, accidents.[1]

—Stephen Jay Gould

One day, back in 1995, before the dot-com boom and bust, before Bill Gates was as widely known for his philanthropy as for his software, and before every bus rider carried a cell phone, Mrs. R. M. Lee arrived for a meeting at her local community foundation. She was scheduled to talk with the program officer about the recent gift her family had made, which had endowed the largest donor-advised fund in the foundation's history. She had but an hour to spend, for she had dedicated the entire day to her family's philanthropic planning and had appointments later on with several nonprofit groups, the family's financial planner, and with the staff of the Lee Family Foundation.

When she arrived at the community foundation Mrs. Lee discussed the family's interest in education, their support for environmental causes, and the challenges of managing wealth. Mrs. Lee occasionally commented on how odd she found it to be rich, having been raised in a struggling immigrant family and scraping by for years with her husband to start the company that was now so successful. She talked of her son and her fears about raising him with money, as well as her fear for his safety if the family's giving (and by inference their wealth) was too well-publicized. They talked about the company's giving, the family's interest in a charitable gift fund offered by their mutual fund company, and the lack of after-school programs in the community.

Mrs. Lee told of how she thought girls needed exposure to business opportunities at a young age, the importance of access to the cultural traditions of one's ancestors, and the creek clean-ups that her son's school often held. She asked the program officer pointedly how her family's interests would be served, how the community foundation staff planned to work with the staff at the Lee Family Foundation, and whether the program officer would personally accompany her on site visits to community organizations. She smiled sweetly at the program officer's cluttered desk, muttered something about "the ridiculous fees this place charges," and excused herself midway through the program officer's reply, "I have an appointment with another advisor," she declared as she left the room, "and then I want to meet with the Venture Partners and their grants committee. I really think we should set that group up as a fund at the community foundation, though the mutual fund company charges much less in fees. . . ."

The events in this story took place in a small town in central California. It might just as easily have happened in suburban Chicago, southern Georgia, central Texas, or Boston. Mrs. Lee could be a second-generation Chinese-American owner of a technology firm, a seventh-generation African-American banker, a Latina retail entrepreneur, a Caucasian fashion designer, or a multiracial wholesaler of auto supplies. She could be any one of the nation's 2 million millionaires, 70 million baby boomers (millions of whom will soon inherit estates from their elderly parents), or one of the hundreds of thousands of immigrants who come to the United States to make their fortune.

The juggling act of philanthropic products, advisors, and issues that Mrs. Lee managed on that day in 1995 is repeated daily all over the country. Philanthropically-minded individuals in the United States now must choose among a variety of philanthropic products, try to make sense of the various fees and advantages of each type of fund, understand the needs of their community, and decide how to give by themselves, with family, co-workers, or in partnership with others. The *dramatis personae* are imaginary, but the tensions of the anecdote are real—these are the opportunities and challenges behind today's philanthropy.

Mrs. Lee represents the future of American philanthropy. She has financial resources to dedicate to her interests, is comparison shopping among the various products and services for managing her philanthropic capital, and is awash with options. While she has ideas about how she wants her funds to be used, she also wants advice—from the community foundation, the venture partners group, and from her professional advisors. She (and all other donors) lacks meaningful measures for comparing the different financial tools other than fees and services costs. She has limited access to research on successful strategies on the issues she cares about, and even less access to information on other interested funders or potential partners. All of Mrs. Lee's decision making would be improved if the market for philanthropic financial products benefited from some of the core qualities of other markets—credible external monitoring, commonly understood standards of quality, access to comparative data and rates of return, and an ability to invest in partnership with others.

The current market for philanthropic products and advice lacks almost all of these qualities. One can compare costs of different funds, but there are few ways to assess the value of a foundation versus a donor-advised fund beyond their different tax ramifications. The industry involves hundreds of thousands of volunteer board members and a few thousand professional staff people. Only these professional insiders have the time to find or use data on the funding preferences and successes of other peer foundations. The opportunity to piggyback on successes or align funds to common interests is limited to a tiny percentage of cumulative philanthropic resources. Designing better systems for moving philanthropic resources will not solve all of philanthropy's problems. However, applying some of the basics of commercial capital markets to philanthropy would make it much easier to aggregate or integrate public and private funds, reduce duplicative spending on research or assessment, apply intellectual capital on a broad scale, and assist nonprofit organizations in accessing a rational and more visible set of financial resources.

Individual donors, advisors to high net-worth individuals, federated fund and community foundation executives, financial service firm executives with responsibilities in private banking or client management, charitable gift fund directors, financial planners, investment managers, lawyers, accountants, and foundation executives are all involved in the same industry of philanthropy. Most of these participants are thinking about how their philanthropy works now and how it could be improved. The opportunity is now here for philanthropy as a whole to take on these same questions.

Philanthropy is a large industry with ambitious growth prospects that is operating within a dramatically shifting external environment. Yet there are few activists, philanthropists, regulators, academics, think tank executives, or nonprofit leaders who regularly stand back and look at the entire industry of philanthropy and envision a more robust future. There are many people and firms working hard to improve the work of individual organizations, but where is the whole endeavor going? What are the real market opportunities, the likely results of competition, and the most useful relationships between commercial and not-for-profit philanthropic vendors? How do we maximize the impact of hundreds of thousands of individual charitable acts and experience the full potential that private giving can bring to our shared society?

The possible futures for philanthropy are very much rooted in its present and the past. These futures will be crafted by all who are involved with philanthropy, those who donate sums large and small, those who occupy professional positions in foundations or other giving institutions, those who provide legal, investment, accounting, and program advice to philanthropists, nonprofits that do the work that philanthropy supports, and individuals who may become more philanthropic in the near future. There are implications for active individual and institutional philanthropists and those who are just about to enter the industry. In fact, emerging philanthropists—those just testing the waters, those who are comparison shopping for giving options or issues to support, and those who have made choices and are a few years into the work—are the industry's key asset for the future as well as its primary challenge. Putting established and emerging philanthropic assets to work in ways that accomplish real outcomes, helping individual philanthropists achieve their dreams and social purposes, and making the entirety of philanthropy a more accessible, effective enterprise is the purpose of this book.

Philanthropy operates in a privileged sphere of ideas, resources, and social concern. It is fundamentally focused on the best possibilities of human endeavor, creation, and concern. While the forces that act upon it—namely, markets and regulation—are familiar to all who participate, the philanthropic industry being shaped by these forces should be ambitious and visionary.

This is a book about the mechanisms and systems of philanthropy. We must ask at the start, and again at the conclusion, "philanthropy for what purpose?" Although it is rare to find philanthropic analysis that seeks to make sense of the industry of giving, it is also all too easy for those who do this work to become too inwardly focused. Philanthropy exists as part of civic life, as part of communities, and as part of all cultural traditions. It can neither survive nor thrive on its own, separated from the public and private sectors; nor can those partners accomplish their purposes without philanthropy and community action. The three-way tango of sectors defines, shapes, and directs philanthropy, just as changes in philanthropy influence expectations for public investment or corporate responsibility. We can look deeply at the industry of philanthropy, and we must. But we must do so with a sure sense that philanthropy exists as part of a system of cultural life, of religious practices and of community improvement, and that efforts to improve philanthropic practice are undertaken in order to strengthen our larger society.

It is important to note that this is not a work about the nonprofit sector as it is usually discussed, although that sector and those discussions provide critical context for this work. The book is focused on philanthropy and basically omits discussion of the larger nonprofit sector because of the good research and writing that now exists on that larger sector.[2] Philanthropy and the nonprofit sector are inextricably linked, and changes in the larger environment are important to changes in philanthropy. This work focuses on the industry of giving—the donors, institutions, financial products, and services that provide critical financial resources to support nonprofit and civic activity.

Research on philanthropy has either been subsumed within the nonprofit literature to such an extent that we cannot really see it or it has consisted of organization-specific studies with few efforts to capture the greater complexity.[3] This book attempts to bring the blurry, idiosyncratic world of philanthropy into sharper focus so that it can be debated, strengthened, and led.

As used in this book, *philanthropy* is the act of giving private resources for public good. It encompasses individual charitable gifts and the strategic investments of foundations staffed by professionals and endowed with billions of dollars. The philanthropic industry includes products sold by commercial banks and brokerages and the activities of nonprofit grant-making foundations. Chapter 1 presents more detail on the components of the industry and the logic behind that which is included and that which was deliberately omitted.

Philanthropy in 2004 is a growing industry, beset with competitive pressures, regulatory revisions, and market innovation. Americans give more than $240 billion annually to support nonprofit activity, ranging from tithing to their churches to cover operating expenses and food programs to multimillion-dollar gifts to endow new halls of science or build "no-kill" pet shelters. The giving comes from individuals and families and is managed through a vast array of financial products. The aggregate amount of philanthropic giving is enormous, yet it is spread across hundreds of issues, thousands of places, and millions of organizations. The strength of American philanthropy is its diversity and personal nature. Its weakness is its dispersed size and diminishing value in the face of ever-widening wealth gaps and public revenue shortfalls.

DESIGNING THE FUTURE

Imagine one could look back on American philanthropy in the latter half of the twentieth century and see it as an intentionally designed set of activities. You would see an industry that operated with the following list of assumptions, processes, and outcomes:[4]

- Foundations would dominate the discussion of philanthropy, even though they provide an average of less than 10 percent of the financial resources counted as philanthropic gifts.

- Foundations that paid for strategy research, program evaluations, and other assessments of their investments would refuse to share that information, as if sharing it would somehow not be in the interest of informing other potential funding partners and the nonprofits doing the work.

- Individual donors would have virtually no access to the research and analysis paid for by charitable foundations, even though they might be interested in funding the same issues. This lack of access would be even more striking in light of the fact that individuals and government account for the majority of financial support for most nonprofit organizations that are more than five years old.

- Foundations would develop all of their operational processes in order to ensure legal compliance for spending grant dollars and expend little time, money, or creative thinking to see if their organizations were set up in ways that might actually achieve their stated social missions. This would result in processes for making grants that keep staff people hurrying to meet false deadlines and nonprofits spending time on reports that never get read. The operations would unnecessarily exacerbate the resource differences between funders and community groups instead of rewarding joint problem solving.

- Most foundations with staff would employ smart people with broad general knowledge. They would then require these generalists to make resource decisions regarding highly specialized areas of work such as healthcare, biodiversity protection, or the legal rights of women in Islamic nations. In another common model, foundations would employ highly educated issue experts, who would produce massive quantities of research, analysis, and synthesized recommendations on hundreds of thousands of nonprofits and not share that research with other funders, thus requiring every potential funder of an organization to repeat the research, analysis, and due diligence process.

- Foundations would concentrate on developing exit strategies for their grant making that were based primarily on assumptions about internal resources and that rarely had any requirements regarding the external success of the organizations being funded or achieving the stated goals of the work.

- Major foundations would undertake an extensive and expensive strategic planning process and refocus their grant-making strategies every time a change in leadership occurred, effectively stating that the needs of the communities they profess to serve must have been radically altered by the transition in their own organizational leadership (or that their previous work had no basis in the needs of the community).

Such a system is so illogical in practice that it is comforting to know that it was not a product of deliberate design. At the same time, as philanthropy has grown this lack of design is seriously limiting the reach and accomplishments of both individual philanthropic organizations and the industry as a whole. Philanthropy is a unique industry in that it—alone among financial service industries—stands to achieve its stated goals only if the individual firms within the sector share information, collude on strategy, pool financial resources, jointly invest in human capital, and build systems for efficiently aligning their individual actions. This is because no single individual or funding organization has the financial resources to achieve its stated social goals. Although the individual entities are set for failure, the industry as a whole invests hundreds of billions of dollars annually in activities dedicated to the public good.[5] If philanthropic resources can be aggregated even in small ways toward common goals, they can be substantial contributors to achieving those goals. If elements of the industry were deliberately designed, streamlined, creatively conjoined, and aggregated we could indeed build new philanthropic capital markets that could significantly improve the quality of community life.

What we have before us is the opportunity to reimagine philanthropy. This book argues that the resources of individual philanthropic players— people and institutions—will have greater impact, provide more satisfaction, and contribute to a better world if the system of philanthropy as a whole is redesigned. If we are successful in this endeavor, we will be able to build an industry that operates in more logical, effective, and robust ways than the one described above. Perhaps, if we take action now, we might look back at philanthropy in 2050 and see an industry that:

- Is strengthened by the diversity and complexity of financial products used to make resources available and to manage philanthropic assets. At the same time, managers of these assets invest in and rely on common, credible metrics to define problems, assess progress, and measure success.

- Takes advantage of the many cultural traditions for philanthropy, and counts all such activities as part of the industry. Philanthropic entities thrive in all communities and philanthropic resources can be easily identified, informed, and aggregated regardless of whether they are held in a private foundation, a donor-advised fund, or a religiously-affiliated trust.

- Makes available philanthropically funded research findings and knowledge to any and all that want access to them. Foundations invest heavily in the use and application of the industry's research findings. Contributions to and use of this knowledge base is a more widely cited ranking of foundation and philanthropic individuals than simply the amount of their gifts or the size of their investment portfolio.

- Uses public problem solving as the coin of the realm. All who have something at stake are invited to help advise the distribution of resources. Philanthropists involve community members and affected residents in the design and implementation of proposed initiatives as part of basic industry standards.

- Includes a public trust that exists where the technical skills of philanthropic decision making can be accessed, so that issue experts and experienced decision makers can help guide the philanthropic resources of many individuals and institutions rather than one at a time. There is also an internationally based and accessible clearinghouse of successful philanthropic strategies that is maintained by public and private investment. It serves as a research and development infrastructure to philanthropists and the public sector.

- Aggregates philanthropic assets by issue and informs them in pursuit of common goals. The greatest professional challenge in philanthropy and the mark of success is the ability to attract other people's money to an issue and apply the joint resources of many to make change happen.

- Operates within a regulatory structure that is informed by experienced philanthropists working in partnership with the monitoring bodies at the state and federal level. The purpose of regulation is to encourage ethical giving and support the use of knowledge and research in conducting philanthropic business. Independent monitoring groups thrive and regularly use publicly available data to advocate for positive regulatory change.

This image seems far-off, but elements of it exist today. Many efforts are made to aggregate resources. Diversity in knowledge, experience, and approach is much discussed. Deliberate efforts are being made to share knowledge and research and develop vital metrics of social betterment and community health. Public/private alliances exist in almost all states around almost all social issues. Networks of funders flourish, organized by joint interest, identity, or geographic location. These are all important steps to deliberately evolving philanthropy into a more effective market of private capital for public good.

Philanthropy is in a unique position to shape itself. Working together, influential individuals and organizations can demonstrate new ways of investing their grant funds, new approaches to the regulatory structures that guide giving, and new ways of defining their goals, activities, outcomes, and achievements. Many of the ideas presented in the book are already in practice in small numbers or in limited ways. The opportunity is to redefine the whole.

Philanthropy is idiosyncratic and, like most systems, it moves in odd ways. In some cases, the points of leverage on the system are counterintuitive.

Some elements of the system have developed for reasons motivated by profit, whereas others are highly personality-driven. The industry of philanthropy can be improved, and this book presents a coherent framework for pursuing that improvement; however, it is presented with the caveat that both evolutionary and deliberate improvements occur in syncopated, sometimes unexpected, ways. We know we can do better, and it behooves us to try. We should eagerly address the potential of unintended consequences, for therein lies much of what we need to learn.

CHANGE COMES SLOWLY

Philanthropic foundations have remained relatively staid organizations even as the world around them has changed dramatically. Although change comes slowly to grant-making organizations, the constellation of players within philanthropy exploded in both size and structural diversity during the 1990s. Foundations are only small players in a complex industry of grant making that includes financial services firms, investment banks, private advisory services, and several viable Internet-based systems and tools. The complexity and diversity of this system is bringing new opportunities for individuals and for the system as a whole.

What new visions and mechanisms are necessary to develop a more organized, more effective philanthropic capital market that strongly and visibly contributes to the public good? How can organized philanthropy change to meet the social and economic challenges of an increasingly global, diverse, and economically bifurcated world? And how can we take advantage of the oddities of philanthropy, its quirks and failures, to inform this effort at improvement?

To answer these questions, we examine how individual organizations, associations, and the philanthropic infrastructure now function and how they are changing to work more effectively. The book draws from previous work on organizational change in philanthropy and pulls together several ongoing but disconnected efforts within philanthropy to deliberately evolve the industry. A critical contribution of the work is the presentation of a complete conceptual framework within which philanthropy can be considered, the forces on it identified, and its opportunities clearly set forth.

Although philanthropy is an industry, it is also a system of human-made and personality-inspired disparate organizations, individuals, and policies.

THE TRILLION-DOLLAR OPPORTUNITY

Recognizing this, the framework that is fit to philanthropy must be modified somewhat from that of a purely commercial industry analysis. This is done by recognizing the naturally evolving characteristics of philanthropy and the forces that drive that evolution. By tempering the industrial analysis with important concepts and timeframes from evolutionary and systems theory, we can identify ways to intentionally design a more effective sector.

THE TRILLION-DOLLAR OPPORTUNITY

Why should we care about changing philanthropy? Simple. Philanthropy in the United States accounts for hundreds of billions—and potentially trillions—of dollars. It attempts to impact every element of human endeavor from the artistic to the zoological. Philanthropy is an ageless human trait and an embedded artifact in American tax codes, public policy frameworks, and community expectations. In short, from religious activity to educational achievement, health care, and business aptitude, the context for success in the United States relies on both public and private financial, human, and intellectual resources. Left to its own devices, philanthropy would probably continue to grow and be a positive force in society. But we cannot assume that the major forces on the industry—markets and regulation—act solely of their own accord. The opportunity to direct and inform the industry's growth, to harness the collective power of available philanthropic resources, and to build a more disciplined, directed system for applying financial, human, and intellectual resources to achieve social good is simply too big an opportunity to leave to chance.

Philanthropy is a growing industry. Annual records document hundreds of billions of dollars in philanthropic activity per year and nearly $2 trillion in the 1990s. It is also an industry that suffers from a dearth of credible, practical, and broadly relevant literature. Presenting a viable vision of a more systematic, cohesive, and mobilized philanthropic industry has implications in several arenas. First, philanthropy and its many participants will find value in (or, at least, much to argue against) the presentation of established and emergent philanthropic entities as players in one industry. This framework will be particularly useful to individuals who are newly engaged in philanthropy on a significant scale. Nonprofit agencies and nongovernmental organizations in all areas of policy and services will find implications for their work with private philanthropic supporters. Leaders of emerging civil systems in other countries will find the book a useful scan of the established, yet still developing, American philanthropic situation. And public policy makers at all levels, as well as media outlets interested in philanthropy, should find the complete industry perspective a useful reference point for their interactions with individual organizations or coverage of specific issues.

The book draws from my previous writing on future trends and foundation philanthropy and the role of knowledge as an asset in philanthropic action. It pushes this work further in regard to designing new structures, recommending action, and seeking opportunity for philanthropy. It also presents exciting new developments for industry resources focused on collective market research and analysis, and proposes several such enterprises. Drawing together the shift in industrial structure, the presence of diverse institutions, and the growing roles of knowledge sharing and networking, the book argues for the potential—and the necessity—for philanthropy to reorganize into a more rational system for social good.

Chapter 1, The Industry of Philanthropy, presents the conceptual framing of philanthropy as a diverse and balkanized industry, with a variety of firms, services, and providers ranging from foundations to financial service firms to individuals. This framework is important for several reasons: (1) only by recognizing their position within the industry are individual philanthropic organizations in a position to drive changes to their favor; and (2) the industrial nature of philanthropy is currently at some odds with its human and social purposes. As the philanthropic industry is increasingly subject to both market pressures and regulatory strictures it will need new strategies for advocating, communicating, and continuing its precious— and precarious—positions regarding tax status and accountability.

The industrial framework allows us to easily see the similarities in various philanthropic vehicles and the profound influence of regulation and markets on how charitable giving works. The framework does not account for the third force on philanthropy—that of its core characteristic as a protector and purveyor of the common good. By focusing on the industrial elements, I hope to shed light on the critical importance of philanthropic individuals coming together to articulate and pursue those contributions.

Chapter 2 posits several examples of how philanthropy could function as a more effective system for social good. By starting with pictures of what is possible, I intend to entice readers to consider the potential of the changes they might lead. The forces of change on philanthropy can be harnessed and directed to make the philanthropic sector more inclusive, more robust, and more effective. But action is needed to direct change in this way, and a vision of a better system is the first step toward galvanizing that action.

Philanthropy is a product of its times. From specific influences such as tax codes and reporting laws to more generalized trends such as demographic shifts and new technological developments, philanthropy grows and adapts and responds to drivers of change at several levels of distance and impact. Today's strongest forces of change on the industry are described in Chapter 3. It includes discussion of demographic changes, wealth and income predictions and disparities, regulatory pressures, new technologies, new corporate structures, and the enhanced mobility of individuals. The chapter frames these drivers within three concentric spheres—organizational, industrial, and societal—to clarify degree of impact and control to assist in understanding how such disparate forces can all conjoin to influence philanthropy.

The roles of markets and market characteristics on philanthropy are presented in Chapter 4. Specific attention is given to the nature of competition in philanthropy and the advent of alliances. Both of these market forces are having a pronounced influence on the actions, values, and goals of philanthropic players. Although some of these behaviors and characteristics have deep roots in American philanthropy, others are more recent and more nuanced. The chapter identifies that philanthropy is now an industry offering only two types of products—asset management products and advisory services—and introduces the implications of this for the future. I also look at the limitations of current business models given this product landscape as well as the roles of collaboration and networking as key steps toward a better system.

The other side of the market coin is the regulated nature of philanthropic endeavor. In Chapter 5 I look at philanthropy as a regulated industry. The potential of the industry model is particularly pronounced in this section. In reviewing the long, mostly arm's-length relationship between philanthropic institutions and their regulators, we see the prevalence of "family myths," the power and reality of direct action by philanthropists, and the many levels at which the industry must prepare itself for regulatory review and action. The chapter proposes a much more active role on the part of philanthropic players in working with regulators and legislators on the public policy of the industry. These are drawn from a set of common-sense principles regarding the role philanthropy should play in civil society. The activist regulatory approach stems not from a commitment to government–industry alliances, but from an analysis of the limited good that philanthropy's more passive stance has achieved over time. A new entity, an international philanthropy research and development enterprise is posited as one type of structural support that would align with the new roles of research and knowledge in philanthropy. This kind of enterprise further contributes to the idea of aggregating and aligning disparate charitable resources, a key element of new capital markets in philanthropy.

Chapter 6 describes the current opportunities to intentionally drive the evolution of philanthropy. The focus is on the industry as a whole because philanthropy can make the most impact as an aggregated force. This chapter looks at the need for a new philanthropic infrastructure, the growing role of hybrid organizations, and the need for leadership that can work within the regulated marketplace on behalf of all philanthropic action. This section looks closely at the development of significant new numbers of philanthropic associations and examines how these alliances can expand the impact of philanthropic investment. It presents a model for a new set of industry enterprises that would capture, organize, package, and distribute relevant market and industry research, share knowledge, contribute to the professional development of philanthropic staff and board members, and lay the groundwork for organizing philanthropic resources into a viable capital market.

Chapter 7 brings the vision of a new industry down to the practical level of revamped philanthropic institutions. Although the industry is what ultimately matters, the individual nodes of this network are the manageable sites of change and improvement. Harkening back to Chapter 2 and "what it could look like," Chapter 7 examines the implications of these changes at the organizational and institutional level, looking at specific new developments such as the role of knowledge, new staff structures, product lines, and revenue streams at community foundations, the changing roles of consultants, and the rise of tangential service providers.

Chapter 8 looks at the opportunity to reorganize philanthropy so that the capital it provides can be used to greatest effect. It draws a model of philanthropy in which the disaggregated individuals and the structured institutions work together in a more deliberate, planned, and interdependent way. The ideas are modeled on private capital markets and the known relationships between various financing sources for commercial enterprise. It posits that philanthropic entities and individuals can be mobilized and connected in ways that allow independent entities to act at their point of greatest value while also developing a more identifiable system of private support for nonprofit action.

Improving philanthropy will take time. It will happen in fits and starts. The whole system may never improve, and it is very possible that regulatory action, budget deficits, and market forces left undirected will further degrade the potential impact of the whole. The forces of fragmentation on the industry are, at this time, far stronger than the forces of aggregation. This book is intended as a clarion call to philanthropic participants that their individual actions occur within a larger system. A system that shapes their success and satisfaction, and one that they, in turn, can help improve.

What Does Better Look Like?

One of the most limiting qualities of the current philanthropic system is the lack of a common, coherent vision. This book and its arguments regarding current forces of change and the opportunity to drive those forces toward something better is predicated on a vision of a philanthropic system that is better than the current one in five specific ways. These five attributes—diverse, aggregated, integrated, well-timed, and committed—underpin all other facets of this book. They build from the best existing qualities of today's philanthropy, but place the emphases in new places and seek to strengthen qualities that some might even argue are deficiencies.

Diverse

The range of philanthropic options, from different financial vehicles to cultural, geographic, and personal diversity, is the great strength of philanthropy. As in a natural ecosystem, this diversity allows for the development of "resilient mutants," the continuation of a vibrant system when some of its parts wither, and an adaptability to new situations that allows for continued innovation and impact. Diversity in philanthropy will engage the greatest number of individuals, present the widest variety of potential strategies, and serve the broadest range of communities.

Aggregated

Philanthropic resources are profoundly limited. Although the hyperbolic attention to the transfer of wealth between generations and the rate of wealth creation would have us imagine nearly unlimited philanthropic assets, the truth is they are both limited and divided among millions of small pockets. To have an impact, these private resources must be aggregated. Philanthropic strategies to aggregate resources depend on aligning the interests of small clusters within the philanthropic whole. Foundations have made many important strides in working together. These need to be encouraged and expanded. The biggest opportunity, however, is to bring the intellectual and research resources of foundations to bear on the many highly-dispersed pools of philanthropic assets held by individuals, donor-advised funds, and small foundations. Designing ways that these independent sources of philanthropic capital can find others with the same interests, can access the research conducted by others, and work collaboratively and in force is the key to building new systems for moving philanthropic resources. Given the overall pool of resources and the generally isolated nature of them, aggregating around issues, identities, or geographies will build sufficient resources to achieve common goals. At the same time, the nature of philanthropy is so individualistic that the threat to diversity one might fear from a strategy of aggregation is unfounded. There is little chance of aggregation on the scale that would do harm and an overarching need to draw resources together.

Integrated

Aggregation refers to aligning and pooling private resources. Even this, however, is insufficient for the philanthropic economy to make major investments. A stronger philanthropic system will integrate private funds with public strategies. Helping philanthropists know where and how to engage with public resources, and when to work in opposition to them is the purview of independent advocacy groups and research groups that can inform the whole industry.

For those philanthropic investments that intend to *advance* existing public priorities, integration involves working with public resources to identify the appropriate size, timing, and quality of investments. For philanthropic strategies aimed at *changing* the public system, the integrating effort may focus only on private resources but still involves starting with an accurate assessment of the public system. The integration in social change strategies will be with minority public positions and revenue sources to effect reform or evolution in the larger, majority structures.

Well-Timed

Philanthropic giving must be well-timed. If the goal is to launch a new approach, the giving must come early and be flexible and in line with identified sources to sustain the effort through its development. If the goal is replication, then the philanthropic investments must come later in the life cycle of the organization or strategy. Being well-timed depends on being part of an aggregated and integrated revenue system. It will help philanthropists make decisions about when to "get in" and when to "get out," based on real information instead of irrational habits.

Committed

One of the greatest challenges for philanthropy is to commit support for the length of time it takes to achieve certain results. Ironically, philanthropy has made great strides in developing investment strategies for its endowments that yield returns aimed at perpetuity. At the same time, the grants made from those permanent endowments tend to have time horizons of only a few years. Philanthropic entities need new metrics and practices that provide incentives for longer commitments.

All five of these attributes represent a new way of analyzing philanthropy. Each of the institutions and individuals in the philanthropic economy that strives to embody these attributes will quickly realize that its work is entirely dependent on the work of others. They are part of a system, a node on a network, and a partner in partnerships. This language has become almost rhetorical in institutional philanthropy, but it has not become a practical norm. As we look at the changes underway in philanthropy today we will see the importance of understanding the balance of asset management and advisory products, the critical role that knowledge sharing plays in building better systems, and the need to aggregate resources to achieve philanthropic goals. These are fundamental characteristics of a new philanthropic capital market.

Throughout this book I emphasize these attributes and the importance of the networked reality of today's philanthropy. The goal is to illuminate for today's philanthropic entities the actual system within which their work occurs and encourage them to reexamine and rebuild their organizations to be successful in that system. The idiosyncratic, independent nature of philanthropic entities can thrive within this networked system, but only if each entity is aware of the dynamics at work. The whole industry of philanthropy, the interdependent whole, will have greater impact as its component pieces recognize their new roles. In turn, these component pieces —individuals and institutions—will derive greater satisfaction and make more meaningful contributions to community and global life as they structure their work to be successful as a piece of the larger whole.

CHAPTER 1

The Industry of Philanthropy

The sweat of industry would dry and die
But for the end it works to.[1]

—William Shakespeare, *Cymbeline*

Philanthropy—at its most basic—is the process of sharing private resources for public benefit. The activities it encompasses range from volunteering time to strategically investing endowed resources in socially responsible index funds to giving time and money together. All of these activities involve "putting something in" to make something better "come out." This can be expressed as an incredibly simple equation:

philanthropic inputs + existing conditions = better outcomes for others

This deliberate oversimplification is important in helping us locate the industrial elements of philanthropy. The equation in its entirety, including the final sum—"better outcomes"—captures both the public purpose of the industry and the extent to which philanthropy is part of its surroundings ("existing conditions"). Philanthropic actions are not about profit or outcomes for the giver, but are actions taken in pursuit of something for others. This public purpose distinguishes philanthropy from other industries and greatly influences the manner in which key components of the industry interact.

The industrial framework applies most specifically to the equation's "philanthropic inputs" variable. While the two most basic forms of input are time and money, applying the industrial lens allows us to see the magnitude of the changing forms, functions, participants, activities, and scope of these inputs. Industries are defined as a set of companies that produce highly substitutable products or services. All financial vehicles for making tax-deductible contributions fall into the philanthropic industry, from charitable gift funds to independent foundations, private banks, corporate giving programs, and social donor networks. Each of these vehicles has a unique set of characteristics from the perspective of tax and estate planning, yet they are all firms or products for the purpose of giving away money. Understanding philanthropy as an industry is an effective aid in better seeing what it is uniquely capable of and what it stands no chance of accomplishing.

Applying an industrial framework to philanthropy is not a futuristic definitional trick, it simply recognizes the changes that have already occurred. The components of an industry, which are detailed as follows, now permeate philanthropy. The market and regulatory forces that shape this industry (and are discussed in Chapters 3 and 4) are profound. They will not disappear simply because many in the industry are uncomfortable with the language I use to describe them or because of some idealistic image of what the nonprofit sector should be.

Pointing out the industrial nature of philanthropy is both an act of accepting the real pressures of markets and regulation and positioning the industry to reclaim control of its future. There has long been a robust debate within nonprofits and philanthropy about what to call the work, some prefer "nonprofit," others like "public benefit," and the 1960s brought us the "independent sector," by which to distinguish the work from government or business enterprises.[2] In contrast, this analysis shows philanthropy and nonprofits as dependent on the public and commercial spheres, especially when the guiding questions are about future directions.

This chapter outlines both the ways in which the industrial framework is useful and the limits of that framework. It also rounds out the conceptual work of the book by presenting components of evolutionary and systems theory that inform the argument.

DEFINING THE INDUSTRY

The literature on business is rife with analyses, exhortations, and primers on industry characteristics, growth, and decline. Industries define themselves through trade associations, the government draws some defining lines while investors determine others, and individual businesses are often active in more than one industry. The work of Michael Porter at Harvard University is particularly noteworthy in defining industries and helping us to see how the standard characteristics and pressures are relevant to philanthropy.[3] The six core elements of an industry are listed as follows and described in more detail in the following section:

- Capital for investment
- Firms, markets, and customers
- Products and services
- Competition and alliances
- Regulation and public policy
- Media attention and public awareness

Viewing philanthropy as an industry provides us with a conceptual framework to hold together these disparate pieces. By thinking of philanthropy as an industry, we can track the influence of capital growth, regulation, product differentiation, and markets. We need to push our imaginations beyond the commonly held vision of a purely commercial industry in order to understand the role that the human and social elements of philanthropy play on the overall shape and size of the endeavor. Lacking a common bottom line, philanthropic action is not as linear, predictable, or quantifiable as changes in the oil, biotechnology, or telecommunications industries.

The various elements of philanthropy are neatly defined by these six industry characteristics.

Capital for Investment

Philanthropy is experiencing an explosion of available capital. The financial resources dedicated to philanthropic action have increased multifold in the last decades, topping out at more than $240 billion in gifts and $476 billion in assets in 2001.[4] This growth is the primary reason that there is so much change in philanthropy. The opportunity to manage and/or advise these financial resources has attracted new types of firms to the market, caught the eye of regulators, excited the media, and created an entry-level for market participation that requires much less wealth than was previously feasible.

As more and more people attain a level of wealth at which managing their philanthropy is an option, they are seeking out a wide variety of giving products. They may choose to establish a donor-advised fund at either a commercial or nonprofit organization. They might partner with peers in creating a giving circle. They may simply increase their charitable giving as part of their overall budget and choose not to invest in a specific philanthropic product. They may simultaneously create a family foundation and become more active in their company's giving program. And, as we will see, many people will choose to use several of these giving products all at once. The growth in giving options—some of which look like products (donor-advised funds) and some of which look like firms (private foundations)—allows broader participation in the industry and encourages a new level of competition between products or firms.

While this growth in philanthropic participation is interesting, it is important to note that more people are purchasing philanthropic products and the actual value of their giving is increasing, but the percentage of individual wealth allocated to philanthropy has remained rather steady (ranging between 1.7 and 2.1 percent of personal income) over the last 30 years.[5] This narrow band of giving is surprising if viewed solely through the lens of the market. There has been no lack of effort to grow the market, as evidenced by the dramatic shifts in the types of firms actively involved in philanthropy and the customers and markets they seek to reach and expand.

The involvement of commercial firms offering charity-related products has drastically affected the role that competitive markets play in philanthropic decision making. As in most competitive markets, there are many players in philanthropy: individuals; financial service firms; private, community, and corporate foundations; giving circles; professional advisors (accountants, attorneys, and investment professionals); and estate planning and fundraising professionals. The various firms and products are simultaneously struggling to differentiate themselves and working together in alliances. They all offer a host of similar products, and several layers of regulation govern them as a single industry.

Firms, Markets, and Customers

Firms in the philanthropic industry include all those who provide or advise charitable giving opportunities. Twenty years ago this would have included foundations, community foundations, community endowments, nonprofit organizations with established donor services and planned giving opportunities, fundraising professionals, banks, and trusts. In 2002, the landscape of firms in the industry included the aforementioned list plus financial services firms, mutual fund companies, independent donor-advised funds, independent consulting firms, professional advisory services, and e-commerce companies that provide Internet technology to manage or assist in fundraising.

The marketplace has become increasingly crowded and diversified. The traditional customers for most of these firms have been individuals with high net worth. One result of the increased activity in the market is that customers with lower net worth are increasingly sought after as target customers, expanding the reach of the market. As the types of firms in the industry continue to diversify and new partnerships and alliances emerge, the old categories of foundation, commercial firm, and donor-advised fund decrease in their utility. As we look to the future, a new matrix for thinking about the firms presents itself, designed more around the services and products being offered than by the host institution selling them (see Exhibit 1.1).

EXHIBIT 1.1   KEY CHARACTERISTICS OF
PHILANTHROPIC FIRMS—2003

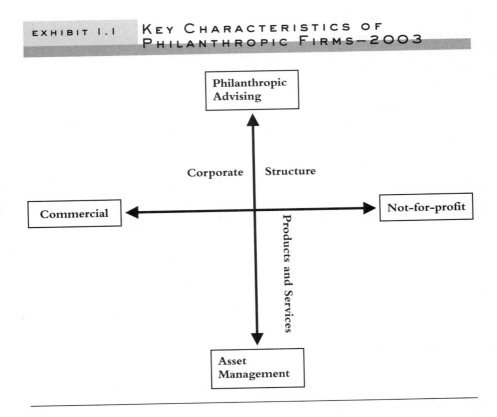

All purveyors of philanthropic services can be categorized on the continuum in Exhibit 1.1. A key trend to track in the industry is where the majority of firms fit along the continuum at any given time. Fifty years ago, it is safe to say that most institutional philanthropy was managed through exclusively not-for-profit organizations (e.g., foundations, community foundations). Commercial banks were involved in the work to a small degree through their trust departments. These institutions provided a mix of advisory services and asset management services, and pricing was based on asset management fees.

Today, the mix has shifted dramatically. Commercial relationships are far more common, either through direct product sales from commercial banks (donor-advised funds) or partnerships between banks and foundations. Many firms that sell advisory services, absent any asset management component, are also visible on the landscape. As we think along these broad stripes of philanthropic firms, it becomes easier to focus on the mix of products and services available to the market, and we are less bound by traditional categorical breakdowns.

Products and Services

The two major products sold in the philanthropic industry are (1) tax-exempt structures for giving funds and (2) advice and research. The available asset management structures include direct gifts of cash or equities to a nonprofit organization, charitable trusts, private foundations, donor-advised funds, supporting organizations, and semi-restricted or unrestricted gifts to community foundations or endowments. Also available are several different annuities, trusts, and estate management tools.

On the advice and research side, the services offered include investment management advice, educational opportunities, reporting to regulatory bodies, grants management, advisory services regarding the structuring of philanthropic gifts, independent research and analysis on issues of concern, family wealth management, board training, peer learning opportunities, and management consulting. Sometimes these services are coupled with asset management products, and often they are sold independently.

Competition and Alliances

One of the most persistent mischaracterizations of this industry is that because it is largely not-for-profit it is also free of competition. As commercial firms have entered the market for charitable giving options, the role of competition has become more obvious. Individual philanthropists have several options for managing their giving. From the standpoint of these donors, the options are in competition with each other. Donors are doing more comparison shopping across products and services. More and more frequently, donors are choosing several options and expecting to derive different benefits from each.[6]

Although community foundations and financial services firms are in competition for managing the assets of charitable individuals, there is also an increasing willingness to form alliances between foundations and other giving vehicles. Several financial services firms work with large numbers of community foundations.[7] Private foundations often work with community endowments. Alliances of private, corporate, and community foundations are nurturing several giving circles around the country. In some situations, private foundations are even turning to the commercial firms' donor-advised funds (and to community foundations) to help them meet payout requirements.[8]

These alliances have several drivers. Most important is the industry-wide recognition that asset management and advice are separate services, available from independent vendors, and that command different pricing structures. This encourages mixing and matching by both consumers and purveyors. Also at work is the recognition that no single philanthropic entity has the assets to achieve its goals alone. This awareness increases opportunities for partnership as philanthropic individuals find themselves choosing several vehicles at once and then seeking ways to make them work together.

Regulation and Public Policy

Philanthropy is a regulated industry. Federal, state, and municipal tax codes govern tax exemptions and regulate charitable giving. Secretaries of state, attorneys general, the Internal Revenue Service, and state departments of corporations oversee foundations and nonprofit organizations. Individual giving is subject to regulations regarding tax deductibility. For institutional giving, additional regulations require public reporting and influence the roles that tax-exempt organizations can play regarding political advocacy and lobbying.

The different firms competing in the philanthropic product market do not share the same interests vis-à-vis tax policy and regulation. This results in conflicting activity on public policy regarding the oversight of the industry. For example, community foundations and private foundations have different opinions on the levying of an excise tax levy on private foundations. Community foundations and commercial financial service firms also have taken different stances on the regulation and oversight of donor-advised funds. The disparate preferences result in several subindustry appeals to regulators and limit the industry's ability to speak with one voice. In general, the industry has tended to be reactionary to public policy rather than proactive in working with regulators.

In his 2002 book, *Wealth and Democracy*, Kevin Phillips attempts a broad history of the relationship between money and politics. In looking over 300 years of government economic policy in the United States, he notes that, "Occasionally public policy tilted toward the lower and middle classes. . . . Most often, in the United States and elsewhere, these avenues and alleyways have been explored, every nook and cranny, for the benefit of the financial and business classes."[9] The preference for policies that help build wealth led to a "wealth gap" at the end of the twentieth century similar only to that experienced in 1929 before the Great Depression. Between 1977 and 1997, the percentage of all income held by the richest 5 percent of the U.S. population grew from 44.2 percent to 50.4 percent (i.e., 5 percent of the population makes more than half of all the money). At the same time, the poorest 5 percent saw their percentage of all income drop even further, from 5.7 percent to 5.2 percent.[10]

Media Attention and Public Awareness

General public awareness of philanthropy is on the rise. The economic boom of the late 1990s led many general-interest newspapers and magazines to profile individuals with high net worth and their philanthropy. In addition, foundations and individual givers have become more proactive in communicating with the public about their work. The competition for donors has led to broad advertising campaigns by commercial services firms and community foundations. Finally, the large-scale scandals that placed philanthropic and nonprofit entities in the news in the past have reappeared recently, and the attention to charitable giving and nonprofit decision making following the tragedies of September 11, 2001 has kept philanthropic issues in the headlines for more than two years.

The increase in advertising that has contributed to and accompanied the growth in donor-advised funds is part of the increased public awareness of philanthropy. From billboards in public transit stops to magazine advertisements to program support on National Public Radio, foundations are increasingly advertising their existence and their activities.[11] This goes hand-in-glove with the advertising done by commercial banks that offer philanthropic services. These ads tend to present the bank's or financial service firm's "one-stop" shop ability for all of an individual's wealth management needs, including estate and trust planning and philanthropic advising.

Heightened public awareness and media attention provides important context for considering the industry in the twenty-first century. Such attention may play out many ways. A greater general awareness may lead to infusions of funds into philanthropy that might not have otherwise occurred. At the same time scandals in philanthropy will play out before a larger audience, and changes in regulatory oversight will draw greater public attention.

The conceptual framework of an industry of philanthropy is a means to an end, not an end in itself. In Chapter 3, as we examine the major drivers of change, the framework allows us to pinpoint ourselves in the current landscape, fix our gaze on the horizon, and identify tangible actions foundations can take to spur movement toward a stronger nonprofit and philanthropic enterprise.

MAPPING THE LANDSCAPE OF PHILANTHROPIC CAPITAL

At the heart of understanding the philanthropic industry is the recognition that all philanthropic giving comes from individuals and is organized by individuals. Some people of great wealth never establish any kind of philanthropic organization, but they give millions of dollars from their checking account on an annual basis, asking for no guidance or input from anyone in their personal or professional circles. Other donors choose to affiliate themselves with as many peers as possible, and so may manage a much smaller annual philanthropic budget through participation in a giving circle, a community foundation donor-advised fund, sitting on their corporate giving committee, and serving as a board member on their family foundation. The dollar value of a person's giving is only loosely related to the number or types of philanthropic products that individual may use.

Recognizing that each philanthropic product is attached to an individual helps us to understand the degree and timing of influence that competition plays in the industry. The following example of Ricardo Jr. shows the sensitivity of different products to customer decisions. Ricardo is the fifty-five year old son of an immigrant father who founded a very successful packaged foods business. Before he died, Ricardo Sr. established a family foundation and named his three children as board members, along with several of his business associates. Ricardo Jr. serves on the board of the foundation, is active in the development campaigns at the university where he was an undergraduate and received his law degree, serves on the board of the local animal shelter, is active on his company's giving committee, and has donor-advised funds with his investment manager's bank, the local community foundation, and through an international community foundation sponsored by his church. He is also considering how to catalyze and inform his adult children's philanthropy.

In terms of his philanthropic assets, Ricardo represents the full spectrum of options. Every year he gives to his alma mater and to the animal shelter, although the amounts he gives fluctuate wildly from year to year. The giving that he oversees through his family foundation is much less volatile—because the budget was determined the previous year and the staff made deliberate efforts to maintain a certain level of giving. The donor-advised funds also rise and fall in size—some years Ricardo advises so much giving through these funds that he nearly depletes them, other times he focuses his own giving on building those funds rather than dispersing them. The new family foundation idea represents the largest possible new philanthropic purchase for Ricardo. He is deciding whether to endow a new entity, direct resources from the existing foundation to a new fund to be overseen by his children, direct his own estate to the existing foundation and bring his children onto that board, establish donor-advised funds for his children, or leave them the financial resources in his will and allow them to choose what to do.

Taken individually, the vehicles that now exist for managing philanthropic assets are discrete financial products. They include charitable remainder trusts, annuities, foundations, donor-advised funds, giving circle contributions, and direct gifts to nonprofit organizations. Yet each of these products is sold or provided by some sort of organization that seeks to manage the donor's philanthropic capital. In the example above, each of the philanthropic entities—from the family foundation to the animal shel-

ter to the community foundation to Ricardo's personal investment manager—has an interest in Ricardo picking their product to manage his resources. In this sense, they are all competitive products even though they
range from free-standing organizations such as the foundation to legal sub-
clauses, such as the estate planning options in Ricardo's will.

One way to look at this is to array the product options according to how
prevalent they are. Recent research out of the Social Welfare Research Institute at Boston College along with IRS data and other survey findings can
be aggregated into the following "topography" of philanthropic products.
In the United States in 2002 there were:[12]

- 6,000,000 charitable bequests in wills
- 150,000 charitable trusts
- 70,000+ donor-advised funds (~$12b)
- 62,000+ foundations ($470 b+)
- 1.6 million nonprofits to which direct gifts can be made
- Charitable gift annuities and retained life estate (uncounted)

The most reliable industry metrics are those that count the most visible
components of this complicated landscape. Thus we know that there are
62,000 foundations in the United States, more than 55,000 of which are
structured as independent foundations, 600 are community foundations,
2,100 are corporate foundations, and 3,900 classify as operating foundations. These entities managed more than $476 billion in assets in 2002 and
made more than $30 billion in grants.[13] The research also shows that almost
half of all people who use one of these products actually use two or more.

These are impressive figures, yet they present an incomplete picture of
the industry. All philanthropic giving in 2002 amounted to more than $240
billion, 76% of which was fueled by gifts from individuals. To further com-
plicate efforts at tracking philanthropic capital, we know that bequests account for about 7.5% of all giving, or more than $18 billion in 2002.[14] Of
the industry giving total, we know that some percentage of it is managed
through the country's more than 70,000 donor-advised funds. It is striking
to note that there are now more donor-advised funds than foundations, yet
we don't have accurate values for either the assets or gifts from these funds.[15]

Nor can we equate individuals with small gifts and institutions with large
ones. As Katherine Fulton and Andrew Blau of Global Business Network
have pointed out, an integrated list of the 100 top givers that counted both

individuals and institutions would include 78 foundations and 22 individual donors. That is to say that these people gave more in that year than 1/5 of the nation's most active foundations.[16] The lines between individual and institutional philanthropy are blurring.

The landscape of philanthropic giving is littered with options, not all of which are easily identified and many of which are very small. Some of the players have been in existence for decades and are endowed in perpetuity, others are less than a year old and will be spent down and replenished each year according to the donor's interests. As products and firms in competition for donor assets, some of the players—particularly commercial entities and community foundations—are extremely sensitive to competitive pressures. For others, such as endowed foundations, the original purchase decision of the donor is the primary point at which the other options stand out as competing choices. The various products for philanthropic asset management are all subject to competitive market pressures, but they do not all experience it equally or at the same time. Exhibit 1.2 shows how the most common products array on a scale of competitive pressures.

A donor seeking to purchase asset management tools for her philanthropic capital must pick among these firms and products—and at this decision stage an endowed foundation is simply one of many product options. Frequently, donors will choose several of the options, including an independent foundation. Eventually that foundation may become home to more (or even all) of the donor's assets, or it may remain relatively small and operate in parallel with other funds, estate tools, or giving vehicles established by the donor. At this point, it starts to look less like a product in

EXHIBIT 1.2		SENSITIVITY TO COMPETITION FOR DIFFERENT PHILANTHROPIC FINANCIAL PRODUCTS	
Product sensitivity to competition	High	• Independent foundation • Community foundation fund • Financial service firm account • Direct gift to nonprofit	• Community foundation fund • Financial service firm account • Direct gift to nonprofit
	Low		• Independent foundation
	Timeline of product purchase	Initial purchase	Established

the market and begins to act more like a firm, especially if it is one of the few foundations in the country to employ staff. Competition in philanthropy has uneven influences, acting as a much stronger force on some entities than on others.

EVOLUTIONARY ADAPTATIONS AND THE LIMITS OF THE INDUSTRIAL FRAMEWORK

> *Man's unique reward, however, is that while animals survive by adjusting themselves to their background, man survives by adjusting his background to himself.*[17]

—Ayn Rand

The uneven responses to competition are just one example of how the industrial framework is not an exact fit for philanthropy. Some have compared philanthropy to an ecological system, whereas others prefer field of practice or sector. In some cases, the difference is purely semantic. Some simply do not want to be tainted by the market overtones that mark industries in general. I prefer to use what works from the industrial framework (which is a lot) and draw from other frameworks as necessary.

There are two other important frameworks: evolutionary theory and systems theory that will enhance the resolution with which we see how philanthropy works. I will highlight some key concepts of these two frameworks that help us to understand how philanthropy works and where it is going.

EVOLUTIONARY ASPECTS OF PHILANTHROPY

From Darwin to Gould, through anthropology, genetics, genomics, and zoology, our understanding of the natural changes that occur over time in animal and plant species is ever-changing. The recent mapping of the human genome has opened up a new world and called into question some old ideas. It also has rejuvenated theories and evidence that had once been discounted.[18]

Noting that nothing is static—even our understanding of evolution—is the first key contribution of evolutionary research. Second is the sense that change takes time. Third, research shows that our preference for a nice, linear story of progressive change that involves clear adaptation to overall environmental stresses is too neat and clean. Change and evolution are messy. They occur sporadically.[19] Certain organisms (and organizations) change only in response to a new niche opportunity, not in line with some overarching predetermined plan. Opportunities for some are often death blows for others. The balance is important, and a diversity of types (e.g., species, organisms, organizations) is generally seen as critical to the health of the individual entities and the whole.

Without digressing into an exhaustive discussion of the state of evolutionary theory, these aspects of the work are indeed immediately applicable to understanding philanthropy:

- Organisms (organizations) adapt to their environment.
- Change is slow, messy, and uneven.
- Opportunities for some can be fatal to others.
- A diverse set of species (organizations) is critical to the health of the individuals and the whole environment.

SYSTEMS THEORY

This question of the whole and its parts is where systems theory comes into play. Although a complex and ever-changing area of study, systems theory is essentially a means of looking at the interactions between and among organisms (or organizations) rather than looking at the individual entities. The theories have evolved and adapted through several academic disciplines, from math to philosophy, and are now usually viewed as inherently interdisciplinary ways of thinking about computers, communities, policies, or other phenomena. One of the key founders of the work, the biologist Ludwig von Bertelannfy, "emphasized that real systems are open to, and interact with, their environments, and that they can acquire qualitatively new properties through emergence, resulting in continual evolution."[20]

Systems theory helps us see how individual organizations can be shaped in very different ways by a shared set of environmental forces. The value of this approach is its emphasis on the interdependence of the whole and its pieces. It allows us to see how changing the philanthropic industry can assist individual organizations and how change at the organizational level can influence industry progress as well. As analysis and research has applied systems theory to fields as far ranging as biological, environmental, organizational, economic, political, and urban systems, several key ideas have become standard. One of these is the idea that there are leverage points at which one can make a small change and have a large effect.[21]

The idea of leverage points has become almost endemic to institutional philanthropy. Grants are often made with either implicit or explicit expectations that, although the funds are small, if well placed they can spark change throughout the organization, the issue, or the system at hand. Grant funds are intended to leverage other funds and to be catalysts of change well beyond their own size. How to assess a system to identify these points, how to measure a grant's success at achieving such impact, and, most important, how to find the points of leverage for the philanthropic system are the harder questions.

In her analysis of how to find leverage points, Donella Meadows of The Sustainability Institute notes that two very common mistakes are made in this work. First, the leverage point is identified and agreed upon, but the wrong action is taken on it (it is pushed the wrong way to achieve the intended goals). The second mistake is that the wrong leverage point is identified. Leverage points, she argues, are counterintuitive.[22]

This would not be such a hindrance if we had good technology or methodology for identifying leverage points. Unfortunately, the science that has introduced leverage points is most robust when being applied retrospectively to data about known systems. It is less useful for analyzing emerging data or applying it to new systems to locate the points of leverage. In other words, systems theory and our understanding of leverage points are at their best when explaining what happened and why, rather than predicting what will happen.

From systems theory we can also draw several concepts to better inform our understanding of philanthropy. These include the following:

- The connections and interactions between entities matter in understanding the system.
- Leverage points are places where small shifts can have large ripple effects throughout a system.
- Leverage points are hard to predict and often counterintuitive.

THE EXCEPTIONS PROVE THE RULE

Having drawn these lessons from evolutionary and systems theory, let us return to the industrial model. Perhaps the most compelling advantage of the industrial framework is that it affords us several comparison models, each of which sheds light on developments in philanthropy. Throughout this book I compare philanthropy to education, health care, the recording industry, movie studios, and financial services. Each sector offers important lessons from history that can inform our understanding of philanthropy's future.

I acknowledge that the industrial framework does not fit philanthropy perfectly. The role of competition, industry growth rates, and the lack of universal bottom-line standards are three characteristics of philanthropy where it is difficult to make the industrial model fit. As important, the human element of philanthropy, its contributions to the social good, and its relationship to the commercial and government sectors distinguish it from purely commercial fields. Some have warned me that to focus on philanthropy as an industry is to invite regulatory and legislative scrutiny and a resultant lack of special treatment. I agree with this point, although I believe the cause and effect are misplaced. Increased scrutiny is already being focused on philanthropy, and industrial standards are already being applied. Those in the industry who believe that philanthropy deserves special consideration because of its contributions to the social fabric of our nation had best find ways to document and account for those contributions, rather than bemoan the industrial analysis thereof.

Let us look quickly at the three exceptions to the industry model—competition, growth rates, and bottom-line standards. First, although many of the charitable fund providers are driven by profit motives, most are not. The short-term effect of the commercial players' entrance into the field has been to increase competition among noncommercial entities as well. The customer—the donor—is the same, and now faces two types of options, one commercial and one noncommercial (and several hybrids are also available). The first ripple of this competitive aspect hit community foundations; it has now expanded to other nonprofit philanthropic institutions, which must continually make their case to their donors.

There are many indicators of increased competition for donors. These include the growth in advertising, an increased (at least rhetorical) interest in demonstrating outcomes or return on investment, the development of distinguishing, value-added services by entities previously focused on price-based competition, and the development of new alliances and hybrids between advisors and asset managers. The form that competition does not take, and that distinguishes philanthropy from purely commercial entities, is that it is rarely acknowledged. Philanthropic publications do not tout market share, and individual entities rarely go public with their efforts to woo donors from a competitor or to their services.

Second, the philanthropic industry does not grow and contract the way other industries do. Restaurants, shoe stores, booksellers, and drycleaners open and shut their doors according to their ability to generate a profit, but most foundations never go out of business. Some may lay off staff, they may suspend grant making, and they may move to cheaper offices, but the effect of an economic downturn is to reduce the size of the foundation; rarely does one go broke. In fact, the foundations most likely to go out of business are those that are deliberately designed to do so, they are known as "spend-down" foundations.

Endowed foundations are, of course, the minority of philanthropic actors. The amalgam of commercial and noncommercial participants is subject to a variety of factors influencing growth or decline, entry or barriers to entry in the business. Commercial firms clearly factor profitability of product into their decisions. It is possible that their charitable services, private banking, estate and trust management, and gift funds may each become so unprofitable as to cease to be offered; however, the motivation for many of these products is long-term customer relationships, and therefore profitability is not even a clear-cut demarcation for these firms.

Growth in philanthropy is greatly influenced by economic good times. The boom in personal income of the late 1990s led to more foundations being created and more donor-advised funds being opened. The bust, however, has not led to the folding of these institutions at anywhere near the same rate. Good times give birth to new philanthropic activity, and bad times slow the growth rate down. Both current regulatory structures and market forces over time have pushed philanthropic industry trends ever upward. In business terms, these factors would be analyzed as the "barriers to entry" for new products (low in philanthropy) and "exit rate" of firms (almost negligible in philanthropy).

Finally, the lack of industry-wide standards distinguishes philanthropy from other industries. This is partly a matter of the different metrics in use by different players: Commercial players track profitability and long-term customer retention, whereas nonprofit entities focus less on profit, can sell services at cost, and focus more on societal impact. The industry is thus not uniformly concerned about market share or profit ratios.

The question of standards runs deeper than just metrics, however. Because of the independent, individualistic nature of philanthropy, there have been few associated efforts to set guidelines on ethical or fiscally prudent standards of behavior. Those that exist are largely self-referential and lack any power of enforcement. The best estimate regarding the percentage of foundations that join existing associations (and must thus meet their standards) is about 10 percent of existing foundations.[23] Government regulators are significantly understaffed when it comes to proactive investigation of charitable activities, and they must rely on whistleblowers or scandal to enforce basic fiduciary standards. There are nascent efforts at reporting performance metrics and developing standards of practice for managing philanthropic assets, but these are woefully basic given the industry's century-plus of operation.[24]

Although the industrial framework is not perfect, it helps us consider the effects of foreseeable future changes on philanthropy in ways that stand stronger than mere speculation. It also allows us to bring into one picture the rapidly changing and disparate elements of firms, products, services, customers, competition, and regulation.

In using the industry lens, we must maintain our understanding of philanthropy as more than a simple subset of financial services. Rather, the remarkably consistent rate of giving and its independence from resources and needs (supply and demand) highlight the very important noncommercial characteristics of philanthropy. Philanthropy is a human endeavor, influenced by pressures as diverse as moral compasses and tax brackets. It can be at once local and global, formal and highly personal, packaged into commodities and defined by human service, guided by religion and community, and subject to regulatory guidance and influence.

THE AGE OF COMMERCIAL CHARITY

Philanthropy is similar to health care and education in terms of its development as an industry. Where once both of these services were provided mostly by the state or private charities, the twentieth century saw a rapid privatization of these services in the United States. Health care in the United States is now a multibillion-dollar enterprise with a complex mix of public services, private commercial enterprises, and public benefit clinics. Education, which is constitutionally mandated as a state responsibility, has been provided through a mix of public and private entities since the nation's founding. For the most part, whether publicly or privately sponsored, education has been offered as a not-for-profit service. Recent decades have seen the rapid rise of commercial ventures in education at all levels from preschool to graduate programs.

The trajectory in these fields has not simply been one of privatization but also that of commercialization. In health care and education, the influence of commercial entities on charitable organizations and government providers cannot be denied. And so it is in philanthropy. Once upon a time, philanthropy was an informal activity of individuals or communities. The advent of the modern foundation at the dawn of the twentieth century began the age of institutional philanthropy. Now in the twenty-first century, the rise of donor-advised funds and the advance of for-profit firms and services mark the beginning of an age of commercial charity. There is no universal equation for the best relationship between the marketplace, government, and nonprofit providers—the challenge is making the mix work.[25] As the balance of players—commercial, nonprofit, and public— shifts, the public benefit sector presents a shocking new environment for philanthropic action.[26]

How do industries with robust mixes of commercial, private nonprofit, and public sector firms develop over time? Which characteristics first bleed into the others, and which fade away in the face of competition, lower prices, newer markets, or higher-paying customers? We have many situations where governments have turned to market tools to enforce public policy, such as in the sale of pollution credits and the auctioning of broadcast frequencies.[27] There is much to learn from these examples.

Consider the pressures on local governments as devolution continues to shift responsibility for services to cities from states and the federal government. Thus cities are attempting several new management techniques and service models to balance the available financing with the needs of their communities. More and more cities make ends meet by encouraging residents "to co-produce public services, such as through recycling and neighborhood watch programs."[28] At the same time, nonprofit contracts with government have become the biggest source of revenue in some spheres, fundamentally shifting the provision of services from the public sector to the nonprofit and employing business systems for their purchase.[29]

We also have experienced decades of debate over how business practices can improve nonprofit operations. Markets, of course, rely on regulatory structure and publicly provided infrastructure. What can we expect to see as philanthropy continues on this developmental course from a cottage industry to a complex system of public and private, commercial and public benefit corporations?

The philanthropic industry includes both the "kitchen table family foundation" and the multibillion-dollar organization with hundreds of professional staff. Both are in the same business, just as the local bookstore is in the same line of work as Amazon.com. Readers are also free to go to their public library to pick up the latest fiction bestsellers. All three providers— e-commerce monster Amazon, small corner bookshops, and libraries—fit a niche in the system. The book industry also relies on publishers, editors, authors, magazine reviewers, distributors, and lecture series. As we consider the changing philanthropic marketplace, we will find ourselves looking not only at the individual firms, but also at the infrastructure that supports them, the secondary and tertiary vendors that sell to philanthropy, and the niches and networks that separate and bind them all together.

Philanthropy is a distinctive industry, set apart from others by its social mission and its elementally human focus. While the financial resources are only one element of the entire philanthropic equation and its final pursuit of public good, the changes surrounding the distribution and management of these assets can best be seen through an industrial lens. Efforts to improve the system as a whole will benefit from a deep analysis of the front end inputs in the system. The experiences of other industries will be instructive in imagining the future. The financial products and services of philanthropy are akin to other industries in that they are subject to both market pressures and regulatory structures.

It is these very products and services—the financial management tools and advisory services for philanthropic asset management—that are the core of new philanthropic capital markets. Just as commercial entities have choices in the types of financial backing they seek, so should nonprofit and civic groups be able to take advantage of a wide variety of capital products.

Donors, whose assets are the engine for these products and services, need to have clear, comparable choices, measures for success, and a conceptual and practical means of assessing the quality of their philanthropic asset allocations. We cannot move philanthropy forward without deliberately designing the system for providing financial resources.

What the Future Could Look Like

Imagine picking up a newspaper and reading the headline, "Tuberculosis Eliminated around the Globe." As you read on, you learn about the hundreds of thousands of lives saved, the anticipated increase in educational and economic development in countries once devastated by the disease, and the decrease in emergency room care costs in U.S. cities. The final strides in eliminating the disease were made by widespread adoption of low-cost medicines, derived from traditional tropical herbal remedies. The work had been ongoing for decades and had met its short-term goal in 2005 of curing 85 percent of identified cases through the joint work of the World Health Organization and the World Bank through the Global Plan to stop tuberculosis.

The article goes on to explain the two key steps in moving from 85 percent to 100 percent disease eradication. The first step was the development of a global regulatory structure to provide oversight of the $60 billion global market for traditional therapies. A coalition of nongovernmental organizations from across the world, funded by significant private support, led the efforts on regulation. The second key act was the successful integration of data on treatment options and outcomes, drawing from both traditional and modern medical approaches, which allowed identification of the most successful, lowest-cost therapeutic strategies. This data exchange involved public health systems, private clinicians, and a mix of financing structures from grants to contracts to licensing deals. Both of these final actions received financial and communications support from an international coalition of private philanthropic resources dedicated to making both modern and traditional medicines safe and inexpensive.[1]

This illustration is intended to focus our attention on what is possible. Imagine a philanthropic system that really leveraged financial investments toward meaningful goals. Imagine that individual philanthropists could make contributions to the issues and organizations they cared about. They would be confident that their gifts were being used appropriately and in conjunction with other resources to efficiently achieve certain goals. Imagine that research on philanthropic activity, investment opportunities, and successes and failures was widely available to inform decision making. Imagine that the billions of small pockets of charitable resources that now trickle through the system could be aggregated into several significant streams as needed and desired. And imagine that the highly personal nature of philanthropic action and decision making remained a defining characteristic of the work and was effectively promoted as a means of encouraging and increasing individuals' generosity.

This is the picture of an evolved philanthropic industry. This would be an industry that capitalizes on the strengths of its current diversity while providing enough structure, support, and feedback to better inform decisions, to document achievements, and to direct resources to the most promising points of leverage. Building such a system will involve each of the players that currently define the industry: philanthropic institutions and individuals, regulators, vendors, nonprofit organizations, and public agencies. It will also involve a joint vision of the improved whole and the understanding that systems evolve slowly and sporadically and that change may come from unexpected sources. The contributions of the current actors will be important, as will the unpredictable effects of actors yet to participate or exist.

The headline in the illustration is dramatically different from those appearing in American newspapers in the first years of the twenty-first century. We have a long way to go before we see such announcements, and at this particular point such good news seems very far off. Rather, the present moment is one of considerable turmoil in philanthropy. In only a two-month period in 2003, headlines across the country instead highlighted significantly less positive characteristics of philanthropy:

> "Nonprofit admits spending charities' money: Donation processor's accounting problems at least 2 years old," San Francisco *Chronicle*, June 5, 2003
>
> "Some foundations spend lavishly on own board members," Baltimore *Sun*, May 13, 2003
>
> "Justices rule charity may be charged with fraud," *The New York Times*, May 6, 2003
>
> "IRS unable to monitor non-profit groups" San Jose *Mercury News*, April 27, 2003

This period of media attention to governance lapses, executive excess, and fraud in philanthropy, as well as the first significant new economy business scandal involving donors' gifts, is happening simultaneously with Capitol Hill hearings on foundation practice and calls for closer legal review of charitable activities in New York, California, and by the Federal Trade Commission. It also follows closely on the heels of the outpouring of giving in the immediate aftermath of the September 2001 terrorist attacks, probably the nation's largest single and fastest charitable response. The confluence of these events is neither coincidental nor conspiratorial, but these times are likely to be a watershed in the workings of the industry. We need not only be hopeful that the turn will be for the better—whether that be defined as greater charitable largesse, more effective giving, or more diverse and accessible philanthropy—but we can also look to history to bolster this hope. The last major revision of the tax laws and period of profound public awareness of philanthropy occurred in 1969 and is an appropriate point from which to date many of the industry's current characteristics.

WHY BOTHER?

Building something new requires upsetting the status quo, and therefore, by definition, will have its detractors. Existing foundations and philanthropists and commercial vendors may not see any immediate advantage in taking on such a challenge. Given this attitude, we can anticipate that the changes will happen in certain nodes of the industry first and may be implemented in pursuit of shorter-term goals (e.g., profit, customer reten-tion) instead of the long-term vision of a new industry structure. At the same time, there are clear and compelling reasons for current actors to in-volve themselves in the work of defining and influencing the direction of the industry changes:

- *Change is certain.* Current industry actors may think they are immune from most external pressures. To a certain degree, some of them are. For example, established endowed foundations are unlikely to go out of business or feel a significant amount of competitive pressure from other financial products. In a philanthropic market cluttered with op-tions, foundations are already eclipsed by donor-advised funds in terms of numbers, and might logically also fall behind in terms of as-sets under management. All other players in the philanthropic market feel the competitive pressures at a greater degree than do private foundations, and so are actively attempting change and differentiation. Philanthropic practice, benefits, and structures will not stay static sim-ply by wishing it so. Foundations face regulatory proposals focused on requiring greater spending, more accountability, and fewer small in-dependent entities. Changes in federal tax law may herald the end of new foundation creation as early as 2010, if estate taxes are not re-implemented. As Tom Lloyd wrote in the early 1990s about the changing interactions between philanthropy and the commercial sec-tor in Great Britain, "There is no going back to the time when com-panies were companies and charities were charities and never the twain shall meet."[2]

- *Market forces will begin to shift from those present in an emerging industry (e.g., price competition, first-tier product differentiation) to those of a mature industry (e.g., differentiating value-added services).* Market forces will begin to drive the development of outcome measures, indicators of effectiveness, research, and aggregation. Typical industries demon-strate their maturation by the increase in numbers of institutions that serve them. This increase signals that the industry or profession has become more complex, typically less transparent, and in need of greater internal management resources.[3]

- *Left undirected, the current forces on the industry push more strongly in the di-rection of fragmentation than in the direction of aggregation.* Further fragmentation of resources reduces the chance that any individual actor will accomplish its goals, limits the overall impact of the industry, and increases the regulatory threats as philanthropy ceases to demonstrate a return on the public tax exemption that underlies the entire industry. As the sector ceases to be purely nonprofit, the question arises: Should the entity receive tax preferences or the public benefit it produces?[4]

- *Community needs and opportunities will continue to demand more effective application of financial, human, technological, and intellectual resources.* If philanthropic entities fail to demonstrate their cumulative contributions to communities, states, nations, and global issues, the regulatory infrastructure that supports the continued enjoyment and expansion of philanthropic privilege will come under pressure from community groups as well as regulators and legislators looking for resources.

GETTING THERE

Such accomplishments as the eradication of major diseases and the restructuring of philanthropy are possible in our lifetimes. The goal of a new philanthropic system should be to demonstratively accelerate the effective application of private resources to achieve public good. This would represent both a radical advancement on the current system and nothing more than an enhanced version of the current structures. The shift is subtle, yet significant.

This goal of accelerating effective application of resources shifts our attention from individual philanthropic players to the connections between them. It requires, in other words, measuring the effectiveness of the industry of philanthropy, not just individual entities. It requires a focus on the interactions, connections, and feedback loops that operate (or should operate) among the disparate actors in the system.

To make these changes happen, we will need to work on two critical levels of the system: the organizational and the industrial. Organizational change within foundations happens in fits and starts. Only recently have shared efforts at organizational change—such as the attempt to develop common performance indicators—really been started.[5] Two other critical sources of organizational-level change are the market and the regulatory structure. For example, the advent of commercial donor-advised funds is a market-driven phenomenon. The regular reporting of grant and financial activity by philanthropic institutions is a response to regulation.

To work at the industrial level is to reconsider and strengthen the systems that currently connect philanthropic organizations. These connections—manifested almost exclusively through voluntary membership associations—have multiplied in number in parallel with the growth in philanthropic institutions. From the formation of the Council on Foundations in the late 1940s to the creation of the most recent lunch network at a regional association, these groups have emerged in all parts of the country and internationally. Several of them have established offices, staffs, independent status, and permanent roles on the landscape. Many of them are intended to be informal, small, and flexible.

We know surprisingly little about these connective organizations, which are generally seen as the infrastructure of philanthropy. Even a complete count is hard to come by, although the most reliable available estimates are between 350 to 400 U.S. associations of grant makers.[6] Although this might imply a best-case ratio of 1:150 (associations to foundations), there is good reason to believe that these 400 or so associations actually represent no more than 10 percent of all foundations.[7] The connections, therefore, are redundant for some institutions and completely absent for others.

What do these infrastructure organizations do? What should they do? What parts of the industry are well supported and what portions are left hanging? *Infrastructure*, in its most literal meaning, in the words of the American Foundation for Civil Engineers, is the result of several deliberate choices and intersects with public and private life on many levels.[8] In contrast, infrastructure in philanthropy has arisen by default rather than by design, extends only a short distance into the industry, and is not particularly well connected to public systems. The metaphor of several private, unpaved roads leading to homes "off the grid" is much more apt than, for example, the interstate highway system.

ASSEMBLY REQUIRED

If we intend to make philanthropy a stronger, more vital participant in social health and problem solving, the most efficient places to focus are on those elements of the industry that broadly affect many individual players. Simply put, the industry is too dispersed and deliberately isolated to effect much influence on it by moving from organization to organization. As we have already begun to argue, there are three relatively direct routes to the tens of thousands of philanthropic institutions: markets, regulation, and infrastructure. We start with a focus on the infrastructure because it is most subject to design and it, in turn, will be in a position to influence markets and regulation.[9]

IMAGINE THIS

Imagine buying a car in the following marketplace: There are sales representatives everywhere; some do lots of advertising while others do none. Some sell bikes, bus passes, and plane tickets in addition to cars, and promise to be the one-stop, low-cost source for all of your transportation needs. Furthermore, in this marketplace there are no independent reviews of cars, no magazines for car enthusiasts, no window stickers that list gas mileage, maintenance costs, and dealer costs, and no such thing as *Consumer Reports* or *The Blue Book*. In such a marketplace, each car buyer would need to go door-to-door, testing every model, haggling over price, and hoping that the promises made about reliability and safety prove to be correct. Or they might even decide to build a new mode of transportation.

As absurd and chaotic as this scenario sounds, it is a telling metaphor for today's philanthropic industry. Every year individuals and institutions donate billions of dollars, yet there is no industry standard for comparing a donor-advised fund to a private foundation. The purveyors of philanthropy products range from large universities to small churches, from private banks to community endowments, from nonprofits to commercial financial service firms. Some do a great deal of advertising, but others do none. There is no annual news coverage of the best and worst returns, no independent web portal providing Blue Book–type analysis of expenses or long-term performance, and the only publicly available trend data are drawn from self-reported surveys of fewer than 20 percent of the industry players.

Individual donors fly blind. The lack of credible, independent analysis of philanthropic trends, social sector revenue streams, and comparative costs and returns will keep some potential givers out of the market. The limited use of industry-wide information sharing limits the return on existing research, hampers efforts to communicate impact, and deters potential investors. Some people get scammed and others are asked to make investments in known failures.

The lack of infrastructure limits the industry's ability to claim results, reliability, or credibility. Infrastructure and independent players that provide industry information are critical to the vibrancy, credibility, and visibility of an industry. The infrastructure supports that an industry builds for itself are the bulwarks of defense against regulatory challenges. They also provide support and opportunity as markets change.

To better understand the composition and roles of an industry infrastructure, it helps to take a look at a mature industry, such as financial services. The financial services industry, which consists of brokerages, banks, mutual fund operators, money managers, investment firms, and the like, rely on tangential vendors such as Bloomberg, Dow Jones, Moody's, and Standard & Poor's to provide independent data, monitoring, and research (see Exhibit 2.1). Financial service firms provide basic "tear sheets" on various commerce sectors for free. Various banking and securities associations weigh in on public policy on behalf of their members, Securities and Exchange Commission (SEC) regulators set and monitor professional standards, and independent analysts at FirstCall, for instance, provide research.

Where are these players in philanthropy? Some organizations have been around for decades, such as the Council on Foundations, Foundation Center, National Center for Responsive Philanthropy, and Independent Sector. These established organizations (and the hundreds like them) are voluntary membership organizations. They rely on member support and meet the shared needs of those members in terms of publications, conferences, representation to national legislators, and industry statistical tracking. These types of organizations, by virtue of their membership structure, are in no position to be critical, independent sources of information regarding the industry or representing it to newcomers.

Such independence is only now emerging in the form of entrepreneurial startups, focused on providing some independent analysis of the industry. These organizations, ranging from GuideStar to Philanthropix Partners, are in their infancy and represent a range of independence and focus. GuideStar, for example, is heavily funded by foundations and focuses on making public information about nonprofits more accessible. Philanthropix Partners, Charity Navigator, and others are attempting to develop nonprofit

EXHIBIT 2.1	COMPARING INDUSTRY INFRA-STRUCTURE: FINANCIAL SERVICES AND PHILANTHROPY-2003		
Industry Elements	**Financial Services**	**Philanthropy**	**Gaps**
Firms	Charles Schwab, Goldman Sachs, J.P. Morgan Chase	Community foundations, nonprofits, financial service firms, individuals	
Research organizations, data sources	National Bureau of Economic Research, Dept. of Labor, Bloomberg Inc.	Foundation Center, AAFRC, Indiana U, GuideStar	Comparative trend data hard to find; research not targeted to individuals
Industry associations/ government relations	American Bankers Association, Securities Industry Association, corporate PACs	Council on Foundations, Independent Sector, Association of Small Foundations	State-level advocacy groups
Regulatory bodies	SEC, Treasury Department	IRS, State Attorneys General	State-level industry groups
Media/press	*Wall Street Journal, Barrons,* trade journals	*Foundation News & Commentary, Chronicle of Philanthropy*	No regular independent, analytic, or critical media
Professional training track exists	MBA programs	—	No professional
Credentialing/ monitoring	Broker licensing	—	No credentialing exists. IRS monitors firms
Independent analysts, information brokers	Hoovers, Datamonitor, FirstCall	—	Some foundations research the industry; no public independent analysis
Rating organizations/ metrics	Morningstar, Dow Jones, Standard & Poor's, Moody's	BBB, GuideStar, Charity Navigator, Philanthropix Partners	No industry standard metrics. Some operating standards in subsectors such as community foundations

rating systems. The market for independent ratings goes hand-in-glove with the increased attention donors are paying to their gifts, both before and after they make them.

This trend can be seen in—among other things—the changes underway regarding legal standing to sue nonprofits. As noted in the *New York Times* recently, "Traditionally, only attorneys general have had standing to hold charities to account in court, but the number of nonprofit organizations has exploded at the same time states have slashed budgets for charity oversight, which was never generous."[10] The last few years have seen donors sue nonprofits, donors sue community foundations, community foundations sue investment banks, trusts sue universities, and residents sue private foundations.[11] If such an expansion of legal standing occurs, we can expect to see legal challenges to everything from a foundation's investment policy to its grant-making decisions. Imagine the lawsuits that could result if the public seeks redress for charitable assets lost by foundation investment managers in 2002!

A new infrastructure will develop not only in response to perceived (or real) threats but also to seize an opportunity. The same opportunity to influence and manage a lot of money that lured commercial firms into philanthropy will catalyze more entrepreneurial efforts to be the *Morningstar*, *Gartner Group*, or *Barron's* of philanthropy. In a 2003 study for the World Economic Forum, the analysts of several new performance measurement efforts in philanthropy noted the need for these independent, entrepreneurial (i.e., semi to completely commercial) players in philanthropy because they are uniquely positioned to provide independent, critical analysis.[12]

To move philanthropy from its cottage industry stage to a level where it can effectively deploy its significant resources, mechanisms that parallel those in other industries need to be deliberately created. The quick comparison in Exhibit 2.1 shows a dearth of independent analysis, little professional credentialing, few strong connections between the industry and the public sector, a nascent media that offers little in terms of critique, and few comparative data sources for outsiders.

New players are emerging to fill those gaps in the infrastructure. In doing so, they will be in a position to promote new regulation, support new product development, and push for standards. Existing entities can either work with these forces from the beginning or respond to them later.

Not Just Newer, But Better

A new industry infrastructure should connect foundations, donor-advised funds, estates, financial service firms, and individual philanthropists. Its products and services should be industry-wide research briefs, independent analysis, and industry standards for making comparisons and decisions. By redesigning and rebuilding the infrastructure, we will arrive at a more accessible, effective, accountable, and measurable philanthropic economy that can account for its cumulative impact and enable individual firms to assess their contributions.

The forecast is for hundreds of billions, if not trillions, of philanthropic dollars to be dropped into our industry, but given the current scattered nature of our efforts, the chances of effectively channeling these resources to substantial public good is like trying to direct the floods of the Nile River by building sand castles along its banks. Only by building better means of coordinating information, sharing resources, and presenting independent analyses to philanthropists and the public can philanthropy expect to be a participant in social policy and change.

CHAPTER 3

The Forces of Change

George Orwell was writing fiction when he sat down in England in the late 1940s to pen his famous thriller, *1984*. But he was tapping into an American obsession with the future. From anthropologists to sociologists to business leaders and homemakers, the questions of what tomorrow will bring are big draws in the United States. America has a mindset of progress and the future, and the publishing industry thrives on providing readers with *Megatrends, Landmarks of Tomorrow,* and *2081*.[1] Alvin Toffler coined the term *future shock* to capture the "disease" of disorientation and stress he believed Americans in the 1970s to be suffering from because of the rapid pace of change. As he noted then, "Future shock is no longer a distantly potential danger, but a real sickness from which increasingly large numbers already suffer. This psycho-biological condition can be described in medical and psychiatric terms. It is the disease of change."[2] Although Toffler's crisis-toned language might speak as much to the tendency to "make medical conditions out of molehills," his book was a best-seller and is still a classic. Of course, if he was correct in 1970, imagine how many of us are ill with future shock today?

Those who claim to predict the future are dismissed as charlatans. Those who can develop powerful, data-driven, graphic options about potential directions are highly valued professionals. Few futurists are ever called to account for their projections. Regardless of the accuracy of their analyses, the value of future prospecting is in providing decision makers today with viable avenues for consideration.[3]

This chapter focuses on major drivers of change on the philanthropy industry. It discusses several key trends and analyzes their potential influence on philanthropy within a three tier framework from the societal to the industrial to the organizational. The trends are organized from the most

external—the society level trends—to the most internal—organizational
level shifts. All three levels are important in understanding how philanthropy is likely to change over the next decades. For example, we will see
that the demographic shifts in the population as a whole creates important
new market opportunities for philanthropic firms such as community foundations and financial service firms. The aging of the population creates new
opportunities for retirement and estate planners, is leading to the creation
of many new philanthropic entities, and is causing several types of organizations to re-examine their core business practices to serve this market.

Of course, these external pressures also influence philanthropy by changing the nature of community needs and opportunities. Aging residents put
different stresses on public systems than do populations of young families.
Global markets inspire a broader awareness of the human condition and
may lead to greater interest in transnational problem solving. The presentation of these forces of change is deliberately ordered so that our examination of philanthropic industry and organizational change cannot be taken
out of the context of these larger social issues. These levels of change are
understood as connected, concentric spheres, as shown in Exhibit 3.1.

EXHIBIT 3.1   **THE LEVELS AND FORCES OF
CHANGE ON PHILANTHROPY**

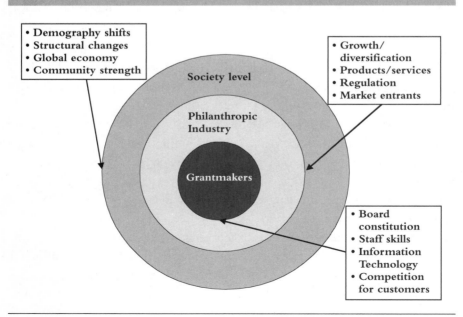

- Demography shifts
- Structural changes
- Global economy
- Community strength

Society level

- Growth/
  diversification
- Products/services
- Regulation
- Market entrants

Philanthropic
Industry

Grantmakers

- Board
  constitution
- Staff skills
- Information
  Technology
- Competition
  for customers

CHANGE DRIVERS ON SOCIETY AS A WHOLE[4]

At the outermost level—the level of society changes—the significant forces on philanthropy are many. Given the diversity of philanthropic action, in fact, it would be easier to assume philanthropic reactivity to all major social, economic, and political trends than to try to narrow the field to just a few. To determine the most influential forces on philanthropy, I focus on a meta-analysis of future studies across many industries and deep analysis of philanthropy in particular.[5]

The following three forces—demographics, new ways of working, and globalization and its backlash—are by no means the only sources of external pressure on philanthropy; however, the changes they represent are so significant at so many levels that they simply cannot be ignored. In addition to these three, a fourth contextual shift that I describe as an increase in community and environmental efforts at sustainability, is discussed in this section. It is important to note that even as these categories of change are distinct, the degree and direction of their influence comes from the interrelated nature of change in general and the components of these forces specifically.

DEMOGRAPHIC TRENDS

The U.S. population is becoming increasingly diverse. The 1990s saw the combined populations of African Americans, Native Americans, Asians, Pacific Islanders, and Hispanics/Latinos grow 13 times faster than the rate of the non-Hispanic white population.[6] The last three decades of the twentieth century also saw a huge increase in the number of foreign-born American residents, growing from less than 10 million to more than 24 million people between 1970 and 1998. About one-third of the foreign-born population has arrived in the United States since 1990.[7] This diversity is not evenly dispersed throughout the country. Three states have non-Hispanic white populations of less than 50 percent, and three states count this group as more than 95 percent of their population.[8]

In addition to racial and ethnic diversity, religious pluralism is also increasing. The largest categories of religious affiliation in the United States are Christianity, secular/nondenominational, and Judaism; however, between 1990 and 2001, the numbers of Americans surveyed who identified themselves as Islamic, Buddhist, and Hindu grew by 109 percent, 170 percent, and 237 percent, respectively. During this same time period, the number of people identifying themselves as Christian grew by 5 percent and the number identifying themselves as Jewish dropped by 10 percent.[9] In addition to these shifts occurring in established religions, the rate of creation of new religious groups continues unabated. Some scholars speculate that the twenty-first century will be one of great religious upheaval.[10]

The people of the western world are also getting older. People are living longer and, in almost all developed countries, the birth rate is below replacement level.[11] In the United States and Europe, the elderly (older than 65) represent 13 and 15 percent of the populations, respectively, while the global average is just 7 percent.[12] As Martha Farnsworth Riche, lead designer of the 2000 U.S. Census, writes:

> The U.S. population is in the midst of a historic shift from a population dominated by the young to one in which there are roughly equal numbers at every age except the oldest old. . . . Census 2000 found a significant increase in the nation's median age, from 32.9 in 1990 to 35.3 in 2000. This is the oldest Americans have ever been, and the country will not be this young ever again.[13]

The aging of the baby boomers and increasing life expectancy in the United States has led to predictions of a doubling of the population older than 65 years of age between 2000 and 2025.[14] Worldwide, the number of people older than 60 is expected to triple between 2000 and 2050.[15] At the same time, a youth bulge is occurring in several of the poorest countries of the world, with burgeoning populations of those younger than 30 in parts of the Middle East, Africa, and Asia.[16] Overall, however, the "graying of the globe" is a major force for societies and economic systems, as demographers estimate there will be more people older than age 60 than children younger than age 15 by the year 2050.[17]

Not only is the population changing, it refuses to stand still. Americans continue to migrate to cities and suburbs, draining resources from rural areas.[18] Immigrants to the country also tend toward the cities, with 10 metropolitan areas attracting the majority of all newcomers in the last decade.[19] Younger people are increasingly mobile, following employment opportunities across the country, not just across town. Although elderly people tend to be less transient, a recent boom in retirement locales in the American south and west indicate that this population may be about to experience a period of large migration.[20]

These changes in the racial, ethnic, religious, and age character of the nation are of tremendous importance to philanthropy. The migration data are already evident in rural areas that consider themselves effectively philanthropically barren. Philanthropic resources are as inequitably distributed as populations and income in general. These demographic factors will ripple throughout our society in terms of social security costs and resources, the role and costs of medical care, migratory patterns, life stages for individuals, business opportunities such as long-term care services and insurance, cultural components of schooling and health care, new communities of vibrant wealth creation, voting patterns, volunteer populations, and faith-based community activities. It is hard to underestimate the many ways our society will change as we live in increasingly diverse and densely populated regions on the coasts, white and underpopulated "ghost towns" in the heartland, and well into our seventies and beyond (for those who can afford the ever-rising costs of health care).

IMAGINE THIS

Potential implications of these demographic changes:

As individuals live longer, they work longer. They cannot afford to retire, nor can they afford individual health care plans. This makes employment and promotion more difficult for younger people. Those who do "age out" of the workforce begin to collect their social security payments, dramatically shifting the balance from those paying into the system to those drawing from it. Well-organized elderly voters continue to go to the polls in far greater numbers than younger, working citizens, therefore shaping election results. This trend shows up in city after city as public resources flow toward services for the elderly and away from schools and preventive programs. In all states except California, school bond issues are repeatedly rejected at the polls. In California, the increasingly dominant Hispanic and Asian American communities come to prominence, winning election to all statewide offices from insurance commissioner to the U.S. Senate.

More adults return to their roles as caretakers, this time for their parents instead of their children. This alters their retirement plans and leads to pockets of mixed-generation communities in need of part-time jobs, social services, and safe, clean, outdoor recreational space. The population of the nation's heartland continues to decline as coastal areas grow increasingly dense, raising anew questions about the electoral college system and the balance of power in the bicameral national legislature.

New financial products are introduced to replace payroll-related retirement investing, and the mega-bank-brokerage companies that emerged after the repeal of the Glass-Steagall Act in 1998 continue to compete for domination of the "wallet share" of their clients. To capture more and more of this wallet, these firms offer a dizzying array of asset management and advising services, including several tiers of allied services with philanthropic experts. Finally, the once-coveted 18- to 34-year-old market that dominated mass culture for decades is passed over for the discretionary spending of the 49+ viewer, and television, news magazines, local cultural offerings, advertising budgets, and product development funds shift accordingly. A boom in age-discrimination lawsuits results in multimillion-dollar settlements against several major corporations, bringing to mind the tobacco wars of the 1990s.

Although all of the preceding vignette may not occur in the next two generations, each element of this situation is plausible. Every community will experience its own particular mix of ethnic groups and ages, but the general impact of the two changes moving together is a shift in the locus of political power. As two scholars of state and local government recently noted:

> Census 2000 data reveal a new set of patterns, featuring a new cast of demographic actors. States and regions have begun to steal the show from cities, suburbs, and countryside. The trend is toward declining heterogeneity across the "borders" of cities, suburbs and their environs and, consequently, toward greater demographic homogeneity within states. . . . Not only does each group of states have its own ethnic mix, but their different sources of growth—immigration, domestic migration and aging-in-place—are giving each group of states its own age structure. . . . While each state's demographic trajectory is unique . . . across the nation, many demographic trends that were once important mainly to city planners and politicians are becoming genuinely statewide issues.[21]

These changes have deep implications for philanthropy. Private giving will need new maps of the public sector. Those interested in youth issues may find it harder to leverage public funds. Donors interested in helping the elderly may find their strategies adopted by the public sector more readily. Philanthropists will need to learn how to work with new vendors of long-term care services and radically altered tax structures. Essentially every element of traditional American institutional philanthropy—its demographic profile, its position as an activity of only the wealthy, the religious ethics and values that underpin much of the work—is in flux.[22]

The age and race of the American and global populations are rapidly changing. For philanthropy, an aging population puts new pressures on public systems, and it creates new opportunities for wealth transfer. The increases in and changing population centers of communities of color are another key demographic change with broad implications for philanthropy.

NEW STRUCTURES FOR WORKING

Although the myth of the new economy has finally been dispelled, there are several lingering offshoots of the boom-boom 1990s that will have long-lasting impact on how we work. For example, the rise of networked organizations and temporal alliances changes where and by whom work is done. As more people stay in the workforce longer, and with many more career changes per individual, we have important new expectations about retirement, work, and commitment. Philanthropy is also changing as a result of new public-private partnerships. There are many catalysts for these partnerships but the devolution of public budgets and decision making from the federal to the local level is a major reason for their growing popularity.

The workplace of the twenty-first century has some notable new characteristics. These include the rise of knowledge workers and a move away from industrial work. Workers now expect several major career changes in a lifetime. Companies and the government have made significant changes in pension laws and retirement benefits. Many people will work well past age 65, and the fastest growing group in the workforce in 2003 was workers older than age 75.[23] Workers can anticipate needing to learn and use new technological tools on the job every few years.

Even as the shift from an industrial to an information economy becomes the common experience, the analytic tools to value these structures and services, and the changes they may require in fiscal, monetary, and social policies, are still unfolding.

IMAGINE THIS

Noting the success of antiwar protestors in organizing through the Internet, several foundations seek to engage these leaders to teach the local nonprofits similar organizing skills. Although several of the protest leaders were profiled in the news during the 2003 U.S. war on Iraq, by 2005 when the foundations are thinking about this work, these antiwar organizations no longer exist. Nonprofit leaders in the community are struggling with turnover, as they always have, but this time the problem has a new twist: Young people won't take the jobs because the pay is too low and none of the benefits they care about are offered. At the same time, the higher-paid senior staff won't retire, at least in part because of their reliance on health care benefits provided only through the workplace. Meanwhile, middle managers can only be counted on to stay in a position for three to four years, before cycling back into the commercial or government sectors from whence they came. The benefit of this change is the ease in finding public and private partners because in any given community the "six degrees of separation" rule means some local public official or private sector president worked in the nonprofit world within the last decade. On the downside, the transience of people and organizations makes it harder for the community to provide reliable social services, a role that nonprofits now fill almost exclusively as contractors to the city agencies. Lacking any working capital to invest in knowledge management practices, each employee who walks out the door takes with her all that she knows about partnerships, local residents, and successful strategies. Several funding agencies—public and private—begin to invest in issue-specific temporary alliances only and end all organizational support.

Some of the predictions about the new workplace point to a growth in networks as a way of working.[24] Others see the demise of corporations as we know them.[25] Still others see rapid growth in temporal alliances between freelance individuals to produce goods or provide services.[26] All of the forecasters agree that the expectations of the workplace are changing, the length of time people will work is lengthening while their tenure in any one job is shrinking, and all of these changes are linked to the global markets and the pressures for efficiency in the workplace. The changes, in turn, are likely to influence individuals' mobility, commitment to community, and expectations for personal wealth management.

GLOBALIZATION AND ITS BACKLASH

This section looks at several contributing elements of globalization and the move to counter it. Changes in job locations, expectations about time and space, and our understanding of the interrelationships among commerce, politics, culture, and stability are all part of these forces. In addition, we look at the role of antiglobalization as a social movement and the changing roles of international politics and transnational organizations such as the United Nations, the World Bank, and the World Trade Organization and some new understandings of the role and potential of international aid.

The era of globalization has been upon us for most of the last decade. Marked by the rapid movement of capital around the globe, shifts in labor markets, and the rising power of international corporations, there have been important shifts in regional and national politics. The U.S.-led war on terrorism has already led to international political alliances both quickly created and quickly rendered asunder. The long-term effect on the United Nations and international cooperation of the 2003 U.S.-led invasion of Iraq will not be seen for several decades, but the sense that a new world order was upon us became prevalent almost immediately following the declaration of the doctrine of preemptive action.

The antiglobalization movement has gained steam among certain populations, particularly the university bound or educated. Both nonviolent activists and violent protestors continue to draw attention to the power of quasi-governmental entities such as the World Trade Organization and the International Monetary Fund and to raise questions about the destabilizing effects of international investment and the escalating gap between rich and poor.[27] As college students in the 1960s came together to protest the Vietnam War and to fight for domestic civil rights, today's campuses are marked by efforts to divest from international diamond mines and tobacco companies and to protest the increased power of American multinational corporations. The role of American youth in these movements is important to consider insofar as they may shape the way this next generation of organizational leaders views the world and thinks about problem solving.

Young adults are not the only ones concerned about the effects of global economic and political action. Peter Drucker warned of a new international order several decades ago.[28] Others who bear direct responsibility have called into question the efficacy of World Bank loans and World Trade Organization policies. From treasury secretaries to United Nations' leaders, there are frequent calls to demonstrate the positive impact of the actions taken by these "nationless" decision-making bodies on the poor and disenfranchised they intend to assist.

Global entrepreneur and philanthropist George Soros has written of the need to balance the power of the markets and the potential of global trade with strong, vibrant social and public systems. From Soros's perspective, not only are markets inappropriate mechanisms for taking care of social and collective objectives, but the key challenges that lie ahead will also rely on new joint efforts between states, markets, and philanthropic actors. In his words, private players, both philanthropic and corporate:

> . . . cannot be counted on to bring systemic improvement. You do need public funds for it. You do need really official intervention—because you need improvement in laws and regulations and public administration that no outsider can accomplish on his own.[29]

IMAGINE THIS

A national nonprofit organization on the Atlantic seaboard is focused on providing health services to low-income communities. Its client population is primarily recent immigrants to the United States. The communities in which the organization operates are served primarily by commercial hospitals, which contract with national health maintenance organizations and insurance companies that rely on lower-cost workers in other countries to manage call centers, process claims, and handle paperwork. The nursing shortage is acute, and services in languages other than English are severely compromised.

A new acute virus is making thousands of people ill and has been found in several of the communities where the nonprofit is active. Global air travel is blamed for the rapid spread of the disease from its source community on the other side of the globe. The nonprofit wants to develop a partnership with the hospital systems to provide translation services and cultural competency training to improve health services to non-English-speaking residents. Several months of effort are

required to maneuver the partnership through the levels of bureau-
cracy of the hospital systems, insurance companies, labor unions, and
affiliates of the nonprofit. In the interim, hundreds of people fall ill.

The increasing connectedness of places and people and work and culture
are leading to calls for new partnerships, new alliances, and new understandings of the roles that markets, states, and the independent sector play.
Individual donors and foundations will seek out ways to work together. As
the lines between sectors blur, there is renewed need to distinguish anew the
strengths, viabilities, and dependencies of each. Although not necessarily
linked to globalization, concurrent interests in corporate social responsibility mechanisms and challenges to the role of international aid organizations
extend this awareness of changing roles.[30]

ENVIRONMENTAL AND COMMUNITY SUSTAINABILITY

Partly as a response to globalization and other forces, we are now seeing a
cementing of interest in and demand for corporate responsibility, sustainable business practices, and community and environmental planning. We
can see these in both practice and attitudinal change. These forces are
changing where and how and by whom community and urban decisions
get made and the factors taken into account. At the same time, they reveal
how our decision-making systems may not be keeping up with these new
forces and the need for regional planning.

Much of the backlash against globalization is seen in the countervailing
growth of emphasis on issues of environmental and community sustainability. These are issues of great importance to young people in America,
as well as many of the new donors who have been profiled in the last
decade.[31] These attitudes and practices are fed by forces as far-ranging as
new science about biodiversity, successful work in restoring connected
ecosystems, research on global warming, advances in sustainable fuel
sources, new materials and processes that demonstrate cost savings in sustainable practices, a rebellion against multihour commutes, and the aging of
former hippies who once again seek a refuge off the grid.

These interests drive new social movements; inform a revitalized re-search and policy interest in regionalism; and inform the work and the in-tended outcomes of social entrepreneurism, socially responsible business, and hybrid commercial–nonprofit ventures.

IMAGINE THIS

Several communities clustered around a major city have seen decades of change from being bedroom suburbs for the city to hosting major corporate campuses to watching those buildings decay as they sit empty, blocking the view of the region's famous lake. Three counties, 27 cities, 22 school districts, six unincorporated areas, five major tran-sit authorities, and five major hospitals (two of which are university-affiliated) serve the area's 2 million people. Services are provided within the boundaries set by the state for public works, environmental pro-tection, employment development, and education.

After decades of boom and bust and the resulting impact on the local infrastructure, several community groups come together to work with an organization focused on protecting green space. They use the nonprofits' experience in working with public systems to plan, advo-cate for, and (after 10 years) create a new regional planning board. The decade of planning and the work itself is funded by individual donors and private foundations, working through a consortium of community foundations.

The new planning board assumes responsibility for regional public transit planning, replacing the five earlier organizations. A plan for con-necting buses, trains, highways, and the city's subway system is de-veloped. Community investment funds are focused on neighborhoods with transit intersections, and the buses and light rail systems are converted to fuel cell energy. Local planners and architects work with university leaders to design mixed-use, medium-density housing and commercial hubs at these transit points. A philanthropic investment in hybrid car engines pays off, and the community chooses to invest in retrofitting two key highways into special transit lanes for a pilot test of these new vehicles.

Significant improvements result from the joint actions. The overall stock of affordable housing increases by 15 percent in 15 years, and the community discovers that it can save a fortune on school buses because more children are walking to school. The abandoned corpo-rate campus that dominates the waterfront is demolished, and a new recreational area is opened, purchased with both private donations and public easements, and supported by a long-term plan that includes low usage fees, educational programming, and rent from the university as well as small businesses.

Philanthropy needs to find new ways to partner on such issues as environmental fragility, sustainable energy, transportation, housing, and communities. As the sustainability movement grows, private donors will need to meet new expectations about financial investment, institution building, and markets for human, financial, and intellectual capital. Coupled with the pervasive reach of new technologies, the focus on sustainability may catalyze creative new approaches to philanthropic problem solving.

Change Drivers on the Industry

> *True evolution is a shift in emphasis. One thing atrophies whilst another hypertrophies.*[32]

The drivers of change at the society level are critical to how we frame problems and solutions. Although the challenges facing young people may dominate our public policy at one point in time, the needs of our elderly may move to the forefront at others. Global trends influence the allocation of resources, the visibility of certain problems, and the interconnectedness of issues. Change is usually slow and subtle, such as intergenerational migration or birth patterns. Occasionally it is rapid and traumatic, as in times of war or rebuilding. At the global level, tracking and identifying trends is complicated and overwhelming, yet important to developing coherent and meaningful strategies and interventions.

At the industry level, change is much more instrumental. Industries in general, and philanthropy in particular, consist of independent firms with substitutable products or services. Markets and regulation influence industries directly and immediately. They rely on information exchange, operate both competitively and in alliance, and generally include several large and dominant signaling players and dozens, hundreds, or thousands of smaller-scale participants.

In philanthropy, firms run the gamut from almost-reclusive family foundations making gifts from a checkbook at meetings around the kitchen table to magnificently housed operations with a hundred professional staff members, identifiable radio tag lines, prominent public figures on the board, and glossy publications. Some are wholly owned nonprofit subsidiaries of commercial banks and mutual fund companies. Each firm sells its donor customer a financial product for managing tax-exempt giving. The qualities of each product determine its appeal to different kinds of customers, and much of the product differentiation happens around such qualities as degree of anonymity, donor control, percentage of tax deductibility, and access to independent research. Foundations rarely think of themselves in this way, but they can clearly be seen as another product in the financial services marketplace.

Even with the level of variability among firms and products, the different players in philanthropy are subject to several common drivers of change. These forces will be felt independently and as a whole. The first driver is the growth of the sector caused by the creation of new wealth, the much-touted intergenerational transfer of wealth, and creation of grant-making foundations as nonprofit organizations increasingly convert to commercial status.[33] If the rate of growth experienced in the late 1990s continued the foundation sector would double in the next decade. That boom period will probably not repeat itself, but even at the more typical 2 to 3 percent annual growth in grant-making organizations and the increase in assets under management, the size of the industry has become a force unto itself.

The second key force at the industry level is the remarkable availability of new tools and services to facilitate philanthropy, including the advent of *e-philanthropy* and the explosion of charitable management by financial services firms. New products and services will continue to develop, ranging from standardized advisory reports to new financial vehicles crafted to take advantage of changing tax laws and demographics. We will continue to see niche products and services emerge. For example, there are now several products for online grants managements, new low-cost tools that claim to help funders measure social impact, and turnkey solutions that allow mutual fund companies to create and administer private foundations for their clients in less time and at lower costs than ever before possible.

The third force is the regulatory structures that shape philanthropy. Under scrutiny in several areas, the framework that defines philanthropic structures and practices is likely to change significantly in the next decade. Pressure can now be seen on the legislative front (the repeal of the estate tax), from the regulators (Internal Revenue Service audits and state attorneys general review), and from the courts (donors suing foundations for misuse of funds).

Changes in public funding practices, primarily the devolution of funding and decision making from the federal government to state and local jurisdictions, constitute the fourth driver on the industry. Finally, the growing public awareness of philanthropy, largely a by-product of the growth in the sector, but also resulting from increased media savvy by foundations and a culture of celebrity that surrounds big gifts, has put philanthropy on the front page quite frequently.

There are several other notable shifts in the industry. The cult of business has made a home in philanthropic practice through both social entrepreneurism and venture philanthropy, two young but vital subsectors within the field. The structures of philanthropy are also in flux, as seen not just in the rise of donor-advised funds but also in the growth of public grant-making charities. These are by no means limited to the traditional geography-bound community foundation but are established now for communities identified by common interest areas, by race, culture, gender, or sexual orientation, and by political affinity. Finally, the center of philanthropy has shifted from the east coast to the west. In 1998 California supplanted New York as the home to the greatest number of startup foundations, and philanthropic assets per capita are also now greater in the west than in the east.[34]

PUSHING ON THE PIECES

Which of these pressures is the greatest? How is the industry responding to these forces? The two most significant forces are markets and regulation, and these are discussed in detail in Chapter 4 and Chapter 5 respectively. Real change will come not from any single force, but from the interactions among these trends. As such, it is important to consider the roles that philanthropic organizations are actually playing in relationship to these changes, ranging from very active to very passive. For example, at the active end of the spectrum, the industry is creating new products and services. During the economic boom of the late 1990s, several large foundations created programs to promote philanthropy, actively seeking ways to channel some new wealth into philanthropy. Examples include joint initiatives such as the national program New Ventures in Philanthropy and independent efforts such as the Annie E. Casey Foundation's Place-Based Philanthropy program. These initiatives are notable for two reasons. First, the endowed foundations funding these efforts are not interested in managing or advising the resulting resources, they are interested in growing the resource pool.[35] Second, these efforts boomed with the boom times and fell with the down times. [36] Oversimplifying, we see an ironic pattern of the industry funding more of itself as it is already growing and less of itself when market forces cause it to begin to shrink.

Economic opportunity and changes in the banking and brokerage industries were more powerful drivers on the introduction of new products and services than were industry-led promotional efforts such as those noted above. Banks, mutual fund companies, and many advisory firms began to offer philanthropic products when their market research showed demand. The success of these products has been handily demonstrated by Fidelity Investments, which began marketing donor-advised funds in 1992 and was, by 2002, the nation's second-largest organization in terms of philanthropic assets raised.[37] Fidelity's success quickly begat competition (the surest way to prove market demand), and by the turn of the century, most of the nation's largest banks and mutual fund companies were offering these products. By 2002, the nation's second largest purveyor of donor-advised funds, the National Philanthropic Trust, was a private label reseller of donor-advised fund services to banks and mutual funds.[38]

Much of the energy for the changes in philanthropy comes from the infusion of wealth that started in the 1990s and is expected to continue, with some variation in pace, over the next two generations. The wealth is both newly created and being passed from one generation to the next. Philanthropic purveyors are actively courting the individuals in control of this wealth. The rush to serve them has inspired the creation of new products and new services.

These new products include the rapid proliferation of donor-advised funds at entities beyond community foundations. Individual nonprofit organizations, independent funds, community endowments, universities and museums, and financial service firms all offer donor-advised funds. Philanthropic advisers now include—in addition to the lawyers, accountants, and investment managers—independent strategy consultants, family dynamic counselors, private firms providing support to family offices, and nonprofit incubators for new foundations. The organization Cool Rich Kids will provide you with both advice and a charitable giving vehicle if you are another "cool rich kid." The e-philanthropy explosion of the late 1990s was one quick-burning manifestation of the interest in providing new levels of services and delivering new types of products to this market.

Facing so many product options, donors often choose not to choose. Many potential donors decide to do nothing. Others find that they quickly become foundation board members, donor advisers, a member of a giving circle, a committee member on the corporate contributions team, or a lead donor to an institution they have long supported. The lines begin to blur between their roles as an individual donor and their work as part of a philanthropic institution. To many of the donors, this distinction does not matter at all. What they do and learn in one arena may inform them in the others. As this shift occurs, they will continue to demand more product selection and services that address a range of their giving options. Purveyors, products, and services that have operated as competitors will need to develop alliances and provide joint services, ventures, product development, and cross marketing.

The new products are being designed to reach and serve the masses. Yet giving is inherently a personal endeavor. The ability to mass-customize philanthropic products and services and to provide the appropriate level of personal touch to high numbers of clients will define success.

All of this is part of what is being called the democratization of philanthropy. More people, at a greater range of income levels, have access to a greater range of giving options. Tax law changes, such as the changes in charitable deductions for nonitemizers, will further expand philanthropic activity.

Philanthropic Commodities

Although these phenomena do allow philanthropic participation by a broader band of individuals, the process is no more democratic than before. What has happened instead is the *commoditization* of philanthropy. Here the similarity to the recent past and present changes regarding Americans and the stock market is a useful analogy. History shows that new regulations allow new products to develop. This is most clearly seen when changes were made in the laws guiding corporate pension plans. One result was the advent of the 401K plan, which led to the birth of a new class of investor. This new investor demanded different services and led to the birth of new firms, a wave of mergers among established firms, and ultimately new industry regulation. The very same cycle may well be underway in philanthropy.

The creation of new philanthropic products and the growth of philanthropic assets are mutually reinforcing. The product development and marketing came about in response to market demand. In turn, the new range of products and services, the broad reach of the distribution channels used to sell them, and the lower costs that first resulted from the competing products grew the market.

On the other hand, several forces of change are now underway on philanthropy that the industry is either practically ignoring or is too poorly organized to actively address. One of these is the very nature of philanthropic structures. Several annual studies and surveys exist of where philanthropic assets are kept. The Foundation Center maintains the largest and most complete database on the numbers of foundations, the value of their assets and their grant making, and the numbers of each type: independent, operating, corporate, and community. At the same time that the industry has witnessed (sometimes bemoaning, sometimes embracing) the rise of donor-advised funds, however, there is no reliable, comparable data set being established of these assets, grants, or number of funds. Nor is there accurate, public baseline data on the numbers of public grant-making charities beyond community foundations or the types and numbers of networks of philanthropists. These data gaps are rather extraordinary, given the broadly recognized role of both donor-advised funds and philanthropic associations. In direct contradiction to the social science maxim that "what gets counted is what is important," organized philanthropy is changing far more rapidly than its own industry measures.

Regulated Change

Of greater importance to the industry is the shifting nature of the regulatory structure that guides philanthropy and the industry's preparedness to respond to, let alone inform, these changes. Few industry organizations exist to represent philanthropy before statehouses or congress, to react to or inform regulatory proposals, or to proactively work with legislators and regulators. Those that do exist operate at the national level, leaving state and municipal governments to their own devices. This is somewhat remarkable, given both lessons from history and the current map of potential regulatory hot buttons.

The historical precedent for institutional philanthropy is that regulation matters at both the national and state levels. The dramatic story of John D. Rockefeller's unsuccessful attempts to obtain a national charter for the Rockefeller Foundation is a good place to start the chronology. Facing pronounced public distrust, caught in both corporate scandal and political maneuvering, the world's richest man finally recognized his limited influence on Congress and abandoned his attempt to obtain a federal charter in favor of gaining New York State recognition.[39] The relationship between government and philanthropy continued throughout the twentieth century, growing slowly but surely and with almost decennial drama in the form of congressional commissions or investigations right up to the present day.[40]

Today's menu of issues under active investigation by the industry's regulators is impressive. Exhibit 3.2 shows that the list is not only long in items but also broad in reach, as indicated by the practical implications related to each of the specific technical items. For example, if the estate tax is permanently repealed, history tells us that it will be very difficult to ever reinstate it. The value of individual estates being left to charities or to endow philanthropic foundations are likely to drop significantly.[41] Without either the revenues from the tax or new philanthropic assets, the revenue pool for nonprofit action will take a double hit. Without overextending one's imagination, it is easy to see a very different philanthropic industry emerging if reform occurs in some or all of the areas identified in Exhibit 3.2.

Despite both historical precedent and the current climate, philanthropy is poorly organized to respond to or inform regulatory changes. The organizations that aim to represent philanthropy—Independent Sector, the National Center for Responsive Philanthropy (NCRP), and the Council on Foundations among them—suffer from two significant structural factors that not only limit their effectiveness, but effectively disable them. First, these organizations operate as membership associations and must serve the

EXHIBIT 3.2   2OO3 REGULATORY ISSUES
FOR PHILANTHROPY

Item Under Scrutiny	Source of Potential Reform	Potential Implications
Donor-advised funds	Internal Revenue Service audits	Technical elements of accounting and grant making
Use of philanthropic gifts/Donor intent	Red Cross Liberty Fund scandal Pending lawsuits	Public outrage Change in leadership
Repeal of Estate Tax	President and Congress	Removal of major impetus for philanthropic giving and estate planning
Governance reform	Corporate governance concerns raised by Enron, TYCO and other scandals; trickles down to how corporate and individual giving decisions are made	Changes in relationships between corporations and foundations, board rules and conflict of interest oversight
Excise tax on private foundations	Proposed legislative changes	Influences donor decisions on structural type (private versus public grant-making charity)
Payout rates	Internal and external calls for change	Setting of real minimums for philanthropic giving
Public accountability	Lawsuits against foundations by communities claiming abuse of the public trust and/or public funds	New oversight, regulation on foundation accountability for grant decisions. New public disclosure laws.
Tax deductions for tax payers who who do not itemize their returns	CARE Act of 2003	Changes in public revenue and for philanthropy resources

interests of all dues–paying members. Policy action has never been a high priority for traditional institutional philanthropy, and therefore resources for it are typically low. Resources require that these organizations serve primarily as watchdogs and research groups, not as advocates or industry lobbyists.

Equally constraining is the nature of the membership for these organizations. In serving both nonprofits and grant-making foundations (Independent Sector and NCRP) or grant-making foundations of several different structural types (Council on Foundations), these organizations must represent the common denominator of their membership before regulators. This is clearly unsatisfactory to both sides when a pending issue—such as the excise tax on private foundations—has very different implications for different members.

Several examples of exactly this split in impact, opinion, and regulatory direction have emerged in the past few years, from the estate tax repeal to payout requirements. The different values and regulatory goals get even greater when commercial entities are considered within the mix. For this reason, these firms have been kept out of the traditional foundation membership groups. The result is an infrastructure in pieces, in which the large umbrella organizations include many, but not all, of the key industry types. The resulting paradox is that the umbrella groups represent too diverse or too small a constituency to advocate for specific positions. At the same time, because of those they exclude, they must contend with more facile and focused groups that represent a small but united subsector of the industry. Whichever way you look at it, you see failure. Either the organized voices intended to represent the policy interests of organized philanthropy are too dispersed and too many, or they are too few and unfocused to provide true leadership.

The result of this piecemeal approach is reactivity. Only when an issue rises to the top of legislative or regulatory agendas does philanthropy mobilize. The better funded, more experienced philanthropic organizations will be better positioned to make a case for their point of view. Commercial philanthropic organizations operating under the aegis of banks or mutual fund companies have the advantage of parent organizations that maintain ongoing relationships with regulators, and who can therefore mobilize more quickly and even proactively.

COLLECTIVELY ISOLATED

Compounding the structural limitations of these organizations is the isolationist culture of philanthropic foundations. The poor quality of the industry infrastructure, plus the deliberate independence of so many actors in the industry, leaves individual organizations disconnected from important issues. Acting on their own, they may remain pleasantly oblivious to legal challenges or regulatory issues at play on peers in other cities or states. That is, until the impact is felt by all. At the time of this writing, there are at least four lawsuits pending against grant-making foundations, from Minnesota to Ohio to New York. The issues at stake range from community accountability to donor intent. The *New York Times* has provided more coverage of these cases than have the two key trade papers, *Foundation News and Commentary* and the *Chronicle of Philanthropy*. Public information sites from the major philanthropic associations at the national and regional levels provide almost no mention of these actions.[42]

Either the infrastructure to inform foundations of these issues is operating underground or it is not operating. Also at question is the degree to which individual foundations seek out this information or care to know. The argument that most foundations do not seek collective information or action rests on the fact that the cumulative, unduplicated membership in known philanthropic associations accounts for less than 10 percent (and probably closer to 5 percent) of all established foundations. Ironically, given their talk of systems change, foundations regularly ignore the extent to which the system that defines philanthropy presents an opportunity to spark massive improvements in the system for financing civil action. One thing is sure, while philanthropy may be reluctant and ill-prepared to influence regulatory systems for its own benefit, changes in those same regulatory structures will force change far and wide.

DRIVERS OF CHANGE AT THE ORGANIZATIONAL LEVEL[43]

The forces of change at the society and industry levels can be seen in specific operational activities and decisions made by individual organizations. At this level, individual decision makers have the most control and influence. They can make choices regarding products and services, marketing, operational structure, and customers on whom to focus. These decisions matter greatly in the life of any single organization. They also affect the organization's ability to achieve its mission. Given the interdependence and complexity of the system, it is also likely that these individual changes could be made in ways that would ripple through the industry as a whole and the larger society.

These levels of connection are critical to understanding and improving the potential impact of philanthropy. Operational decisions directly influence an organization's ability to collaborate with peers, partner with the public sector, or distribute what may be useful research. The organizational implications are key not only in and of themselves, but also for the role they play in philanthropy's potential to add up to more than its parts.

Every philanthropic organization is directly influenced by the industrial components described earlier: (1) capital for investment, (2) products and services, (3) firms, markets, and customers, (4) competition and alliances, (5) regulation, and (6) public awareness. Yet the different types of philanthropic organizations respond in different ways. The next section briefly looks at the different ways that independent and community foundations react to change.

Some organizations are actually a result of the choices made between products. For example, independent endowed foundations represent one choice in the marketplace of philanthropic products, and once created, these organizations have fairly limited choices about capital, products, and customers, especially when compared to their community foundation or commercial fund counterparts.

Community Foundations Innovate First

Community foundations and commercial donor-advised funds are the most sensitive to the competitive pressures on the industry. These entities are involved in stewarding existing resources while attempting to grow them through both investment strategies and gifts. The most successful of them therefore make decisions about products and services, assess their markets, customers, competition, and potential allies frequently, and pay a good deal of attention to public accountability and regulations. For example, community foundations offer several lines of products and services, ranging from chartered family foundations to donor-advised funds to unrestricted endowment pools. They should make operational decisions about staffing that advance their progress and reflect their decisions about customers, markets, products, and competition.

Given this variance in reactivity to the industry, it is not surprising to note that community foundations, commercial donor-advised funds, and public grant-making charities have been the most innovative and persistent in terms of philanthropic market research, product development, operational structure, marketing, regulatory action, competition, and alliances.

At the topmost level, the drivers of change for community foundations are represented in operational decisions about product and service development, staff and board structures, and marketing. Chapter 7 presents more detail on how community foundations are responding to the new industry opportunities.

PRIVATE FOUNDATIONS AND CHANGES IN THE INDUSTRY

Independent endowed foundations are most sensitive to industry dynamics at the point of creation. After they are established, it is so cumbersome to take them apart that very few are ever put out of business. Rare as this is, it is not unheard of. Richard Goldman, a San Francisco scion, has announced his intention to dismantle his family foundation by distributing some assets to other foundations and spending the rest of the endowment before he dies. In other cases, such as happened with the Culpepper Endowment, one fund is folded into another to achieve operating or mission-related efficiencies.

Private foundations, like all others, do have a responsibility to steward the financial resources that they control. Recent studies have found that this is the one area in which executives actually believe they have the appropriate tools available to them.[44] For independent foundations, the capital they have available to them is usually embodied in a single corpus, and the focus is on managing growth through investment strategies. For some the prospect of an additional gift to the endowment upon the death or transition of the founder is also an important issue in considering its capital resources. Independent foundations represent a choice in the philanthropic marketplace that, once made, mandates little attention to the issues of customers, markets, products, or publicity. It is entirely possible—indeed, it is the most common approach in organized philanthropy—for an independent foundation to focus on pleasing no one other than the donor, meet the minimal reporting requirements through use of outsourced professionals, give no consideration to issues of competition or alliances, react only to regulatory changes brought upon it from outside, and avoid publicity and marketing of any type.

Of course, many independent foundations structure themselves so that the issues of customers and markets, competition and alliances, publicity, accountability, and products and services are more visible than in the previous example. These foundations may hire staff to facilitate alliances, conduct research to assess potential partners and barriers in achieving its goals, seek publicity for its own work or those of its nonprofit partners, and actively assess and revise its use of different products (e.g., grants, communication strategies, convening, operational projects, research contracts) on a regular basis. In other words, endowed foundations are themselves a philanthropic product as much as a firm, and therefore have the rather unique opportunity to choose how actively they engage the rest of their industry.

THE TIES THAT BIND FOUNDATIONS TOGETHER

Despite their organizational independence, a new phenomenon in philanthropy effectively ties the different structures together and reinforces the ways in which they are each influenced by changes in the others. The Giving Portfolio (see Exhibit 3.3), which is generated from the types of giving options available, also causes us to reconsider the relationships between giving vehicles and the effect of the whole.

The Giving Portfolio reveals several important facets of philanthropy. First, donors are at the center of a very crowded market. They often

EXHIBIT 3.3   THE GIVING PORTFOLIO

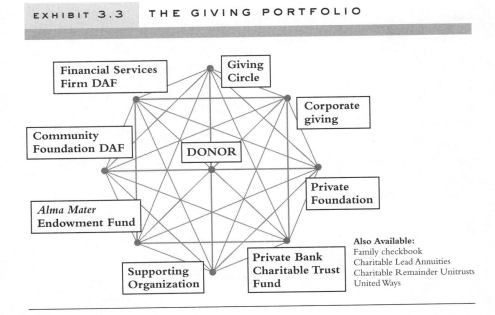

Financial Services Firm DAF

Giving Circle

Corporate giving

Community Foundation DAF

DONOR

Alma Mater Endowment Fund

Private Foundation

Supporting Organization

Private Bank Charitable Trust Fund

Also Available:
Family checkbook
Charitable Lead Annuities
Charitable Remainder Unitrusts
United Ways

choose multiple options, as in Exhibit 3.3, which was first drawn to represent an actual family. Each of the vendors trying to serve the donor customer needs to be aware of its competitors; they will sometimes work in partnership and other times be in direct competition. Each of the vendors will need strategies to serve donors in complementary ways. Each vendor or product needs to:

- Define their unique contribution to achieving the donor's goals.
- Define their complementary value in relationship to the others.
- Provide a means of measuring their contribution (in terms of fiscal management, knowledge assets, and social impact).
- Work as part of the whole to expand the market for the individual and collective services, and contribute to the measurement thereof.

These are big changes for many of the firms and products represented in the portfolio. They call for new alliances and joint approaches. The new Merrill Lynch Community Foundation Initiative, the work of Community Foundations of America, and some of the joint partnerships that undergird the Calvert Fund for Giving are good examples of what new philanthropic alliances will look like. This network of vendors and products also shows the ties that bind, the routes that influence will follow, and the ways in which all of the products are subject to the same set of forces.

IMPLICATIONS OF THESE CHANGES

These trends have numerous implications for philanthropy. The exponential growth of the sector has produced an era of affiliation and association, with foundations aligned in a crazy quilt of common characteristics ranging from geography to interest areas to demographic identities. Individual giving, which has always dwarfed institutional philanthropy, is the target market for e-philanthropy and a force that harbors changes for institutional givers as well. Internet-based giving and Internet services for nonprofits, donors, and foundations have grown significantly.

Donors read about private foundations in the newspaper, giving circles in the airline magazines, and community foundations in the major business weeklies, they are aware of the choices that exist. And as they learn of these different options, they are choosing all of them, not one of them. They are managing Giving Portfolios, and this change is important for the donors, advisors, and purveyors of these vehicles, the nonprofit and public sectors that interact with private philanthropy—for all of us. The use of many giving vehicles by many people represents a major change in the ways individual givers and philanthropic institutions interact and the ways these institutions need to think about the donors who fund them.

The choice of many vehicles instead of just one mirrors a larger trend noted in recent studies of Internet commerce. These articles comment on the fact that most new-car buyers now come into dealers' showrooms having first done extensive Web research. These buyers are getting better prices, refusing expensive add-ons, and playing one dealer's offer against another's. The same behavior is seen in patients coming into doctors' offices with reams of medical information and customers bringing online book reviews into local bookstores, looking to get their book now and save delivery fees.

The Internet has made it far easier for consumers (and philanthropists) to learn about the choices available to them. Armed with this information, the philanthropists are doing the same thing they do as consumers—they are looking for value. Just as consumers' behaviors have implications for car dealers, doctors' offices, and bookstores, philanthropists' behaviors have implications for the institutions that serve them—banks, brokerage houses, private or community foundations.

Knowing that a donor is already using several different giving vehicles to achieve her philanthropic goals changes the landscape for all parties involved. It is not a purely competitive decision between one option and another. A much more nuanced set of factors is involved, and good advisors can help donors see the complementary nature of the choices they are making. The trend toward multiple giving vehicles has several implications for philanthropy. These implications are crosscutting, but for clarity's sake they are broken down according to interest groups within the whole.

DONORS
- Comparison-shop across options, structures, and vehicles
- Seek metrics that can help them assess impact across structures
- Use some vehicles temporarily, rather than in perpetuity
- Continue to mix-and-match, creating new hybrid structures that best fit their needs

PURVEYORS OF DONOR-ADVISED FUNDS

- Operate in an increasingly competitive field, watching out for new purveyors from both the commercial and nonprofit sectors (witness the rise of university-based donor-advised funds)
- Offer complementary services to keep donors as repeat customers
- Need to continually educate their advisers about changes in the industry. Cross-sector educational opportunities will be important.

NONPROFITS AND PUBLIC SECTOR PARTNERS

- Seek to map the connections between vehicles and the donor networks
- Leverage connections with one node of a donor's network

INSTITUTIONAL PHILANTHROPY

- Need metrics to assess impact of different vehicles, as well as ways to articulate the roles of complementary strategies and networked giving
- Need to reconsider standard definitions of philanthropic activity when measuring entities, and may need new categories for philanthropic networks or hybrid structures
- Benefit from deliberate cross-pollination of ideas between financial services firms and the nonprofit sector as donors seek hybrids
- Will see the impact of the late 1990s boom in new fund creation five to ten years from now as the startups settle in

The boom of the late 1990s is just beginning to show its impact on institutional philanthropy. We have seen (and are still seeing) an explosion of new giving vehicles coming into the market. We can find many examples of hybrid entities being formed by creative philanthropists. And donors are choosing multiple giving vehicles, creating new networks of funds, and looking for both differentiated and complementary value from each of their choices. All of these changes mark the beginning of new terrain for philanthropy, one that calls for keeping one eye on the horizon, one in the rearview mirror, and both hands on the wheel.[45]

IMAGINE THE INDUSTRY ANEW

Given the uncertainty of the market and regulatory pressures, and the tremendous changes in behavior that alliance marketing, knowledge packaging, and shared technology infrastructures will demand, it is difficult to predict how the future will play out. The mix of external and rather un-controllable pressures from the economy and legislatures, and the demands of the internal and manageable pressures of partnering and reorganizing, makes for a heady set of variables.

There are enough variables in flux to demand that we consider the con-tours of a very different philanthropic industry within 25 years. The once-marginal commercial firms may become central and dominant managers of philanthropic assets. Alliances may come to predominate, spreading donor management across several firms and requiring whole new mechanisms for and attention to customer management. Individuals may become less en-ticed to participate in philanthropy because of new tax regulations, and the marketing push will shift to maintaining an industry of $200 billion rather than growing one of trillions. Co-production of social services may be-come the norm, as municipal governments scale back and individual resi-dents and philanthropic entities band together to provide core community services such as recycling, safety, and recreational services.

A rash of mergers and acquisitions, focused on building the most com-prehensive big bank approach to philanthropy could occur. In response, new products and service developments would be done by nationally fo-cused research and development firms or industry alliances, rather than at the local level. An example of this change already in action is the National Community Foundation Research & Development Incubator, located at the Michigan Council on Foundations and working with support of the Community Foundation Leadership Team and 56 Michigan community foundations. Other developments would include education services and advisory products becoming as common in philanthropy as they are in fi-nancial markets. Industry-standard indicators of philanthropic success might be found in the Sunday business pages. Shared online databases of expert research, proposal reviews, and philanthropic mutual funds could be created. Relatively rare philanthropic tools such as program-related invest-ments, bond issuances, nonprofit bank loans, and new financial products will be common, and grants will be rare.

CAN PHILANTHROPY CHANGE ITSELF?

The drivers of change described in this chapter break down into two easy types. First, there are those coming from outside, over which the industry has limited influence, although we believe the industry could have greater influence on these pressures, especially the regulatory ones, than it has wielded in the past. Second, there are the forces that lie within the industry and its component organizations over which significant influence is held and much has been done in scattered, disconnected islands of the industry.

The confluence of these forces, the advent of these industrial changes in relationship to public sector deficits, political pressure, and a rising sense of disenchantment with corporate structures (including nonprofit corporations), and the emergence and establishment of a first tier of successful early innovators makes the timing right for organized philanthropy to actively attempt broad change within the industry. We have passed the point where the impact of commercial vendors, technology backbones, partnership philanthropy, or a competitive environment can be dismissed as inconsequential. We are in the midst of a public revenue crisis at every level of governance that will not allow philanthropic assets to remain unaccountable or disconnected. Finally, the leadership within philanthropy, the heads of large foundations, infrastructure groups, new vendors to the industry, and important individuals are calling for change and promoting new visions of better-connected, more accountable, more public, and more influential uses of philanthropic resources.

This time will pass, and the industry may have experienced only slight tweaks to technical details of its operating procedures. If this is the case, an enormous opportunity to restructure the work so it can attract, channel, and account for the potential trillions of dollars of investment capital will have been lost. We should not assume that an unchanged industry will automatically attract those resources because it has failed to do so in the past.[46] Only by actively attempting to innovate and improve on the industry level will we see what philanthropy is truly capable of achieving, at the level of individual participants, communities, the industry, and society as a whole.

CHAPTER 4

Philanthropic Marketplaces

Change is one thing. Progress is another.

—Bertrand Russell

Philanthropy is both a product of and a player in markets of many types. Individual success in the commercial marketplace is a precursor to the creation of most philanthropic institutions. Once an individual chooses to act philanthropically, he must shop within the marketplace of philanthropic giving options. When those choices have been made, most philanthropic assets are invested in the financial markets in some fashion, making the available assets fluctuate in response to those economic cycles. There is a marketplace of ideas for philanthropic pursuit, market choices to be made among nonprofits to support, and several tangential industries serving the philanthropic markets, from publishing and trade presses to legal services and technology solutions.

Some of the markets that influence philanthropy act in classic fashion. Competitive bidding, supply and demand, and profit margins all play their usual roles in these vectors. This is not true across the board, however. Competition plays a strange and varied role in philanthropic markets, serving to inspire innovation and keep prices down in some cases and stifling innovation and mission achievement in others. The odd nature of competition affects the role of alliances, partnerships, and networks. Both of these market forces are having pronounced influence on the actions, values, and goals of philanthropic players. Whereas some of these behaviors and characteristics have long roots in American philanthropy, others are more recent and more nuanced.

This chapter focuses on two specific elements of philanthropy and markets: competition and alliances. These are distinct yet related elements of the philanthropic industry. Making them explicit will afford us a better platform from which to identify points of leverage to improve the industry.

PHILANTHROPY AND FINANCIAL SERVICES: PARALLELS AND DIVERGENCES

It is useful to consider how the philanthropic industry works in comparison to other mature industries. In particular, the observed parallels between philanthropy and the mutual fund industry over the last 20 years are compelling. If we consider the major changes that have occurred in the financial services industry—including commercial and investment banking, brokerage services, and financial planning—we can find some touchpoints for tracking developments in philanthropy.

If we consider the commoditization and mass marketing of stocks and bond mutual funds, we find an analog for the strongest drivers of change in today's philanthropic market. Starting in the late 1970s, new tax laws, new rules about pensions, and new retirement savings vehicles (i.e., IRAs and 401(k) plans) led to a massive increase in the percentage of Americans participating in the stock market.

That these products were designed to assist with retirement planning was particularly appealing to the baby boomers—70 million Americans born between 1945 and 1964, the eldest of whom were now in the job market and facing decisions about long-term financial planning. The confluence of a surging age group, new regulations about retirement, and new products sparked a boom in America's stock market activity. The amount Americans invested in mutual funds rose from $49 billion to more than $100 billion from 1980 to 1995. This growth pattern set the stage for the stock market boom that followed, the initial public offering (IPO) craze, and the so-called new economy.

This example illustrates the effects of three of the same forces identified as active in philanthropy now—major demographic shifts, a changing regulatory environment, and new products. The explosive growth in the financial markets was fueled in part by the expanding market for the products it had long offered. The regulatory changes in retirement law put individuals in charge of their long-term planning. The quick move by so many to take advantage of this new control was accelerated by the simultaneous introduction of discount services that made the markets accessible to small investors. The role of new, lower cost product options and services that put the customer in the driver's seat is especially interesting when we compare the development of discount brokerages to the new players and products in philanthropy.

In his analysis of the catalytic impact Charles Schwab and Company has had on the financial services field, John Kador tracks the revolution in that industry to the passage of technical provision by the Securities and Exchange Commission (SEC) to deregulate the commissions charged to clients for investment management services. Implemented on May 1, 1975—ironically known as May Day in the industry that is perhaps most emblematic of capitalism—this change influenced the creation and success of Schwab & Company. Also ironically, the innovations that Schwab would introduce were made possible because the bulk of the extant investment firms chose to ignore the possibilities created by the new law and refused to reduce transaction costs for their customers. Schwab stepped into the fray, providing brokerage services focused exclusively on executing trades at the lowest possible price, and releasing customers from the bind that most firms held on them.

With some notable ups, downs, and reversals of fortune, the narrative continues on to describe the rise of discount brokerages, the disaggregating of services and products once seen as permanently tied together, and the subsequent drawing of millions of small investors and billions of dollars into the equity and mutual fund markets. Following the story from 1975 to the present day, Kador shows how Schwab & Company first rent asunder such services as trading and research, then began to slowly reconnect them, only to make advertising history in 2002 by focusing on the independence of those products at Schwab compared to the blurred lines of research, retail service, and investment banking that snared Wall Street after the boom.[1] Although Schwab was not single-handedly responsible for the boom and busts of the 1980s and 1990s, they did play a role in setting the stage. Their innovations started out as fringe offerings in the brokerage business and have—after almost 30 years—induced significant changes in their competitors, led to new product creation, fueled the application of the Internet to financial services, and influenced corporate relationships to employee retirement plans.[2]

In a parallel fashion, we are now seeing the impact of an aging population, new products, and new regulation on philanthropy. America is older now than it has ever been and younger than it will be for the foreseeable future.[3] By 2004, the youngest baby boomers will be 40, and retirement and estate planning will take on new meaning for them. Many stand to inherit significant wealth from their parents.[4] Many new products, services, and advisors have emerged for managing that wealth and the associated philanthropy. A repeal of the estate tax effective in 2010 is now on the books. Given the challenges of reinstating repealed taxes, the likelihood of the repeal being made permanent is high to begin with and increased dramatically following the Republican Party's victories in the midterm elections of 2002. We have seen the number of philanthropic foundations double between 1980 and 2000, a frenzy of new lower cost product creation ranging from automated foundation creation to donor-advised funds, and a blur of advertising for philanthropic planning.

Just as companies encourage employees to invest in the stock market through their 401(k) plans, they also encourage employees to be philanthropic. Although this has long taken the form of workplace giving campaigns and employee community service days, the last years of the 1990s saw the rise of company-sponsored philanthropic advisers at Cisco Systems; the promotion of community investment plans at Charles Schwab & Company; and the creation of stand-alone foundations dedicated to corporate giving, such as the Entrepreneurs Foundation. The 1990s also saw the first rapid-fire "franchising" of a philanthropic vehicle, the growth in Social Venture Partners chapters from one in Seattle to almost 30 by decade's end. While not officially connected to particular companies, the original SVP grew largely around Microsoft employees and alumni, and subsequent chapters tended to be based on social networks built around the workplace. Armed with more sophisticated communications technology and marketing techniques, the Calvert Funds and giving circle organizations such as SVP, the Taproot Foundation, and the Full Circle Fund are just the latest example of aggregating and sharing philanthropic services across small donors, just as Schwab and e★Trade were able to do with small investors.

How closely the next 10 to 20 years of philanthropic activity will mirror the changes underway in American stock investing and retirement account management is pure speculation; however, the similarities between the two industries certainly suggest the utility of monitoring the well-researched and documented histories and developments of the financial industries.

COMPETITION IN THE PHILANTHROPIC MARKETPLACE

The parallels between the role that regulatory change and market forces played on the developments in financial services cannot be carried over directly to philanthropy. Whereas competition (or the lack thereof) led to the passage of the May Day fee deregulation, the rapidity and extent of discount brokers' response to that opening would likely not be replicated exactly in philanthropy.

This is because the role that competition plays in the commercial sphere in terms of spurring product development, price wars, and value-added services does not map across to traditional philanthropy. For endowed foundations, there has been virtually no need to compete for donors. Once established, these organizations are in business; only a market cataclysm, donor decision, or criminal activity can force them to close up shop. This is most important for historical reasons, since for decades independent endowed foundations were the primary institutional form for philanthropic giving. As the number of options for new donors increases and includes products or services that are both more malleable than endowed foundations and more sensitive to competition, the landscape of philanthropic vehicles is changing.

Selling Philanthropy

Since 1991, when Fidelity Investments sought and received an Internal Revenue Service determination letter recognizing the tax-exempt status of its Charitable Gift Fund, to the present day, the role of competition in philanthropy has become more pervasive and more complex.[5] Discussion still rages within philanthropy as to how exactly Fidelity succeeded in launching this product line. An article in the leading legal journal for nonprofit organizations notes that, "The exemption application for the Fidelity fund apparently flew beneath the [Internal Revenue] Service's radar screen, being approved by the Brooklyn District office without any review by the

National Office."[6] Subsequent efforts by Fidelity's traditional competitors in the mutual fund business, include American Guaranty & Trust Company and the Vanguard Group, were reviewed by the national office and restrictions placed on them that had not been imposed earlier when Fidelity had applied.[7]

Within the commercial sphere of mutual fund companies, banks, and brokerage services, the race to sell charitable gift funds has followed a fairly predictable path. By 1999, Fidelity was managing more than $2 billion in these accounts and drawing the asset management fees accordingly. This success served as proof of concept to Fidelity's competitors, and by the end of the twentieth century all major fund companies and banks were offering fairly similar charitable giving products.[8]

Also now in the competitive sphere of these banks and fund companies were the more traditional sellers of these types of funds, namely community foundations. In 1991, the landscape of community foundations was drastically different than it is today.[9] Many community foundations were members of the regional associations in their states and of the National Council on Foundations, but they were hardly organized in a formal fashion to either work with the commercial firms or mount a united challenge to them. As important, there was no single perspective of the community foundations about the entry of commercial firms into philanthropy. While some of the largest, such as the California Community Foundation, commissioned a review of the legality of the tax-exempt status determination, others saw these firms as potential partners and distributors more than competitors.[10]

The relationship between community foundations and financial service firms provides us with a useful entry point into understanding competition in philanthropy. First, there is no single story. The relationship includes partnership and competition, support and exclusion. Second, the management of assets is at the core of both institutions. The business models of both financial service firms and community foundations rely on asset management fees, which increase slightly the more additional service is attached to managing the investments. Third, philanthropic activity at both institutions tends to rise and fall with the larger economic systems and is particularly sensitive to financial market cycles and changes in personal income. Fourth, the increased competition has led to more public service and product differentiation and contributed to the establishment of several subindustry trade associations to focus on the particular issues of the subsector structures.

It is important to note that there is no single community foundation opinion or stance regarding financial service firms and vice versa. Some have actively opposed the commercial firms' involvement in philanthropy, whereas others have seen them as worthy competitors and adapted practices to better meet the challenge. They have taken advantage of the large marketing budgets of the commercial firms as promoting philanthropy and differentiated themselves on service and products for donors in their local communities. Some community foundations have worked from the beginning to build partnerships with the commercial firms and have adjusted their services and fees to facilitate such changes. There has been no single voice for community foundations, either formally or informally.

The Limitations of the Business Model

The business model reliance on asset management fees has worked to the benefit of individual organizations but has been an obstacle to greater partnership, either within the sector of community foundations or between community foundations and financial firms. Assets under management not only determine core operating revenue for many community foundations and commercial firms' charitable funds, but the size of assets under management is also a key cultural indicator in philanthropy. Foundation reputations are often at least partly made by the size of their endowment, lists and industry trends are kept and made public, foundation executives and boards are assessed by their ability to grow the endowment, and presidents and staff of foundations with large endowments are more widely regarded in the industry than those of smaller organizations.

As long as the fees for the asset management model reign supreme, it is difficult for two organizations to share a single customer. First, a viable alternative revenue source is needed. Value-added services such as advising, convening, educational publications, staff support, and family advising are not explicitly "costed out" by most foundations. They are not charged for on a fee-for-service basis or provided in a single product revenue-generating way. Finding ways to do this would have several important implications for philanthropy. First, new revenue streams would follow from expertise and excellent service. Second, the revenue streams and products

associated with knowledge and solid community performance are complementary to those hinged on asset management and would allow for more
natural alliances. Finally, the presumed added value of these activities
would become "real value with a real price." From a business standpoint,
such feedback on services (will people pay for them?) is absolutely critical
to product and service development. Second, quality matters in such product lines. By building new revenue streams hinged to community knowledge, social impact, goal achievement, coalition building, fund leveraging,
or any of the many other things community foundations do for donors, the
industry would be able to balance the assets under management marker
with indicators of social good achieved.

Because market forces beyond the control of any foundation executive
often determine the size of the endowment or assets under management,
the development of these social good indicators would provide important
marketing information during difficult economic times. Not only would
the foundation be able to provide quantifiable evidence of its impact on the
local community, but it also would be able to market that information in
economic good times and bad. This could begin to counter one of the
most frustrating elements of philanthropic relationships to the markets—
that when bad times befall the economy, philanthropy tightens its belt
along with every other source of economic support. It is likely that that
trend would continue with new metrics, but it is also logical that the development of indicators of social good accomplished would inform foundation strategies and guide their decision making in ways that might stem
the flow of funds a bit.

Finally, the rise of commercial firms in philanthropy has been partly responsible for the development of an increasingly complicated and dense
mix of industry associations. As the commercial firms first entered and then
became successful in the donor-advised fund marketplace, community
foundations began to see the need to coalesce and share ideas in more substantial ways than they were then organized to do. At the time, community foundations mostly met and shared ideas either through local informal
groups of CEOs or at the Council on Foundations conferences and events
targeted to community foundations. In the mid-1990s, several of the nation's largest community foundations made their desire for a more permanent national focus known. The strategic planning process of the Council
on Foundations in the last decade provided the opportunity for community

foundations to create a Leadership Team under the auspices of the Council. In 1999, several community foundation leaders also came together to create Community Foundations of America, a stand-alone nonprofit membership and trade group focused exclusively on developing large-scale marketing, technology, and information products for the community foundation market.

Community foundations were not the only ones to begin creating national associations to focus on their needs. Once a field inhabited only by the Council on Foundations, by 2000 there were separate national membership professional and trade associations focused exclusively on the interests and needs of foundations with few or no staff, family foundations, community foundations, and foundations with an explicit political point of view, either conservative or progressive.[11] Of course, with the exception of the last category (political perspective), none of these categories are mutually exclusive, and so many foundations found themselves deciding to join several of these new organizations. This quickly had financial implications for both the foundations and the member organizations because the former worried about increasing dues bills and the latter worried about cannibalizing each other. The diversity of organizations also makes philanthropy difficult to access from the political perspective because so many associations now speak for the industry that once again there is no single voice.

How does all of this relate to competition? First, the pressures on community foundations as financial service firms began to market donor-advised funds led to some immediate changes in business practices, product and service delivery, marketing, and industry associations. These reactions are not surprising and are very similar to what happens when a serious new competitor enters any market. As happens in the recording industry or bookselling, a new entity spurs the established players to reconsider their prices, their product lines, their marketing budgets and strategies, their use of technology or distribution channels, and the ways they work together or apart. Confined to the subsector of community foundations, the impact of the financial services firms on philanthropy were textbook reactions to new competition.

Pushing out beyond community foundations, however, we see more distinctive reactions and ripple effects. First, community foundations— especially small ones—began to seek support in their cause from their independent and corporate foundation relations. In some places, there were large private foundations with a distinct favor for the community foundation model, and they initiated new funding programs to strengthen community foundations. Some of these efforts in the 1990s were statewide (Indiana and California) and were premised on providing every resident of the state with access to a local community foundation.

Other private foundation/community foundation relationships were focused on issues (e.g., health care, neighborhood development, or education) and had roots in the more traditional relationships between foundations in which the community foundation serves as the local expert and distribution channel for the larger private foundation's program missions. What changed in the course of the 1990s were deliberate efforts to simultaneously strengthen the community foundations themselves as well as work with them on social issues.

This partnering of independent and community foundation, in the face of the increasing presence of the financial firms, had two results. First, it put independent foundations squarely in the community foundations' camp "vendor of choice" in the business of donor-advised funds. Second, it opened a door for the pressures of competition that the community foundations felt directly to seep, rather indirectly, into the private foundations.

This seepage is important. Private endowed foundations feel few sources of external pressure or competition. Changing the business practices of these entities from outside is very difficult. As they became more and more aware of the changing business landscape for their community foundation peers, private foundations slowly began to consider the implications of that changing landscape for them. Although there were many other causes for changing organizational behavior in the late 1990s, some of the newer business practices of private foundations were generated in some small part by the newfound competition for resources represented by the financial firms.

For example, the financial firms upped the ante quite significantly in terms of marketing. At the same time, more private foundations began to invest in communications departments, catchy slogans to follow their name when announced as supporters of public radio, new media strategies as part of their program work, and a general increase in proactive public awareness. This was by no means a direct response to Fidelity or Schwab's advertising, nor did it have the same purpose (to bring in donors), but it was an effort at increasing awareness of the presence and work of these endowments, as if to say, "Don't forget we're here too."

Another area of seepage occurred in the pressures to be cost-efficient. For community foundations, this was a direct result of the financial firm's low costs for donor-advised funds. For private foundations, these low-cost options made board members more aware of the high costs of doing business as an endowed foundation (generally seen as the most expensive philanthropic alternative). As community foundations increased their marketing, and the commercial firms ran huge advertising campaigns, private foundations were being presented far and wide as an expensive, grandiose, old-fashioned solution. In response, some boards took an even harder look at administrative budget lines, executives made investments in tools to boost efficiency, and suddenly almost all foundations had Web sites, even if they sought no proposals, no donors, and no publicity.

Another indirect effect of the increased competition is the current interest in performance measurement and effectiveness. Again, the direct impact was felt immediately by community foundations, many of which sought private foundation support to help develop meaningful indicators of their effectiveness. Because community foundations were primarily distinguishing themselves on the basis of their community knowledge and impact, the need for indicators was preeminent. Private foundations helped invest in these efforts, found out how difficult it is to track social impact, and turned the lens on themselves, beginning to wonder how they would measure up.

The culmination of these influences is an indirect and diffuse competitive pressure on private foundations. At the level of established, staffed, and endowed foundations, where we would expect to see the lowest level of change (assuming they would perceive the least amount of competition), we see the results of this pressure in new business practices such as greater public communication, efforts to document impact, and a focus on streamlined operations. At the level of the key customer—the potential philanthropic donor—we see the competitive landscape between giving vehicles much more clearly (see Exhibit 3.3, The Giving Portfolio). The choices from supporting organization to donor-advised fund to private foundation to community foundation fund are arrayed and displayed on countless Web sites from community foundations and regional associations, and one can find extensive efforts to educate professional advisors about the pros and cons of each vehicle.[12]

One emerging irony of the role of competition in philanthropy is that while private foundations once supported community foundations in their early-stage differentiation efforts from the commercial funds, the community foundations now fairly actively promote themselves as positive alternatives to private foundations. GiftPlan.org, for example, is a collaborative effort of several California community foundations to market their services—in partnership with financial service firms—as the cost-effective and results-oriented alternative to private family foundations.[13] One immediate response to this action was a cry of negative campaigning by a commercial consulting firm in the same region that makes its money by providing outsourced staff to family foundations.

The Changing Landscape

The anecdote about the consulting firm and the marketing campaign raises the role of tangential vendors in the industry. Although foundations and financial service firms are the purveyors of giving choices, the environment in which they operate has changed considerably in the last two decades. Independent consultants abound who will manage foundations for families, provide program research and evaluation, or handle the family dynamics associated with managing money across generations. Academic research centers, nonprofit business divisions of the nation's largest management consulting firms (McKinsey and Co., Bain and Company), and publishers, training programs, software vendors, technology consultants, and investment managers all focused specifically on the philanthropic market now abound. The competitive environment for these organizations (even the noncommercial entities) first seeped into philanthropy slowly but is now a dominant cultural element, as these firms vie for the business of every type of philanthropist.

Competition Creep

One way of understanding the complicated dynamic of competition in philanthropy is to see it as a slowly creeping reality. Taking some liberty with the concept of early adopters, we can easily organize the philanthropic entities in a hierarchy from first influenced to late-comers where competitive pressure is concerned (see Exhibit 4.1).

EXHIBIT 4.1   COMPETITION CREEP

First influenced	→	Middle carriers	→	Latecomers
Commercial firms				Independent, endowed foundations
Community foundations		Nonprofit vendors		
Public charities (non-endowed)		Trade associations		Academic research centers
Commercial consulting firms				
Commercial vendors				

The different sensitivity to competition of these different players distinguishes the industry from purely commercial ones. It is a distinction that at its core relies on the independence of the endowment—the more central to an organization the existence of such an endowment, the less susceptible it is to competitive influence. This applies, however, only to existing endowments. We must remember that from the donor's perspective, an endowed foundation is just one of many products in the philanthropic marketplace.

PRODUCTS IN THE MARKET

Today's marketplace of philanthropic options runs a gamut from low cost to high cost. Within the market there are essentially two types of products being sold and used: (1) asset management tools and (2) advisory services. At one end of the cost spectrum, the asset management tool is a direct charitable gift of cash or appreciated assets, which are then deductible at certain levels. Moving to the other end of the spectrum, an independent staffed foundation sets aside cash or appreciated assets and the donor(s) receive tax deductions. Once consultants or staff are hired to advise the foundation's giving, the donors or board members have moved to the next tier of product—advisory services. These then may take a wide range of forms, from bare-bones administrative support to full-fledged investments in professional staff, researchers, technical support providers, and evaluators. The products now available in philanthropy can be divided into two classes, which can then be mixed and matched in many ways (see Exhibit 4.2).

We know that these products respond differently to competitive pressure (see Exhibit 1.2, Sensitivity to Competition for Different Philanthropic Financial Products). In addition, these two product lines—financial

| EXHIBIT 4.2 | PRODUCTS, SERVICES, AND DELIVERY MECHANISMS |

Products

1. Asset management tools
   Remainder trusts
   Annuities
   IRA rollovers
   Endowed funds
   Non-endowed funds

2. Advisory services
   Legal services
   Investment management
   Accounting and reporting
   Mission and goal setting
   Issue research
   Technical support
   Evaluation

Delivery Mechanisms
Foundations
Community and federated funds
Commercial firms
Direct gifts to nonprofits

Pro bono
Consultants
In-house staff

asset management tools and advisory services—are independent of each other and can be purchased separately or bundled together. Because we tend to think of philanthropic products as existing organizational forms, it may be easier to see this by mapping those forms on a grid that shows the range of high and low for both asset management tools and advisory services (see Exhibit 4.3).

Exhibit 4.3 oversimplifies somewhat the degree of management and costs for each of the two products—financial asset management tools and advisory services, and a more nuanced scale would be helpful for fully understanding the range of product mixes. But the simplicity of the table helps us to see just how the existing organizational forms mix these two products. Commercial donor-advised funds, for the most part, market their value in managing the money and leaving the decision making to the donor. Community foundation funds, on the other hand, emphasize their range of investment options as well as access to their professional staff as the distinguishing feature of their donor-advised funds.

Independent foundations with staff represent very high investments in both the administrative structure for managing the funds and in the full-time employment of professional issue advisors. Independent foundations without staff or consultants, on the other hand, are an option for donors

EXHIBIT 4.3   COMMON PHILANTHROPIC PRODUCTS MAPPED BY INTENSITY OF ASSET MANAGEMENT AND ADVISORY SERVICES

Financial Asset Management	Advisory Services	
	Low	High
High	• Commercial donor-advised fund • Charitable bequests • Charitable trusts • Charitable annuities	• Independent foundation • Community foundation donor-advised fund • Philanthropy advisors (e.g., Rockefeller Philanthropy Advisors)
Low	• Individual checkbook giving	• United Way or other federated workplace giving

who wish to invest in that particular asset management tool but don't see the need for professional advisors.

Drawing again on the analogy of financial service industries, the upper right hand cell on the table represents the pre-1974 full-fledged brokerage account model and the upper left-hand corner represents the discount model that Charles Schwab & Company introduced. And just as Schwab has continued to roll out more highly-managed and advised levels of service, we are seeing a great growth in new products that provide new mixes of services and costs.

This is an entirely new way of thinking about philanthropy. These two products dominate the market, yet most players in the industry are more concerned with the current organizational alignment of them than with the products themselves. By this I mean that foundations are concerned about foundations, donors with donors, and gift funds with gift funds. A whole subindustry that calls itself donor education has emerged within the advisory services area. A great irony of this is that its leading proponents decry the use of the term *donor education* even as they call themselves by the term.[14]

Business gurus relate a mythical anecdote about how the nineteenth-century railroad barons chose not to invest in developing the internal combustion engine and went on to lose out to both the trucking and airline industries because they thought they were in the railroad business when they should have realized they were in the transportation business.[15] Apocryphal or not, the railroad industry's short-sighted understanding of its business should serve as an apt reminder to institutional philanthropy. This chapter looks at how the marketplace is changing the subsectors of philanthropy from foundations to individual donors. Many of these changes are for the better. But as we will see in this chapter and the next, the failure to understand this basic change in product lines may well doom institutional philanthropy to the same fate as the railroads.

PHILANTHROPIC ALLIANCES

As the role of competition morphs and ripples, the use, maturity, and effectiveness of philanthropic alliances in the marketplace also changes. Foundation staffs have been working in networks with each other in several forms for many years. The most formal representation of this networking is found in the infrastructure membership associations previously discussed. With 28 regional associations, dozens of affinity groups, and several major national associations, the structured opportunities for organized philanthropy to work together abound. These membership organizations are the most visible but by no means the dominant form of joint work in philanthropy. There are at least three different types of alliances in philanthropy that warrant discussion: networks, syndicates, and joint ventures. Each type has different strengths and weaknesses, and each plays a part in the overarching market of philanthropy.

Foundation Networks

Although neither a comprehensive map nor a directory of existing funder networks exists, the affiliation options for institutional philanthropy range from local to international, from informal to formal (see Exhibit 4.4).

There are, in other words, hundreds of ways in which the puzzle pieces of foundations work together. The most common approach is to be no part of any alliances. Most foundations are not members of any of the existing associations (represented by Foundations A and B in Exhibit 4.5). If they do have any connection to other foundations, it is likely to be informal personal connections and requests for ad-hoc advice (represented by Foundation X).

EXHIBIT 4.4   A CONTINUUM OF ALLIANCES

Informal
Lunch groups
Issue committees of regional associations
Peer reading groups
As-needed meetings on issues
Jointly funded projects

Formal
Committees
Regional associations
Pooled funding collaborative
National membership associations
Issue or identity based affinity group

EXHIBIT 4.5   THE PUZZLE PIECES OF PHILANTHROPIC NETWORKS

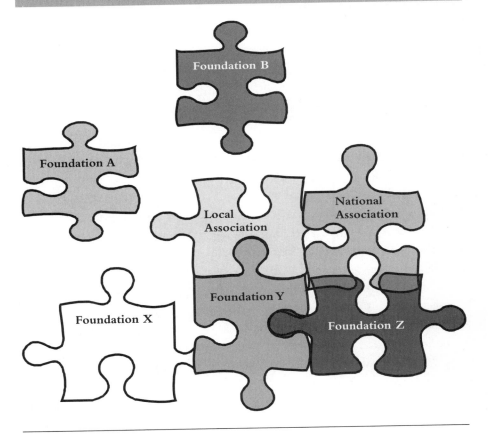

These ties are temporal and relationship based; they require no exchange of fees and produce no definite joint action.

Foundation Y represents a common arrangement for larger staffed foundations. It is directly involved in the work of a standing local association, is close to (and may be a member of) at least one national association, works in partnership with Foundation Z on several areas of joint interest, and occasionally advises or interacts with Foundation X. These pieces can be rearranged in countless fashions, and on very few issues is there a clear, commonly understood sense that one particular configuration is the right one.

The different types of alliances and networks serve different purposes. National associations focus primarily on broad membership-specific services, publishing, networking, and peer exchanges. They also manage some professional development responsibilities, representation before national governing bodies, and some standard setting. They rarely manage actual joint work by foundations. Rather, they are independent entities built to serve foundations, supported by dues and fees, and provide common ground for actual work.

Funder Syndicates

When foundations actually try to accomplish something together, the informal, nonmembership structures have proven most effective. These ad hoc groups of four or five funders interested in school reform in a major city, in health insurance in one state, or in launching new national technical support efforts are driven by committed leaders within individual organizations who are actively seeking funding partners. Examples abound of both successful and unsuccessful efforts at this kind of joint work. As one foundation senior manager said, "If I stopped to count the number of failed efforts at funding collaboratively, I'd be so depressed I'd leave the business."[16]

Experienced program and senior staff work the system in other ways. Vincent Stehle, of the Surdna Foundation in New York, has become a master driver of what he thinks of as "funding syndicates." Focused on a single nonprofit partner, dedicated to building the organizational capacity of that organization to provide its services on a national or international scale, these funding efforts involve an enormous amount of work with consultants, colleagues, and the nonprofit. Over time, the efforts that have yielded successful joint funding have demonstrated the need for patience, investment in building managerial and financial platforms, expert coaching in presentations, and the hosting power of one or more committed foundation partners.

In the experiences of the two most successful such efforts, Surdna and several foundation partners came together to work with Philanthropic Research, Inc. (GuideStar) and VolunteerMatch. Investments started individually and small, and built toward system-building grants for management consultants who could help build scalable technology platforms, sophisticated financial controls, and excellent governance and operational capacity. Time and money were spent by the early investors to help both GuideStar and VolunteerMatch develop first-rate investment cases, and then the early funders took on the responsibility of bringing their peers to the table with the nonprofit partner to hear the pitches, work out the investment strategy over time, and stay at the table for the next few years. As Stehle notes, this approach is perhaps more similar to the work of venture capitalists than the individual efforts of venture philanthropists because it is built on primary and secondary investors organized as a group of investors from the beginning.[17] The group of investors and the nonprofit partners has agreed to quarterly and annual goals and works together to track and report progress. The early-stage funders are also deeply involved in positioning the nonprofit to attract second and third round support, as well as building out revenue-generating strategies to address longer-term sustainability issues.

Several elements of this type of relationship are notable, when thinking about the role of alliances in philanthropy. First, they are not only issue-based, they are targeted joint investments in a single organization. They require no infrastructure outside of the participating foundations and nonprofit (consulting services are contracted for by mutual agreement and as part of an investment in the nonprofit). The allied work is organized along the timeline of accomplishing specific goals. Membership, ongoing alliances, and dues or fees play no role in doing the work. When the goals are accomplished, the alliance disbands although strong relationships can remain.

An example of this is an initiative focused on capacity building that was led by the Sobrato Family Foundation, Peninsula Community Foundation, and Charles and Helen Schwab Foundation. These funders came together with 16 human service agencies to develop a learning and funding initiative focused on building organizational capacity. Over the course of three years the partners and independent evaluators met repeatedly, developed customizable funding strategies for each agency, and built a system for sharing what worked, didn't work, and ways to plan for future investments. This experience was so valuable that Alexa Culwell, President of the Schwab Foundation credits the initiative with catalyzing significant changes in how the Foundation operates today.[18] These activities are somewhat similar to the movie production company approach to work: Bring together the necessary partners for a specific film, make and distribute the resulting movie, and disband for individual partners to move on to other projects. As in the movie business, some teams will remain in touch and go on to work together again, others will part ways.

The downsides of these arrangements are the insider nature with which they work. The lack of permanent alliance means that the next capable nonprofit cannot access this same kind of support. The projects are foundation driven. These alliances are strong because of the personal relationships that make up their base, but they are also limited by this structure because they have no means for reaching beyond their known circles. They are deliberately operating under the radar screen. To date, these efforts have done little in the way of "making method from their madness," nor have the funders taken a role in bringing in other key players in the long-term revenue picture for the nonprofits, namely public sector and individual partners. These criticisms, while important, are by no means limited to these types of alliances. In fact, the structures of the more visible foundation networks makes them no more accessible to the external circles of nonprofit organizations, government, or individual philanthropists.

Joint Ventures

Another common form of alliance in philanthropy is the joint venture. In this structure, two or more grant-making organizations partner to co-produce a set of tools, products, or services. These arrangements are becoming increasingly common among similarly structured organizations. For example, community foundations have come together to develop common marketing strategies, jointly trademark certain giving vehicles, and share programs.[19] These ventures also occur between foundations or grant makers of different types. There is a long history of ventures between independent foundations and community foundations, sometimes focused on developing a regionally specific solution to a certain problem, or in other cases seeking to bring a set of ideas and approaches to several communities at once.

In other cases, regionally-focused private foundations will partner with national funders on a mutual interest. The work of the Robert Wood Johnson Foundation and The Charles and Helen Schwab Foundation around substance abuse prevention in California is a good example of this. The Johnson Foundation brings deep expertise in health financing, policy and systems, while the Schwab Foundation has very strong relationships and partnerships with program providers, local university experts, and state policy makers. The two foundations formed the core of a funding initiative on substance abuse prevention and the evaluation of various efforts that now includes several other partners as well.

In the best case, foundations will find a way to learn from peers through an alliance, find investment partners and forge a syndicated or joint venture approach, and build relationships that inform the work of the field. Several foundations point to the work of the Youth Transition Funders Group and the Funders Network for Smart Growth and Livable Communities as examples of membership-based, issue-focused associations that have actively catalyzed joint investments and learning. A key to the success of these efforts seems to be the mix of national and local partners, a strong leadership commitment, solid research, and a mutually-identified action agenda.

The challenge for successful joint action among foundations is this agenda-setting. The idiosyncratic nature of foundations results in many organizations with broad common interests, but each with such specific lenses onto the issue that they can't all come together. Successful strategies for working around this have included the deliberate creation of complementary issue agendas. In southern California, for example, Los Angeles Urban Funders (LAUF) developed a poverty-reduction strategy that included specific complementary avenues such as transportation, workforce development, childcare, education, and housing. The leaders of LAUF then sought partners who brought funding interest and expertise in each of those areas and worked to focus their resources on the complementary pieces of an overall agenda to reduce poverty in three areas of Los Angeles County.

As commercial firms have entered the market and the focus has shifted to product lines, such as donor-advised funds, an interesting shift has occurred in the types of joint ventures commonly found. In the early 1990s (and for decades before), community foundations and independent foundations were partners on issues and product development as discussed in the section on networks. The early response to commercial firms entering the market was an alignment of independent foundations and community foundations working to promote the unique value of the traditional non-profit approach to philanthropy. These were essentially efforts to align against the newcomer commercial products.

As donor-advised funds have become increasingly common products and are made available by commercial firms, universities, nonprofits, and community foundations, a remarkable shift is occurring on the landscape. Seeking a share of the perceived pending wealth, community foundations and commercial firms (both vendors of donor-advised funds) are developing a wide range of joint ventures (see Exhibit 4.6). These include the Merrill Lynch Community Foundation Initiative, regional partnerships between several community foundations and regional banks, and independent partnerships involving a single community foundation and commercial partner. As they do so, they share a marketing message about the advantages of donor-advised funds. Those advantages are most evident in terms of tax deductibility of assets, the lack of excise taxes, and the relative freedom of public charity grant making compared to private foundations. In

EXHIBIT 4.6   COMMON JOINT VENTURES

Early 1990s		Early 2000s	
Dominant alliances	*Loners*	*Dominant alliances*	*Loners*
Community foundations and independent foundations	Commercial vendors	Community foundations and commercial vendors	Independent foundations
Characteristics of alliance		*Characteristics of alliance*	
Built around complementary programs Common bond: nonprofit status		Built around complementary products Common bond: product cost	

other words, community foundations and commercial firms are now in joint ventures, aligned as alternatives to independent foundations.

The Power of Joint Action

All three forms of alliance are important in the philanthropic landscape and represent major strides toward aggregating resources. Each is best at accomplishing specific goals: networks help share information, syndicates can move money, and joint ventures help create new products and distribution channels, although in some cases one form can lead to several desired outcomes. What is missing is any means of being more systematic about either the structural option for collective action or real connective tissue between the alliances.[20]

As more philanthropy occurs in some kind of joint fashion, the opportunities for changing the whole system open up in exciting fashion. First, there is a tremendous need for a system map of institutional philanthropy. This is more than a listing of members of various large associations (although a cross-referenced, nonduplicative list would be an important first step). As the 1970s brought forward directories of foundations, it is time to think about developing maintainable databases of funder networks. Such a public access database would serve two important purposes: it would connect the connections and it would provide point of entry for newcomers. By connecting the connectors, the individual networks are strengthened. By presenting a navigation tool of the system to newcomers, such a database could help attract new members and reduce duplicative efforts.

Second, the networked power of philanthropy is currently vastly underused. For starters, the networks, syndicates, and alliances we have identified only connect institutional grantors. Given the small percentage of the overall philanthropic industry this represented, these organizations are deliberately excluding the largest and most consistent source of philanthropic capital: individual donors. Before examining this missing link in more detail, however, it is helpful to look more closely at the power and potential power of the networks as they are now constructed.

TIED TOGETHER AT THE TOP

There are more than 62,000 foundations in the United States, managing $45 billion in financial assets and making grants of more than $450 million

per year. Add to that the 40 or so commercial donor-advised fund purveyors and their $5 billion in assets and you are still capturing less than 25
percent of the $212 billion in U.S. giving.[21] Although small in proportion,
these sources of philanthropic revenue are easy to find, share some institutional characteristics, and are therefore significantly easier to aggregate than
the remaining 75 percent of the market.

One way of imagining the philanthropic industry is as a pyramid of institutions and individuals (see Exhibit 4.7). At the top, you have a relatively
small number of relatively large institutions. They are large in terms of assets
managed, grant funds disbursed, and (possibly) professional staff.[22] Constitut-
ing the bulk of the pyramid are the many (millions) individual donors, who
each account for relatively small amounts of giving but who together are responsible for three-quarters of the annual philanthropic revenue stream.

Exhibit 4.7 is a convenient, but somewhat misleading picture. In actu-
ality, the size of most foundations is relatively small (less than $1 million in
endowed assets). Operationally, these organizations look more like wealthy
individual donors than they resemble their institutional brethren—large,
staffed foundations. We also need to incorporate into this picture the hundreds of individuals and families who have invested more than $6 billion in
philanthropic assets through commercial donor-advised funds. Although

EXHIBIT 4.7   THE PHILANTHROPIC PYRAMID
ORGANIZED BY NUMBER OF UNITS

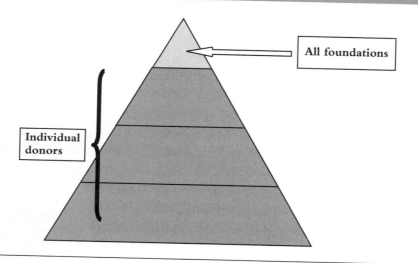

these assets are held in common at the commercial firms' gift funds, individual donors are directing their use.[23] The interesting problem they represent for our philanthropic pyramid is this hybridized nature of pooled yet individual. There are approximately 40 commercial firms managing this $6 billion asset pool, which offer a potentially powerful organizing tool for informing and networking their donors.

Looked at from the perspective of capacity for networking, we see the pyramid in a slightly different way (see Exhibit 4.8). The bulk of the 56,000 foundations that might otherwise rest in the top quadrant move to the bottom tier. The hundreds of individuals who give through commercial funds move to the top.

The assets that the organizations at the top manage are privileged in many ways. Regardless of the structural form in which they are held, they have already been exempted from taxation and marked for charitable use, so from a planning perspective there is an opportunity to forecast potential revenue from this stream. Philanthropic funds from institutions are by no means available to nonprofits without strings attached, but they do often go to support new ideas or allow new initiatives to be tried. Unlike government funds,

EXHIBIT 4.8   THE PHILANTHROPIC PYRAMID SHOWING POTENTIAL CONNECTIVITY

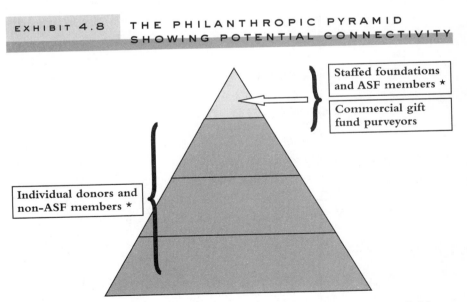

Staffed foundations and ASF members *

Commercial gift fund purveyors

Individual donors and non–ASF members *

*ASF (Association of Small Foundation) membership is used here as a proxy for unstaffed foundations (of any size) that have already connected to the larger system through the association.

philanthropic assets are not contracted for certain services, nor are they as dis-aggregated as individual gifts. The managers of these institutional assets are often full-time professionals, whose responsibility is to identify opportunities, share information, and measure results. They have goals to meet and (in some cases) are held accountable for their success. In other words, at the rar-efied level of the top of the pyramid, there is both the capacity and a small degree of responsibility to work together.

This, no doubt, is why this smallest sector of philanthropy has done the most to organize itself, even with little external pressure to do so. To date, the commercial firms have been kept from these networks and have been relatively isolated from the rest of the field and from each other. Nor have they shown tremendous interest in organizing or connecting their individ-ual donors, although they see those services as potentially valuable additions down the road.[24]

Even with these relative advantages, however, organized philanthropy cannot rest on its laurels for grand achievements in working together. Most networks exchange information with little or no responsibility on members to apply that resource in any particular way. The independent nature of the member organizations trumps the collective pull of the network in every imaginable case. There is a trend toward aggregate action in the weak hi-erarchy from network to joint venture, as there is a tighter degree of part-ner-to-partner accountability as you move from membership association to funding syndicate to joint product development.

EMERGING CONNECTIONS

By adjusting our vision of who and what constitutes the top tier of this pyra-mid, we actually begin to see new types of connections. Three of these have passed the proof-of-concept phase and are windows onto the shape of things to come. All three use information and knowledge resources to di-rect financial capital. They are described in the following sections.

Sharing Knowledge

The knowledge that informs philanthropy takes two essential forms: tacit and explicit. *Tacit knowledge* refers to personal interpretations, relationships, and undocumented experience. *Explicit knowledge* includes reports, evalua-tions, data, research, analysis, and written grant reviews or proposals. In

1999, the Ford Foundation, one of the country's largest and longest-term staffed foundations, launched GrantCraft, a collection of documents, videos, audiotapes, and workbooks that capture both explicit and tacit knowledge on several areas of grant making. The information for the series comes from staff and consultants to Ford and dozens of other large staffed foundations in the United States and abroad. The materials are carefully edited and compiled to be useful to both professional and volunteer staff and board members at other foundations. Many of the materials are available in Spanish as well as English. To date, GrantCraft represents the most comprehensive effort by denizens of the top of the pyramid to share practical information and research with the rest of the industry. GrantCraft provides derived knowledge, repackaged and made easily available to any who wish to access it. The materials are mostly free and are available online at *www.grantcraft.org*.

Jan Jaffe, the founder and project manager of GrantCraft, notes that this effort has produced materials that can be used for self-guided learning, as part of the curriculum of informal or formal training programs, and they mark the beginning of an industry knowledge base that unleashes some of the secrets from the top and makes them available more widely. The challenges are many, she notes, and include quality control, pricing, and definitions of best practices, market feedback, and branding. It is very difficult to know to what ends and effects the materials are put. These are important questions—as is the issue of achieving self-sustaining revenue—and the GrantCraft team is actively investigating ways of knowing the impact of the materials and the degree to which they are actively pushing on a point of leverage within the industry.

The trade-offs between broad reach and access and direct interaction with an opportunity for feedback and improvement is faced by several other material-driven programs and products now on the market. These include case studies in philanthropy, modeled after the use of cases in the teaching of both law and business. Although the professional training that employs these cases in the fields of business and law have not yet been institutionalized, the cases developed at Harvard University's Kennedy School of Government are being widely distributed for use in less formal ways. Again, the trade-off here has been broad reach for less in-depth application. Industry standards in this market include the more operation-focused workbooks, guides, videos, and publications from the Council on

Foundations and The Foundation Center. The Association of Small Foundations launched an online repository of edited materials called "Foundation in a Box" in 2002, which markets a selection of materials to board members and professional advisors to philanthropists.

Taking this type of written material one step further, an online resource called GrantPartners.net is attempting to serve as a connective database for funders and nonprofits working on health issues in Southern California. A consortium of foundations in Orange County built a publicly accessible Web site (*www.grantpartners.net*), where registered grant makers can search for posted proposals in their areas of interest and nonprofits can post proposals as well as search for potential partners with whom to collaborate. This site is in its first stage of use. To date it has been designed to ease the workload on nonprofits and allow staffed foundations to accept applications online. Eventually, the platform will be available to nonprofits, donors, and foundations from anywhere in the world and will help them find each other. The originating partner foundations are building the platform, but other than that, they provide no endorsement of the organizations that post applications.[25]

This effort mirrors several failed dot-com approaches to online grant matchmaking that burned bright and quick at the end of the 1990s. One professional grant maker remarked—at the height of the boom—that he feared that grant making would become simply a marriage of two huge databases—one of funders and one of nonprofits, electronically trolling through each others' contents to make online matches.[26] Of course, the idiosyncratic nature of funding ensured the failure of such depersonalized tools. Modifications of the model, involving significant human interaction and subjectivity, have continued with some success, as seen in GrantPartners.net and similar efforts such as DevelopmentSpace.org and the Global Exchange for Social Investment (*www.GEXSI.com*), which describes itself as "a collective initiative of individuals and organizations from both the for-profit and not-for-profit sectors focused on creating a market for social investment and development assistance."[27]

In addition to databases of information on grant making or prevetted proposals, several foundations have taken to building repositories of their research, position papers, and informant contacts so that peer funders interested in issues need not re-create these wheels. The source information in these repositories varies from grant reports and evaluations provided by the Robert Wood Johnson Foundation to research and position papers on homelessness used and shared by the Charles and Helen Schwab Foundation. Communities of nonprofits are also recognizing the value of compiling and cataloging this kind of information. The Eureka Learning Fellows Program, which focuses on leadership renewal in the nonprofit sector, has a robust online source for program evaluation. The Annie E. Casey Foundation uses the Web to share its KidsCount data and other commissioned research.[28]

Many foundations are beginning to invest quite heavily in knowledge management and knowledge sharing techniques. The Schwab Foundation emphasizes knowledge sharing as part of its key mission, and sees these investments as critical to informing the field, building partnerships, and ultimately seeing a "multiplier effect" on the foundation's investments of funds.[29] Efforts to invest in knowledge management and sharing can be found at foundations as varied as The Enterprise Foundation in Baltimore, which has seven full time employees managing and sharing research, outcomes, and online databases of the foundation's work in affordable housing. The United Nations Foundation dedicates one senior manager, an intern, and a consultant to working across all departments of the foundation to disseminate research findings within and outside the organization. The Fannie Mae Foundation has a Knowledge Initiative, a new company called KPublic seeks to serve as the technology provider and clearinghouse for research in the nonprofit sector, and The William and Flora Hewlett Foundation regularly posts commissioned papers on its web site, sponsors a research fellow who publishes extensively, and convenes learning clusters of peer organizations.[30]

Portfolio Advising

As with many big ideas of the late 1990s, the emphasis on rational action on enormous scale improving the efficiency and effectiveness of philanthropy proved to be simultaneously visionary and short-sighted. The essential human element of philanthropy—the individual interests, passions, irrational interest in certain ideas, and the personal relationships between nonprofit leaders and their causes and philanthropists and their colleagues—cannot be erased from the picture. Attempts to replace this subjective element of philanthropy with the latest whiz-bang technologically-driven,

objective, information-based tools fell flat. The important lesson they provided was ironic. In failing so poorly, these attempts to make philanthropy systematic only highlighted the pervasive importance of the irrational and human elements of the philanthropic markets.

The models that recognize the need for human contact and guidance are now showing some success. These efforts preserve the funders' interests in learning more information when they want it, while not subjecting them to a deluge of unsorted material. These models use technology and rational information provision and management to inform the process, not to overhaul or replace it.

The commercial firms' charitable gift funds, which focus on asset management and provide barebones, do-it-yourself access to additional information, have shown tremendous success in using the technology to lower product costs, while not exposing customers to more than they have asked for. These models represent an enormous step in attracting philanthropic funds but much more modest (if any) progress in informing the deployment of those resources.

One mutual fund company, The Calvert Giving Fund of the Calvert Group, has taken the largest step in providing philanthropists with both low-cost, online asset management tools for their giving and a credible, focused body of information that can help them direct those resources. The Fund works by partnering with other grant makers to develop Giving Folios of organizations that Calvert's donors can access and support. Some of the portfolio advisors and issues include the Global Fund for Women (global women's rights), Roberts Enterprise Development Fund (social enterprise in the San Francisco Bay Area), and the New Schools Venture Fund (education reform).[31]

This folio approach allows individual donors at Calvert to access the research and vetting expertise of staff from both public and private grantmaking foundations. Once clients have purchased charitable gift funds at Calvert, they gain access to both low-cost asset management services and information that can inform their giving. The folio managers get involved in exchange for the opportunity to inform others of their work and draw funds to the organizations and causes they support. The nonprofit organizations in the folios gain exposure and credibility at virtually no cost to them.

This model works for Calvert for several reasons. First, the Calvert Group specializes in socially responsible mutual funds, so its client market has already self-selected by interests to some degree. This is an important distinction because it allows the Calvert Giving Folios to be selected within a more narrow band of activity and political spectrum than would be possible with a more diverse market of customers. Since the launch of these products, the Giving Folios have distributed close to $1 million to the featured nonprofit organizations.

This approach is not entirely new. Community foundations have been managing similar approaches through field of interest funds for years. Other public grant makers, such as The Tides Foundation, have also attempted various ways of informing donors to try to pool their resources for greater impact. There are two important differences in the Calvert approach. First, the scale is much larger because Calvert can reach socially responsible investors anywhere in the world through its advertising for its mutual fund services. Second, the human relationship is mediated in a way that allows that broad reach, but it remains extant. Whereas community foundations tend to personally know their donors, build relationships, and then provide advisory services and information, Calvert has sliced its market into a manageable demographic, leads with the sale of fairly impersonal asset management tools, and then provides an opt-in function for Giving Folios. The staff of Calvert, the Folio Managers, and the benefiting nonprofit may never lay eyes on the donor, yet all feel served.

Peer-to-Peer Outsourcing

At the other end of the spectrum lie several peer-to-peer efforts at sharing information to aggregate financial resources. Here again, community foundations have led the way. Although many (most?) still offer donors tiers of services that are fairly distinct and disconnected, more and more community foundations are trying to make the expertise of their staff and the information they use and generate available to a broader slice of their clients. Some do this by sharing staff proposal reviews and recommendations with donor advisors. Others convene regular meetings between program staff and donor services staff so that the people in contact with the donors know what is going on in the community. Others bring forward their dockets of recommended grants to donor advisors at some time before grant funds are awarded to supplement unrestricted grant funds.

Some foundations now recognize that using their staff people to attract other resources to the nonprofits they support is a positive element of the foundation's work. Job descriptions and performance reviews are now written to encourage and reward leveraging of other funds. Two private foundation CEOs, Alexa Culwell at the Charles and Helen Schwab Foundation in San Mateo, California, and Julie Rogers of the Eugene and Agnes Meyer Foundation in Washington, D.C., see their efforts in this regard as critical to the success of their foundations. They actively promote the organizations they fund, they advise other foundation presidents and take calls from individual donors and volunteer board members, and they provide information and guidance to foundations with fewer staff resources.

Both foundations also are considering ways to share their staff's time and expertise with foundations or grant makers with similar interests. Schwab has successfully done this in the past with both The Emily Tremaine Foundation and Alan Parker and the Oak Foundation. In the formative years of the Tremaine and Oak Foundations, Schwab staff presented research, met with the foundation trustees and advised their early grant strategy development around learning differences. The staff from Meyer worked with the webMethods' Foundation to prepare the company's staff for grant making, review proposal requests, and provide support and training to the webMethods' employees when they moved into this community work.

The Annie E. Casey Foundation has focused on reaching "downstream funders" of local initiatives. To reach the smaller, locally focused foundations that make up the vast majority of U.S. foundations, Casey has launched a place-based philanthropy initiative in which the research and expertise of the Casey Foundation's staff—especially on children and family preservation issues—will be provided to small family foundations, which tend to have an interest in their immediate communities.[32] Such efforts bode well, both for sharing information and reducing the percentage of foundation funds spent on internal administration. The Meyer Foundation, like the Roberts Enterprise Development Fund in San Francisco, has joined with Calvert to serve as Folio Managers for CalvertGiving.com, thus bringing this relationship to the level of private foundations informing individual philanthropists. Meyer staff members also advise individual donors, have taken a lead in launching TouchDC, a regional web portal powered by Network for Good, and partnering with the Harman Family Foundation to pilot a Washington area "Catalogue for Philanthropy."

And these efforts pay off. The Meyer Foundation staff estimates that their efforts in 2002 helped to move more than $19 million in national and local philanthropic resources to the organizations and causes the Foundation supports. This is significantly more than the $6 million the Foundation made in grants that same year. Similarly, the Schwab Foundation staff measure and are held accountable in regard to the funds they help direct toward the Foundation's issues. In addition to significant public resources that Schwab staff have helped their substance abuse provider partners access for more adolescent treatment beds, the Foundation can look to the $5.5 million in giving for learning differences from the Oak Foundation and several other examples to quantify the payoff for its strategic emphasis on partnering and knowledge sharing.

The Meyer Foundation's commitment to these approaches is particularly interesting. As a relatively small regional foundation, Meyer has traditionally supported small, grassroots groups in the Washington D.C. area. These kinds of groups have the hardest time attracting attention beyond their immediate reach, and Meyer successfully draws in newer regional funders, large national foundations, and aggregated individual donors to support these organizations. As President of the Meyer Foundation, Julie Rogers takes it on herself to seek funding partners and she requires her staff to do so by serving in leadership roles on national and local commissions. The Foundation's board has gone so far in supporting this work to amend the Foundation's mission statement to include a statement that the Foundation is to "serve as a resource to other donors who want to make effective charitable investments in the region."[33]

The Foundation Incubator represents another version of this model. The Incubator provides shared office space to emerging foundations as a means of lowering overall administrative and operational costs while providing workshops, educational programming, and opportunities for donors to share ideas. Another model has community foundations maintaining a bank of consultants who can work with individual donors or families with significant funds at the foundation in a semi-staff fashion, providing the donor with many of the advantages of paid professionals as well as the benefits of the community foundation. The Acumen Fund creates pooled issue funds for donors interested in international issues, allowing several donors to benefit from a single expert staff and their networks.

DIVERGENT TENSIONS

These various examples of partnering, sharing knowledge, and using the staff of a foundation to advise a company giving program or an individual's grant making are exciting and valuable efforts at aggregating resources. It is important to note that the best examples of joint work—those that actually result in aligned and aggregated grant making—are built most solidly on the relationships and knowledge sharing that foundation staff can bring to the table. These are powerful forces of collaboration, alignment, and aggregation. Those that work for peer organizations such as large staffed foundations have tremendous potential. Those that find ways to use foundation knowledge resources to inform and guide individual giving are the basis of an evolutionary new philanthropic capital market.

It is also important to note that the forces of fragmentation on these resources are far more numerous and far stronger than the forces of aggregation. The pressures to continue operating philanthropic resources in small, isolated pots include the fundamentally personal nature of philanthropy, as well as the traditional financial structures, some new ones coming online, and the regulatory nature of the system.

The existing regulatory structure (to be discussed in detail in Chapter 5) and the traditional financial structures—ranging from community foundations to private foundations to donor-advised funds—provide neither carrots nor sticks for donors to work together. There are no requirements for pooling funds, collaborating on issues, or sharing information. The efforts to do so have been borne purely from the experience and expertise of those who have worked in philanthropy long enough to understand that no individual or foundation has the resources to achieve lofty goals on its own. At the same time, the new products that have been introduced in the last decades, including the widespread marketing of donor-advised funds as well as newer products, actually contribute to the continued disaggregating of financial resources. These newer products include online grants management systems for small foundations (CyberGrants), private-labeled, low-cost foundation administrative services (FoundationSource), and full-fledged foundation management services provided by commercial money management firms (Fidelity Investments Private Foundation Services).

The market pressures on philanthropy are thus immense. An increasingly dispersed and isolated set of products is now available to manage the enormous pool of financial resources. At the same time, the industry and its established institutions are ever more cognizant of the need to aggregate resources in order to achieve impact. In this marketplace, with its uniquely featured competitive nature and the ever-changing landscape of alliances, the two key resources—financial and informational—are moving in opposite directions.

CHAPTER 5

Public Support for Philanthropy

These funds should be so large that to become a trustee of one of them should make a man at once a public character. They should be so large that their administration would be a matter of public concern, public inquiry, and public criticism.[1]

—Frederick T. Gates to John D. Rockefeller

Regulation is the third leg of the three-legged stool that shapes philanthropy. Balanced by market forces and the public benefit that it exists to produce, philanthropy also operates as a regulated industry. The relationships between private philanthropy and the public sector are multidimensional. Philanthropy is legally bound to the public sector by the regulations and laws overseeing the nonprofit sector. It is bound to the public by virtue of its public benefit purpose: Philanthropy has a moral and structural commitment to serve the public good. Philanthropy is thus a product and a producer of public benefit. Regulations tie private philanthropy to the public sector by setting legal definitions, prescribing structural limits, and providing for public oversight. Philanthropy, in turn, ties itself back to the public through its contributions to public purposes and services.

Public regulation → Philanthropic activity → Public benefit

Proud of its independence, philanthropy often chooses to ignore the relationship it has with the public sector. Truth be told, philanthropy only exists at the whim of the public sector. As Lawrence Friedman notes in his scan of philanthropy in American history,

> At no point [in American history] was there anything approaching an autonomous voluntary sector. America's experiment with philanthropy, therefore, exposed the vicissitudes in the purported distinction between the public and private sector. Indeed, the term Independent Sector was more the prescription of contemporary figures such as [John] Gardner and [Virginia] Hodgkinson than a grounded historical reality.[2]

Philanthropy as we know it exists within the bounds of state and federal tax codes. This chapter presents the current state of philanthropy as a regulated industry, providing a quick review of the twentieth century trends that brought the industry to this point. It also presents an analysis of the sources of external pressure and identifies the points in the regulatory structure under the greatest scrutiny.

The value of the industry conceptual framework is particularly pronounced in this section. In reviewing the long, mostly arm's-length relationship between philanthropic institutions and their regulators, we see the many levels at which the industry must prepare itself for regulatory review and action. The chapter proposes a much more active role on the part of philanthropic players in working with regulators and legislators on the public policy of the industry. This stems not from a commitment to government–industry alliances, but from an analysis of the limited good that philanthropy's more passive stance has achieved.

By choosing to be responsive and reactive to the regulatory structures that guide it, organized philanthropy has chosen to play defense with regulations as opposed to offense. At the same time, having failed to communicate broad, industry-wide contributions to the public good, the industry cannot rest on the goodwill and support of either overseers or the general public. At certain times, the simultaneity of public budget deficits, media scrutiny, and industry growth have created a ready platform for close examination of foundation activity. The first and second quarters of 2003 are such a time.

What is remarkable about the industry's approach to regulation—generally summarized as fear, loathing, and defensiveness—is that this attitude continues relatively unabated even though the environment around philanthropy has changed dramatically. For example, the current deregulation of the banking industry is leading to rapid new product and service development within financial institutions as banks seek to control more elements of their customers' financial lives. From insurance to annuities to stocks, bonds, and checking accounts, banks are now developing and offering product suites that will help them manage an increasing share of each customer's wallet. Philanthropic activity and charitable giving are at the center of that product suite.

The leading edge of this charge by financial institutions was to push for changes in the regulations on their industry. Even as corporate accounting and governance scandals dominated the news media in 2002, the banks' decades-long push to dismantle the Glass-Steagall Act of 1933 was finally successful. By working with legislators and regulators, the banks pushed for a set of laws and rules that would allow them to reach new business goals. They could then dedicate their research, development, and marketing staffs to track changing tax codes, conduct market research on their client's needs, and market new products aggressively.

Meanwhile, in comparison, the nonprofit philanthropic community mobilized late in the game to attempt to stall negotiations on legislation aimed directly at charitable giving. Working with their lawyers and members, national, regional, and issue-based foundation groups mustered a last-minute push to remove unwanted regulations from Senate and House bills.[3] The strategy was to stall these bills and keep them from a conference committee. Unlike the banks, there had been no proactive promotion of alternatives, and the effort came to a head just as the general and trade media unleashed a flurry of negative stories on excessive expenditures at foundations and the Supreme Court released new decisions on charitable fraud.[4] With attention focused exclusively on the CARE ACT in the U.S. Senate and The Charitable Giving Act in the House of Representatives, it is safe to say that foundations and their affiliate bodies were not paying attention to developments in bank regulations, financial firms' product development, or the implications for nonprofits of new corporate governance restrictions, such as those created by the Sarbanes-Oxley Act of 2002.

Examples such as those cited previously abound. Philanthropy, unlike other industries, is profoundly unprepared to use regulation as a tool to further its own mission. Although this is true, the competition in the philanthropic marketplace has brought banks and insurance companies into direct competition with nonprofit endowments, just two rival industries with far more active approaches to shaping regulation to their benefit. As Emmett

Carson, CEO of The Minneapolis Foundation, noted in a speech to foundation board members in April 2003:

> Additional government regulation should not always be viewed as a negative development to be avoided. For an industry that relies on the strategies of partnering with government to provide services, influencing government to engage or not engage in particular activities, and encouraging government to adopt programs that have been successfully piloted by foundations, philanthropy's fear of any added government oversight or regulation seems somewhat counter-productive. We should be open to the possibility that, in some cases, reasonable government oversight could be beneficial and might help to clarify otherwise gray areas of accountability and minimally acceptable best practices.[5]

For philanthropy, the defensive approach to regulation has implications beyond just the immediate scope of restrictions and guidelines on practices. It has profound implications for the strength of the nonprofit set of players in the industry. Unlike decades past, when these nonprofit endowments and community foundations were the majority of the firms in the field, the presence of commercial firms has forever altered the dynamics in philanthropy. They are far better positioned to take from the nonprofits the mantle of new product developers. Their national and international networks allow them to move resources seamlessly on a common technological platform—a rival for which is only just now being built by community foundations.[6]

While nonprofit firms in philanthropy can point to their social missions as their distinguishing value, they have proved oddly inarticulate at selling that value. Some rely on the dominance of the nonprofit endowed firms as compared to the commercial firms and refuse to see the upstart commercial firms as real threats. This is a false comparison when looking to the future. The nonprofit endowments, which manage more than $450 billion in assets, have the benefit of having had the field to themselves for decades, allowing those assets to accrue over time. In the decade since the commercial firms entered the marketplace, the rates of growth for foundation endowments as compared to commercial donor-advised funds have been practically the same, and at times the commercial firms have grown faster.[7]

The regulatory environment for philanthropy influences the marketplace. Both the regulatory and market forces are hot enough that the nonprofit element of the philanthropic industry should be reconsidering how it operates and how it promotes itself. The opportunity for philanthropy is to work both ends of its public relationship, to inform and guide the regulatory structure in ways that can improve and expand philanthropy's contributions to the public good. Failing to do so is an abrogation of the industry's public benefit responsibilities.

REGULATED FROM THE START

We often think that the modern foundation was born at the start of the twentieth century. This is true, but the philanthropic and charitable regulations and the legal relationship between private and public resources that allows these institutions dates back to the first decades of the new Republic. The U.S. Supreme Court, in an 1819 decision involving the ability of the State of New Hampshire to dictate use of funds at Dartmouth College, codified the philosophical underpinnings for protecting private resources that can still be felt in today's philanthropic industry.[8] The Court ruled that voluntary associations protected by corporate status cannot be used by the public to provide those services that the public sector must provide. The decision made practical the Constitutional protection of corporations and helped define both responsibilities and limitations of government.

Thus public entities must set priorities and provide for basics such as health, education, and infrastructure. The private sector would thus be in a position to enhance, complement, fill gaps, or provide alternatives; states and municipalities would not be allowed to rely on private benevolence for the core services.[9] As McGarvie notes, "The real importance of the *Dartmouth* case is not simply the delineation of private and public, but also the perpetuation of the alternative visions of American society by the legal recognition of public and private spheres."[10]

The Supreme Court thus set the stage for philanthropic corporations, and 200 years after the Dartmouth case, the chambers of the New York State Legislature guided into being two of the most influential examples of institutional philanthropy. It was there that the two formative American foundations, the Carnegie Corporation of New York and The Rockefeller Foundation, came into existence. These institutions have roots in earlier organizations, particularly the Peabody Education Fund and the General Education Board, but these were the first truly general-purpose permanent philanthropic endowments in the United States.

Andrew Carnegie established his foundation in 1911 with an endowment of $125 million worth of Carnegie Steel stock. Two years later, after three years of trying and failing to obtain a federal charter, John D. Rockefeller endowed The Rockefeller Foundation in New York with an initial gift of $50 million in shares of Standard Oil.[11] One year later in 1914, Cleveland banker Frederick Goff, who was looking for a better way to distribute the funds held in estates and trusts to the community, created the first community foundation.[12] All three examples required state charters, and the activities they could undertake and the degree to which they would be monitored was established at the start.

These early years also saw the emerging relationship between the tax code and foundation philanthropy. A populist outcry against the great fortunes of the late nineteenth century led President Woodrow Wilson to sign into law a national income tax in 1913. Much like today, this first tax was graduated, home mortgage interest and state and local taxes were exempt, and in 1917 charitable contributions were made tax deductible.[13]

One immediate impact of this new tax structure seemed to be the way John D. Rockefeller—the world's wealthiest man at the time—chose to distribute his personal wealth. Rockefeller faced choices between children and charity that would look familiar to today's donors, in structure if not in size. Before 1917, his son, John D. Rockefeller Jr., and his daughters had all received generous allowances but had inherited relatively little of their father's fortune. Rockefeller Sr.'s contributions to charity (including the new foundation) before 1917 had exceeded $275 million, while his children had received an estimated $35 million.

From 1917 to 1922, Rockefeller reversed this ratio and gave an additional $200 million to charity and an astonishing $475 million to his children, the vast majority of it to John Jr.[14] Rockefeller was aging, public opinion of him was low and dropping, and his children were now grown, so tax laws were not the only influences on his distribution decisions. But his ability to deduct gifts to the foundation (of which John Jr. was President), provide for his children, and reduce his own tax bill (while also removing himself from the public eye in regard to his philanthropy) were all important factors to the elderly Rockefeller.[15]

The factors in these kinds of calculations—the ability to provide for future generations, the opportunity to build (or continue) a family tradition of philanthropy, avoidance of income, estate or inheritance taxes, the exemption of assets, pursuing a social purpose or making contributions back to a community—remain the key elements in philanthropic decision making today as they were in Rockefeller's time. The balance of these factors continues to depend on individual circumstances, and we have seen how the universe of products to meet those needs has blossomed. At the same time, the body of law that informs these decisions, the regulatory requirements, and the public sector's oversight of the resulting entities have also expanded since the turn of the twentieth century.

INDUSTRY GROWTH AND PUBLIC OVERSIGHT

The twentieth century saw three clustered periods of active philanthropic endowment (the teens, the 1950s and 1960s, and the last two decades of the century). The foundations created in the second decade of the 1900s inspired dozens and then hundreds of peers. The first half of the century, dominated by war and economic depression, saw a single rapid period of foundation creation and then a period of dormancy. Following World War II and the generally strong economic periods of the 1950s and 1960s, a new boom occurred in foundation creation. Similar to the first boom, this second rush came into being as a result of family transitions where great wealth had been made. The riches of industrial giants in oil, steel, and banking fueled the initial foundation boom. The second boom, in the decades after the war, saw endowments created from automobile and consumer goods wealth. The further reaches of wealth became apparent in this second boom, as foundations sprang to life in all areas of the country and across a wider range of asset sizes. These dimensions would characterize the third boom of the century to an even greater degree. In the last two decades of the twentieth century, the pace of foundation creation, the dispersion of these assets, and the types of wealth that fueled them would reach new heights.

These growth spurts in institutional philanthropy led to a similar pattern of public investigation and oversight. These investigations took the form of congressional committees, independent review boards, or investigations by state attorneys general. Starting about a decade after Rockefeller and Carnegie endowed their legacies, jumping ahead to the late 1950s and then again a decade later at the end of the 1960s, we find three significant inquiries into philanthropic activity.

Past periods of public inquiry all have had their own unique contextual roots, but there are some striking parallels in the conditions leading up to them. Public revenue shortfalls—embodied by decreases in taxes—shine bright lights on alternative sources of either public revenue or revenue for social services. Philanthropic entities and endowed nonprofit organizations always attract attention in such an environment. The booms in philanthropy tend to follow periods of marked wealth creation, such as the start and end of the twentieth century and the immediate postwar period. Of course, these same periods of wealth creation highlight and expand the disparities of wealth, another form of pressure on the philanthropic system. With these largely external and unguided forces aligned, the more predictable forces of ambitious legislators, media attention, and scandal are all ready to send calls for reform and review into overdrive. The public reviews of philanthropy in the halls of congress and state legislatures have usually resulted from the alignment of more opportunistic and less purposeful forces.

Oddly, philanthropy has tended to allow this pattern to continue by taking a consistently passive stance in terms of its work with the public overseers. Shaped perhaps by the spectrum of political approaches, a business world sense that less government involvement is more, or by its own stubborn determination to remain outside of or above public decision makers, organized philanthropy has never adopted a common, proactive strategy of attempting to improve the system that shapes it as a means to improving its own effectiveness.

OPERATING IN THE PUBLIC EYE: GROWING PUBLIC ATTENTION

While it has been reactive in relation to regulation, philanthropy has been more active as an industry when it comes to communicating with the general public. This stems both from an internal commitment to community benefit and the growing public awareness of philanthropy. The 2001 Annual Conference of the Council on Foundations was titled "Preserving the Public Trust: Responsible Use of Private Wealth for the Public Good." This is only one recent manifestation of the industry's recognition of its responsibility to the public. There has been much talk of accountability and transparency in philanthropy, and most foundation executives will go on record as standing for these two characteristics. Many have invested heavily in communicating about their work, hiring communications experts, building robust Web sites, and publishing materials far in excess of that required of them by law. At the same time, thousands of foundations are more interested in anonymity and staying behind the scenes.

The industry's interest in communicating its work is occurring in concert with a growing public awareness of the field. Philanthropists must recognize that the general public's awareness of their work has changed forever. The general and business media feasted on philanthropic cover stories in the last years of the 1990s. From a boom of celebrity philanthropist profiles to the wide-eyed wonder of how quickly billions of charitable dollars flowed to the direct victims of the 2001 terrorist attacks, the media "found" philanthropy at the end of the twentieth century. The media also quickly found a more sordid side to the story as well. The *New York Times* headline on September 14, 2001 read: "After the Attacks: Charity: A Range of Donors Helps those in the Rescue Effort," and it was followed one day later by "After the Attacks: The Profiteers: A Tragedy Spawns Charity Fraud and Oil Price Gauging."[16]

Media coverage of charitable giving related to September 11 looked closely at how funds were to be used and how philanthropic decisions were to be made. This was an uncomfortable spotlight for philanthropy, which found itself defending its lack of alignment with the public systems, its closed-door decision making, its endowment practices, and the meaning of donor intent. Over the course of the next two years, the once celebratory picture of philanthropy that filled pages in *People, Business Week,* and *Forbes* would be replaced with stories of excessive compensation, board perquisites, inadequate industry monitoring, community mistreatment, and egregious fundraising expenses.[17]

THE POTENTIAL FOR INDUSTRY ACTION

Philanthropy has an opportunity to use the regulatory structure to advance the potential of philanthropic investment. This chapter has sketched out the long history—philosophical, legal, and financial—between the public sector, private resources, and public benefit in the United States. Institutional philanthropy in the twenty-first century must be willing to examine its relationship to public structures in terms of partnerships for social purposes, legislation and regulation for future investments in philanthropy, and guidance in the marketplace as competition continues to increase. Promoting appropriate regulatory oversight will confirm the industry's commitment to accountable use of tax-exempt resources. It can reinforce the public commitment to private partners by demonstrating enviable corporate oversight, public disclosure, and freedom from conflicts of interest. As a partner with the public and commercial sector in addressing community needs, philanthropy can position itself to lead by promoting high standards of practice and working with oversight agencies to enforce those standards. Perhaps most important, the industry needs to promote more deliberate regulatory action to ensure that it remains a sector defined primarily by its social contributions and not by its role within the financial service marketplace.

This last point is the most difficult to articulate and the keenest source of pressure on the field. The commercial marketplace for financial products is rapidly changing, as every related industry from real estate to luxury services to travel to professional counseling seeks a piece of the "wealth transfer market."[18] This competition places philanthropy firmly in the midst of one of the most competitive and diverse marketplaces ever. The commercial industries excel at product development, marketing, and regulatory influence. Without a joint effort by the nonprofit endowments within the philanthropic industry, their emphasis on social mission will be pushed to the back burner by these other forces.

As donors comparison shop among philanthropic options—as well as the many other markets for their money—they will continue to balance the same decision factors as did the Rockefellers, as well as newer considerations such as price, efficacy, and efficiency. These donors are also a regulatory force to be recognized because they are also voters. While foundations wait to work with legislators, donors are the ones voting the legislators into office. The pressures on institutional philanthropy to find a political voice are a result of the divergent yet related political power of its constituents; its commercial partners are based within industries with extraordinary political experience and its individual constituents are voters who cover the political spectrum. Regardless of their partisan position, it is safe to say that individual voters bring to the polls a range of preferences regarding tax rates and social expenditures, but they do not bring a strong commitment to promoting the robustness of the philanthropic industry.

As a counterweight to external forces of pressure on philanthropy, the industry must develop a more articulated, proactive approach to philanthropic regulation. Moreover, internal commitment to ethical standards, public benefit, and the achievement of social purpose also provide good reason to pursue certain legislative and regulatory agendas. The delineation between public and private that the *Dartmouth* case began to clarify in the early nineteenth century has several twenty-first century counterparts. Philanthropic problem solving, institutional grant making, and individual charitable giving still flow to issues defined by public systems and revenue streams. Whether individual participants seek to function as an alternative source, a gap filler, or a partner to public support, philanthropic resources cannot replace public investments over the long term.

The philanthropic industry is guided by a complex set of regulations and regulators, and the diversity of firms within the industry adds to the complexity. Exhibit 5.1 provides an introductory picture of the regulatory players for philanthropic firms (including individuals). The first point to note is that both individuals and institutions need to act within two or three tiers of oversight. In many cases, the alignment between federal and state

EXHIBIT 5.1	PHILANTHROPIC REGULATORY FRAMEWORK AT A GLANCE					
	Federal		**State**		**Municipal**	
	Codes	**Monitors**	**Codes**	**Monitors**	**Codes**	**Monitors**
Individuals	Income tax	IRS	Income tax	State tax boards	N/A	N/A
Institutions	Corp. and sales taxes	IRS; Federal Trade Commission; House Ways and Means Committee; Senate Finance Committee; Banking and financial service regulators	Corp. and sales taxes	Dept of Corps.; Attorneys General; State tax boards	Property taxes	Local Assessors' offices

regulations is quite close; in others, they are completely out of sync. For example, until recently, the State of Minnesota did not allow residents to deduct charitable contributions to out-of-state organizations from their reported income, although they could be deducted for federal income tax purposes.

Similarly, the state tax regulations for different types of foundation contributions vary, as do state regulations on corporate structures, and national commercial vendors must also account for state variation in banking regulation. This hodgepodge of regulators and regulations provides ample opportunity for confusion or ignorance, not to mention abuse.

PRESSURE POINTS IN THE REGULATORY FRAMEWORK

Given the abundance of regulatory bodies involved with some piece of the philanthropic industry, there are seemingly innumerable opportunities for regulatory revision or action. Several of these have received significant attention in the general media, such as presumed excesses in administrative expenses or violations of donor intent.[19] Others have been long-term areas of contention within the industry, such as the minimum distribution of assets that foundations are required to pay out in grants each year to qualify for tax exemption, a requirement first implemented in 1969 and revised in 1984 and 1990.[20]

At the same time, however, some areas of the regulatory framework are much more obscure yet still wield significant influence and could effect substantial changes if they were revised. The variability of local property taxes and the frequent challenges to tax exemptions at the municipal level could force large property-holding foundations or nonprofits to operate in new ways. Examples of such entities include universities, hospitals, and many foundations, although the impact is felt most profoundly on those entities that own property in several jurisdictions. Another less visible point in the framework is the issue of who has legal standing to sue a nonprofit or a foundation. The recent Supreme Court decision to allow charities to be sued for fraud revolved around specific elements of commercial fundraising practices, yet may provide fuel to the fire to expand the scope of who can sue whom.[21] Other cases pending in Texas, New York, and Illinois focus more specifically on the issue of who can sue a nonprofit or a foundation. Changes in this question of legal standing have considerable philosophical implications for how these organizations view their public responsibilities. They also could have significant practical implications for how nonprofit and foundation decisions on everything from investments to grants get made, documented, and publicized.[22]

Replicating a pattern familiar in other elements of American life, the inability to obtain satisfactory action from regulators or legislators may signal a move to court action. As noted in a *New York Times* article on individual oversight in philanthropy, "Traditionally, only attorneys general have had standing to hold a charity to account in court, but the number of nonprofit organizations has exploded at the same time states have slashed budgets for charity oversight, which was never generous."[23] Should these cases be successful, we can safely presume that a shift in practice will occur regarding how nonprofits and foundations interact with their donors, partners, and the general public.

WHAT THE REGULATORY FRAMEWORK SHOULD DO

Having examined the regulatory structure for philanthropy and the industry's attitude toward it, we are left with the question of what the regulatory framework should do. What should the position of the philanthropic industry be regarding public disclosure, requisite financial practices, payout rates, corporate board structure, appropriate expenses, and accountability? Clearly, these are the issues for industry leaders and participants to act on, but what conceptual framework should guide them?

The industry framework gets complicated here. Most other industries are guided by the pursuit of profit at member firms. Philanthropy should be guided by the pursuit of the common good. There are many definitions of this—as there should be. There are many ways to pursue it—as there should be. This expansiveness can inform a common agenda regarding regulatory action. Key to action is the recognition that the variable for determining regulation, however, is not the benefit of the firms within the industry, but the benefit of the public that serves and is served by the industry.

There are several areas in which guiding principles for philanthropic regulation can be developed. These can be drawn both from the historical place of philanthropy in American society and from current challenges. At the very least, guiding principles should address (1) the freedom to act philanthropically and (2) the public obligations of private philanthropy.

The Freedom to Act Philanthropically

Philanthropy and charity have a long history, religious, cultural, and within the United States. The motivations for philanthropic giving are many, and all should be promoted. All individuals and institutions should have the opportunity to give their private resources as they see fit. This must apply both to the quantity of giving and the direction of the resources. Tax codes should encourage all individuals to give and afford them credit for their charity. Similarly, the breadth of choices for charitable giving should remain as great as possible—from direct provision of help to an individual to global policy research, analysis, and advocacy—because philanthropy and charity are critical contributors at all levels of the systems in which they operate. Restrictions or limitations on political perspective or the type of charitable activity should be avoided.

One key opportunity here is to examine tax codes and regulations with regard to the development and sale of products and services to encourage philanthropy. Philanthropic vendors—nonprofit and commercial—have a vested interest in continuing to encourage philanthropic and charitable giving. In this part of the philanthropic landscape, market forces work well. New product developments, marketing, and value distinctions are all important to maintaining a range of giving options that can serve the broadest set of communities.

Giving is a critical element of American tradition, it is important to communities in its many forms, and it continues to promote precisely the many alternatives to government action that it was designed to do in the early years of the Republic. Some will argue that tax-exempt funds are ultimately better used as tax receipts. The tradition of individuality and community in the United States, the religious and cultural aspects of philanthropy, charity, and tithing, and the Constitutional guarantees to free speech, assembly, and the right to contract argue otherwise. A system of laws that encourages philanthropic activity—at all levels—is an inarguable public benefit.

The Public Obligations of Philanthropy

Philanthropic funds must be used responsibly, ethically, and for the benefit of the public. Regulatory structures that enforce the public's right to know how these funds are being used are an important part of that accountability. New technologies and new markets for philanthropic information are further opening the doors on nonprofit and foundation finances, governance, and staff structures, and this is a positive move for the industry as a whole. Publishing or posting this information promptly and providing easy access to it is a baseline requirement.

In addition to the reporting requirements on financial activity, the oversight obligations of philanthropic board members and decision makers need to be set at the highest possible standards, and these standards must be enforced, within the industry and by its overseers. These decision makers need to be accountable for the financial activities of the organization, the social contributions pursued and achieved, and the public purpose of the funds. Above all else, the public-purpose obligation must be enforced to avoid self-serving relationships between the funds and those who manage them.

The 1969 Tax Reform Act laid the groundwork for public reporting of basic financial and grant information. In the 34 years since the Act was passed, the philanthropic sector and the public sector have become far more sophisticated about the impact of their financial actions. It is no longer enough to allow basic financial reporting to suffice in regard to the billions of philanthropic dollars now in play. After all, financial reporting tells us how much money is at stake but nothing about its purposes or its impact.

Monitoring, calculating, and reporting on results is treacherous work in the social and cultural circles where impact is more nuanced than bean counting. Yet tracking the results of the philanthropic investments (of both capital and grants) is key to actually preserving an appropriate role for the sector. The complex relationships between government agencies, public funds, commercial enterprise, and philanthropy make it even more difficult to clearly distinguish which funds or actions achieved which goal or the extent of causality. The key to reporting on public purpose may not lie in trying to tie monetary contributions to social outcomes; in fact, decades of experience with evaluation may be showing us that exactly the opposite is true.

So how do we capture and represent the public purpose and obligation of philanthropic action? The current regulatory structure guides only the resource decisions—it essentially tracks revenue flows—however, when a donor or board of trustees chooses a structure or strategy that costs more, it should logically return more to the public good. Measuring this only in terms of the actual expenses, and then deducting those expenses from the total grant distribution, makes little sense now (although it might have in 1969 when the options for giving were fewer).[24]

NEW MARKETS, NEW APPROACHES TO REGULATION

The regulatory principle here should be guided by the changes in the philanthropic marketplace since the 1969 Tax Act. It may have made sense to equate operating expenses with qualifying distributions when a donor's choices were effectively limited to private versus community or federated funds, but this is no longer the case. As we consider the public reporting obligations for philanthropic vendors, we must approach the regulatory issue with full recognition of the new market forces at work.

What should philanthropy report on to accommodate the changing market and to address this question of public mission? The answer will vary depending on how much "more than money" a philanthropic entity is intent on providing. For those individuals who manage their giving from nothing more than a checkbook, little can be expected other than reporting those financial contributions. For the more complex and supported versions of philanthropy—ranging from donor-advised funds at commercial firms to private foundations—more is expected and more should be reported.

For example, the current debate in Congress over the qualifying distributions of private foundations centers on whether staff, office, research, technical support, and other expenses should be counted as part of what the foundation contributes to the public good. The current structure only allows these contributions to be counted insofar as they are assessed as part of the total distribution requirement of the foundation. As such, there is no means in this structure for these investments to accomplish anything. They could do nothing other than offset funds for community work. And thus the debate has come down to counting those investments against the amount "due" to the public. But do the same regulatory structure and applications that mattered in 1969 still make sense today? Given the changes in the philanthropic marketplace, one has to consider a new approach to regulation.

Given the marketplace of options for philanthropic giving, it is logical to assume that those that require more infrastructure and support should and do cost more. Now that the industry is clearly made up of two kinds of products—asset management tools and advisory services—regulatory decisions and market choices should be seen along those lines. The most basic choice to be made is the asset management decision; once this decision is made, the additional advisory and assessment services can be added on. The current regulatory structure is focused on the asset management products and reporting. There is no real public oversight of the advisory service role, other than the prohibitions against self-dealing.

In choosing to go beyond the basic asset management tools, donors or board members are spending some portion of the core philanthropic assets on additional services. There must be some expectation of return on those costs: greater recognition, better results, professional management, or simply someone to do the work. Because these services are paid for from the core of philanthropic resources, a public obligation must be met in how they are spent. In fact, the very things this portion of philanthropic resource pays for can be considered public good, if they are in fact made publicly available.

As we imagine a more effective system, we must keep in mind the new role that relationships and knowledge are playing in philanthropy. The previous chapter highlighted several ways foundations are working together and with individual donors. In almost every case, the currency of those relationships is experience and knowledge. Regulatory support for cost effective ways of distributing knowledge or building an industry-wide knowledge base are two possibilities to consider.

New ways of maximizing the financial return on research and learning supports the goal of encouraging giving. This can be done in many ways. The marketplace can continue to morph toward centralized, accessible exchanges of explicit information while also building alliances and networks for relationships between donors and foundations.

On the other hand, the industry itself and the public sector might collaborate on developing a public/private philanthropic research and development organization. This would be a forum for vetting research findings, providing information to donors, and accessing publicly-supported research. Just as independent environmental advocacy groups are responsible for analyzing and advocating policy and action based on public data, a new

R & D organization for philanthropy could focus on making public credible, comparable data on community issues. Individuals, donor advisors, and foundations could use the data as they saw fit, but a single accessible source for broad based social data and metrics would be available. This kind of organization would serve as a research support service for the common good, consolidating research and knowledge sharing for use in complementary, cost saving fashion by the full variety of philanthropic organizations. Such an entity might have several departments, to focus on the two key products—new financial tools and advisory services. Standards of quality, leveraged investments in research and evaluation, and a central role in making information accessible, useful, and meaningful to donors would be the hallmarks of such a resource. It would streamline the process of entering philanthropy, advise institutions in their ongoing work, and relieve existing organizations of the burden of document distribution and research commissions.

The regulations that are passed to promote giving, which in recent years have included significant changes to the tax code, could focus on promoting informed giving or provide incentives for partnerships that reduce overall administrative costs and result in more dollars to communities.

MEANINGFUL METRICS

The industry needs a commonsense means of assessing and reporting the value of these knowledge-based investments. Assuming these additional investments result in higher-quality work, they should be rewarded. In other words, philanthropic vendors (e.g., staffed foundations, commercial firms, community and federated funds) that commission research, use evaluation, and employ staff to conduct due diligence should be recognized for these investments, insofar as they can demonstrate an improvement in the quality of the financial work of the foundation.

Given the variability of philanthropic purpose and the inaccuracy of most metrics for social welfare, how would this be done? Other industries that include both a mix of nonprofit and commercial enterprises rely on market incentives, prestige, and peer accountability. It is possible to establish structures that recognize and provide incentives for positive action. Education, health, and environmental groups have come up with both regulations and market incentives for promoting positive results from their actions. These range from peer accrediting agencies to reduced insurance costs for healthy behaviors to tax credits and refunds for using sustainable resources.

The challenge in developing incentives for results in philanthropy is that the incentives need to be provided on an individual or organizational level, whereas the results are most likely to be seen at some aggregated level. In addition, the impact of charitable investments is accomplished by the organizations they fund, not by the foundations, federations, donor-advised funds, or remainder trusts that hold the financial resources. The key then is to create incentives for philanthropy that tie them to the results of their partners' activities.

These ideas can already be seen in practice. Philanthropy is—in the best cases—holding itself accountable for the quality of the work of its partners. What is missing here is (1) any influence on that accounting by those same partners and (2) real incentives for working this way. Tiers of incentives are clearly needed. Tax deductibility of charitable giving at all income levels is a start. Encouraging joint action—participation in community philanthropy, joint funding, or federated giving—could be encouraged by increasing the deductibility of these gifts.

For institutions, developing and applying useful information, sharing staff expertise, creating partnered investments, and consistently monitoring and reporting results could be encouraged through reductions in the excise tax on private foundations. Community or commercial funds that can show their contribution to positive community results could be recognized as such and allowed to market themselves as meeting a certain standard. Such recognition is possible through peer review, by assessing the quality of the funds' issue or community knowledge through a process similar to assessing professors and universities, or through an independent ratings board that uses publicly understandable criteria and reviews philanthropic accomplishments.

Small steps toward these last two systems have already been taken. Several online ratings agencies exist for checking nonprofit financial information. These already include philanthropic organizations and could be expanded to reveal the accomplishments achieved through the financial activity. Similarly, the movement toward information sharing and knowledge building in philanthropy is a positive force for many reasons. Among other values, it opens the doors to formalizing and expanding the peer referral network that is so prevalent in philanthropy today. Funds, staff members, or boards that develop and distribute material could be assessed based on the use of that material by others. This information would be very useful to new donors, who are trying to choose among competing philanthropic options.

CHAPTER 6

Evolving the Industry

You have to be willing to see beyond the point.[1]

—Maira Kalman

Philanthropy must evolve from the current imbalance of market mentality and regulatory panic to a new system, one that is capable of inspiring and applying privately held resources to public good. Several significant changes have already occurred in the market but have not necessarily been noticed by all who will feel their effects. This chapter looks at four aspects of the industry where collective innovation and influence will create a more diverse, aggregated, and committed philanthropic industry. These four leverage points are the following:

1. Aligning products and services to aggregate resources
2. Using knowledge as a philanthropic resource
3. Promoting hybrid organizations and strategies
4. Redesigning the industry infrastructure

These are areas in which a dramatic amount of growth and excitement has already occurred. More important, they are areas where manageable changes can be made that will ripple throughout the industry and may thus be examined with an eye toward their tremendous potential.

Given the nature of these changes, bringing them to the forefront of thinking for industry decision makers and the communities served by philanthropy is critical. Philanthropy is one of the few industries in which collusion by disparate participants is both possible and positive. Actively sharing ideas, resources, research, development and assessment, and working together with other philanthropists, community partners, government, and business are key components of successful philanthropic strategies. To do this, we must share a common understanding of who and what matters in philanthropy as it now functions, so that our evolutionary goals are not drawn from outdated perceptions of the industry.

The industry needs to see itself in the aggregate as a set of remarkable assets—both financial and intellectual—to be used to make life worth living. As it now stands, philanthropy is an afterthought for most of those whose wealth is involved and a comfortable status quo—with few risks—for professionals in the sector. The current regulatory debate, the difficult market dynamics, and the public distrust for organized philanthropy and nonprofits may be—in the longer term—exactly the turning-point events that spark real evolutionary change in philanthropy. In the near term, however, wouldn't it be exciting to consider how to deliberately move the industry to a new standard, rather than relax into the hands of fate?

ALIGNING PRODUCTS AND SERVICES TO AGGREGATE RESOURCES

Chapter 5 ended with a presentation of the two key products currently available in the philanthropic marketplace: asset management and advisory services. This product-based view of philanthropy is a significant change from the common landscape of individuals, foundations, bequests, and corporate giving. By pointing out how these product lines have been separated—and distinguishing the products from the purveyors—we get a sense of the myriad of realigning and evolving elements that come into play.

When we take this view to the world of philanthropy, we see the more familiar elements of philanthropy as simply combinations of these products. Exhibit 6.1 presents a small sample of the product suites.

By turning our view from philanthropic giving organizations to product combinations, we see the potential for new suites of offerings, the entry points for new purveyors, and the opportunities for new product development. We can also see the likelihood that donors of significant wealth will be using more than one product or suite of products. As noted in Chapter

EXHIBIT 6.1   PHILANTHROPIC PRODUCT SUITES NOW AVAILABLE

Individual or family giving from bank account	→	Asset management
Family foundation, no staff	→	Asset management Advisory (legal, accounting)
Corporate foundation with staff	→	Asset management Advisory
Donor-advised fund, no additional support	→	Asset management Advisory (legal, accounting)
Donor-advised fund with program support	→	Asset management Advisory
Individual giving with contract program research	→	Advisory
Bequest including direct gift to nonprofit	→	Asset management

5, one of the product lines—asset management tools—is well-regulated, and innovation in product development for managing philanthropic assets seems to be quite sensitive to regulatory change. As tax codes, banking laws, and financial management regulations shift, the impetus for creating new asset management tools will be rekindled. In fact, because of their experience with product development, sensitivity to the bottom line, and regulatory changes, the commercial sector is likely to be the source of the most exciting new philanthropic asset management products in the future. How well the nonprofit sector of the industry will participate in this development or deploy these products once they exist is another issue.

At the same time, we recognize that the other major product—advisory services—is only partially regulated. The legal, accounting, and investment services provided to philanthropy are part of well-monitored industries and operate under the professional standards and guidelines of those fields. The program advisory piece, however, stands out as a separate entity. There are no standards of practice, no recognizable profession or credentialing requirements, no oversight bodies (self-maintained or otherwise), and no common definition of what the product line is. Elements of these advisory services include mission setting, strategic planning, grants management, due diligence, issue research, evaluation, and technical assistance.[2] Given how vast these services are, there are also few barriers to entry for potential providers, a good deal of room for innovation, few accountability measures, and no professionally certified standards of quality. At the same time, we know there are more than 17,000 paid professional staff in American foundations, several hundred if not thousands of consulting firms, more than 1 million nonprofit organizations (that advise individuals about their giving all the time), and countless individual relationships that inform a potential donor of how and where to give. These services—and the potential purveyors and purchasers—are on the edge of change in the industry. By recasting our perspective on the instruments of philanthropy, we see just how incredibly dynamic the market is. The questions of philanthropic evolution are not if it will happen or when, but how and led by whom?

This division of product and service has already occurred, and we must look to the future from this perspective. There are several key elements to building a new system of philanthropy: (1) sound commitments and meaningful definitions of public benefit must be expressed, rallied around, and pursued by viable networks of resources; (2) the changing dynamics between individual and institutional philanthropy need to be capitalized on to the advantage of communities; (3) the role of networks and temporal alliances needs to be raised up, over and above the marquee role now given to independent entities; and (4) the intellectual resources of the industry need to be amassed, applied, and assessed just as their financial counterparts are now.

Aligning for Public Benefit

The parameters around public benefit are quite broad. One source of this definition is set forth in Section 501(c)(3) of the tax code, which spells out what types of organizations are included, what activities they may participate in, and how they should be structured.[3]

It is important to note that several of the activities described in this tax code section are also routinely provided by public agencies, including schools, child and family welfare departments, public health providers, animal care and control, public works, and the police. Public benefit might mean any of these things, or it can also be seen as meaning "not private benefit," a point also made in the tax code that requires "none of the earnings of the organization may inure to any private shareholder or individual."

So how can a common definition of public benefit be achieved, if all of these activities and goals qualify? The process of defining a clearer, more cogent definition of public benefit will not occur at this broad level, nor should it. To seek to organize all of philanthropy around a single definition of public benefit would be both futile and ill considered. Promoting complementary or alternative views and services to those provided by the public's representative entities (i.e., democratically supported government agencies) is a core value of the philanthropic enterprise.

But what can be done—and must be done if philanthropic financial resources are to make a noticeable impact on difficult issues—is the alignment of like-minded philanthropists around common goals and visions. The reason is purely arithmetic: The kinds of benefits described as public—child welfare, arts promotion, education—are enormous pursuits requiring the resources of many, not just the resources of a few. To the degree that individuals, organizations, and foundations committed to a certain set of environmental goals can aggregate their financial and intellectual resources, they will advance their opportunity for success.

This need for aggregation and alignment has become both reality and rhetoric for one small corner of philanthropy: professional foundation staff. The reality can be seen in the proliferation of associations and alliances for information sharing and networking. The rhetoric can be seen in the lack of actual joint strategy and resource investment done by most foundations. Professionals may sit at a table with their peers, but their organizations will rarely make actual resource decisions together, fund the common research, or actively work together to pursue a mutual agenda.

The most well-known exception to this rule is the success of several conservative foundations in setting a common policy agenda and funding it for many years. This work, documented by the National Center for Responsive Philanthropy, involved several foundations acting on common principles, making decisions across organizations, and employing a broad strategic approach that included funding think tanks, policy analysis, communications strategies, leadership development, and grassroots activism. The second-stage analysis of these activities noted that the 20 groups studied spent $158 million in 1996, or $20 million more than the Republican Party collected and spent in that same election year.[4] Both studies note that these mutually defined and pursued funding strategies resulted in achieving the specific goals of the individual organizations participating and in influencing political debate at the state and national levels.

What is astonishing about this research today is not its findings so much as the degree to which they have been ignored by other funders. With exceptions for those practices noted from the Charles and Helen Schwab Foundation and the Eugene and Agnes Meyer Foundation in Chapter 4, there are very few examples to be found of independent foundations deliberately defining and endorsing a course of action and actively seeking other philanthropic resources to achieve common goals. Imagine, however, that the strategies used by the conservative foundations in the 1990s were to be replicated by groups of funders interested in social justice, biodiversity conservation, human rights protections, or promoting individual artistic creation in a metropolitan region.

What It Probably Looks Like Now

The current process involves aggregation primarily at the level of a particular nonprofit organization; all of the foundations in an area interested in promoting individual artists may find themselves all funding one presenting organization, for example. The funders will not have worked together to determine their common (or mutually exclusive goals), nor is the nonprofit likely to have the resources to spend on trying to bring these funders together to strategize about more efficient ways of working. Over time, some funders may move into other interest areas, leaving the rest holding the burden and the nonprofit desperately seeking replacement resources.

What Other Processes Would Look Like

Example 1   Several foundations meet and identify their common goals for artistic development over the next 10 years. They meet with local artists, nonprofit partners, public funders, commercial galleries, and individual philanthropists. They agree to a long-term goal involving the number of artists to support and the disciplines on which to focus, noting the respective sources of revenue for each type. Several aligned commitments of funding are made by the foundations and individual philanthropists, as complements to the predictable directions of the public funds. The artists, gallery owners, and nonprofit presenting organizations set the criteria for grants and assist in the selection process. All of the partners meet regularly over the course of several years to assess progress, identify new gaps or challenges, and bring new partners to the table. Ten years later, dozens of local artists have been supported, their work shown nationally, and the local art scene is thriving. All involved get credit for the success.

Example 2   An independent foundation is focused on prenatal health in low-income families. Having commissioned extensive research on the extent of this problem in the local region, the foundation makes the research available to a variety of social service providers in the community and all of the foundations in the region that address any related issues. Through a series of facilitated meetings, the foundation presents a set of goals, possible strategies, and complementary approaches, allowing all who participate to comment and disagree. After several such meetings, a core group of local foundations and individual philanthropists decide to commit several million dollars to the issues, in concert with the existing public agencies and revenue available.

In addition to addressing the specific challenges of providing preventive health care, the consortium agrees that all involved parties will be responsible for raising the funds necessary. To streamline the process, the private funds raised will be pooled together, managed by the private foundation, and allocated according to the mutually developed plan. An online communications system and regular meetings will keep the partners in conversation about progress and challenges, and the local university research librarian will provide weekly news and policy clippings on relevant issues. Regular tracking toward three goals is reported out quarterly: (1) families served and healthy babies delivered; (2) progress on changing the reimbursement protocol at several local clinics so that public and private funds are more evenly distributed; and (3) progress toward raising additional funds. Over time, significant gains are made in healthy births, and the network of providers has in place more outreach mechanisms, a quicker reimbursement process, and more readily accessible care for families.

Example 3   Several identity-based, progressive philanthropy associations find an opportunity to rent a large shared office space. After moving in, they learn more about how each group defines its work and identify several common principles of progressive action they hold. They develop a joint initiative to increase the culturally specific, transnational philanthropy they each care about. Working together, they obtain foundation support to contract with a product-development firm to prototype new financial services to facilitate individual giving and make the transactions less expensive.

Working with several prototype products, and supported by their extensive market research on the populations they serve, they seek a partnership with a financial service firm to jointly build and market the product to their local community, with the intention of taking it nationwide eventually. Five years later, each of these associations can point to the growth in transnational philanthropy within their communities and the savings produced by the lower cost of the new financial services. The financial service firm points to its expanded customer base among the various communities and the revenue stream from the new products. The supporting foundations point to the additional philanthropic resources now available in these communities. The associations also note the growth in their numbers and types of members, as they now boast individual, commercial, and nonprofit philanthropic entities as active members of their networks.

Alignment and aggregation of resources is possible when common goals are identified and success does not rest on independent causality. In other words, private organizations bound by common interpretations and commitments to a public good can achieve it. Private organizations intent on independent pursuit of their interests—even if those interests are to the benefit of a broader public—are less likely to accomplish their goals.

Individuals and Institutions

One of the largest chasms to cross in the industry is the separation of individual charity and institutional philanthropy. The relationship between individuals and institutions reflects the two-product structure of philanthropy perhaps better than anything else. Ironically, while donors are increasingly connected to multiple giving structures and are choosing a variety of asset management and advising options, institutions are attempting to maintain the old walls between their assets, their advice, and all other resources. In other words, the asset management tools bridge the chasm, connecting individuals to multiple institutions. At the same time, advisors for each of the institutions rarely operate in ways that facilitate aligning these resources, nor are they always aware of all of them.

IMAGINE THIS

Four brothers and sisters constitute the board of a foundation created by the wealth of the previous generation. The foundation has three paid staff people. Each of the siblings has funds at the local community foundation: one has a commercial gift fund, and three are on the corporate giving committee of the inherited family business. Each sibling has a spouse and children, and each of these families also contribute generously to the community and have a variety of estate planning tools in place.

When the family foundation staff members recommend a particular set of strategies regarding early childhood education in the community, the board acts on those recommendations with no thought of involving the community foundation's staff. They continue to make individual gifts from their donor-advised and gift funds to other early childhood initiatives. The family's giving goes in several other directions. After several years, the board is frustrated by the lack of success in their early childhood education initiative. None of the programs they supported has been able to raise funding to keep the projects alive.

At an annual community foundation event, one of the siblings mentions the initiative and its failure to a staff person at the community foundation. Intrigued, the community foundation staff member calls the private foundation staff to learn more. In the course of the conversation, the community foundation representative informs the foundation director that an alternative set of programs was launched at the same day care centers at the same time. That initiative is funded by virtually all of the other local foundations (including the community foundation). On hearing this, the family board gives in to their discouragement. They ask the staff to develop a new set of grant-making priorities for something other than early childhood education.

The preceding story reflects the strange truth of fiction. Although this example is entirely imagined, real examples of the exact scenario are probably present in every community with more than one foundation. Community foundation staff members are generally well aware of local initiatives, but only a few are focused in such a way that they can inform their donors about these options, seek out interested local foundations, or help align local funding toward a common goal. If one were to try to calculate the wasted funds in this example, it would have to include the foundation staff time spent in researching, developing, and implementing the initiative, all of the time and expenses of the day care centers associated with the program, and the money taken out of early childhood education by the discouraged foundation board.

The independent actors in the story were connected through several asset management tools, but that alone was not enough to align resources. The advisors in the story were ineffective in identifying the alignment opportunities. The day care centers were doing their best to find multiple means of support and probably could not even imagine that the funders were not aware of each other. Just as important, the individuals involved—the sibling board members, donor advisors, and charitable givers—seemed incapable of wearing multiple hats at once. They did not see the possibilities of aligning resources over which they had decision authority, so imagine how hard it is to align disconnected resources.

Aligning resources across individuals and institutions is key to capitalizing on the financial strength of philanthropy. At $25 billion, the cumulative giving by foundations is not small change; however, when compared to the $161 billion given by individuals, the potential for influence is profound.[5] Foundations and other early-stage funders need to actively involve the decision makers who will provide program funding three, five, or ten years in the future. In most cases, the sources of that funding are private payments (fees for service), individual donors, and public agents, either through government grants or contracts for service.[6] Foundations have not been particularly good at aligning with their peers, and the challenges of working with these downstream funders are even greater. They also are even more important to ensuring the ongoing viability of the organizations involved.

What continues to keep the institutional funders and individuals apart? Given the changing product mix, it is fair to predict that this traditional distance may begin to decrease; however, several obstacles must be overcome to make this happen. As the example shows, some of it is simply communication and information challenges. For both volunteer philanthropists and professional philanthropy staff, there never seems to be enough time to know all there is to know about any given issue. New uses of technology, new organizational structures at some foundations, and even new incentives for foundation staff members to track the "other money" they influence are all positive influences in changing this situation.

Much of the distance, however, comes from self-imposed organizational bias, an institutional focus on complex problem solving as opposed to direct service support. Charity has a distinct Judeo-Christian set of roots, and its American tradition draws heavily from the early colonists' aversion to big government and their commitment to serving their own communities.[7] Philanthropy, however, has roots in the Enlightenment and seeks to provide rational solutions to complex problems.[8] Through the institution building of the twentieth century, the more structured, formal, and informed mechanisms of philanthropy have come to look down on the more prevalent, disbursed, democratic forms of charity. Philosophically, this may be because, "By eliminating the problems of society that beset particular persons, philanthropy aims to usher in a world where charity is uncommon—and perhaps unnecessary."[9]

A quick glance at the data on giving in the United States and at prominent social indicators tells us that we are in no danger of philanthropy making charity unnecessary. The same analysis also begs the question, rather than answers it, about whether philanthropy—if that is equated with institutional giving—is really focused on root causes of social problems, but that is another issue. From at least two perspectives—that of the nonprofits doing the work and that of the donors making the initial asset management decisions—the distinctions between charity and philanthropy may be fading away. And that is a good thing because the potential for alignment of resources depends on systematically bringing both ends of the revenue stream together.

USING KNOWLEDGE AS AN INDUSTRY RESOURCE

The role of knowledge as a philanthropic asset has been explicitly discussed within the industry for the last few years; however, even before the terms *knowledge management, information economy,* and *intellectual capital* came to the fore within the foundation world, the recognition that good philanthropy depends on good information was well established. American foundations have long traded on the prestige their support lends an endeavor, hired knowledgeable professionals to guide their grant making, and invested specifically in research on issues of concern.

Foundations are now literally awash in information. They glean information from research; learn from community partners and colleagues; commission reports and studies; evaluate grants; and retain consultants to analyze issues, conduct meta-scans of research, and synthesize information into usable resources for their staffs and boards. Many foundations are now trying to find ways to manage the sea of information they generate and access; others are looking for ways to share what they know; and many are simply stuck trying to determine what knowledge they have, what information they need, and how to be more efficient in managing these resources.

All of this has happened in the context of a broader societal trend in which communications and information technologies have unleashed a flood of data and information into the workplace. Although this is a boon for the most part—providing people with easy access to information that can help them do their jobs more productively—it also brings to the forefront four key issues: applicability, duplication, time management, and quality control.

Philanthropy as an industry presents challenges to thinking about knowledge as a resource that are distinct from those within the commercial sector. First and foremost, most research is commissioned and used by large, staffed foundations with the resources to invest in analysis, commissions, consultants, evaluations, research scans, and so on. Other research resources in the field—from independent institutes, think tanks, research libraries, and academia—also are used most often by the foundations with the staff resources to locate, analyze, consider, and apply this information.

Second, the commissioning institutions are the primary users of these research products. Thus a foundation study on environmental justice is, more likely than not, only going to be distributed within the commissioning foundation and to a small circle of its peers. This is true even though the report may be of tremendous interest and applicability to community and environmental organizations, to other foundations, to policy makers, and to the media. Even as large foundations are increasingly investing in distributing their information, they do so in rather haphazard ways, they have fairly limited reach, the public must know which foundation covers which issues, and the general sense among most foundations is that distribution of knowledge is not a priority for their staff.

These factors result in an artificially low return on investment for the research; the only value the research is likely to generate is within the commissioning foundation. In this context, limited return means that foundations sponsoring research miss out on important strategies to develop sustaining resources for their work. Their ability to develop partnerships is limited, and their success in positioning their causes and grantees with other philanthropists is compromised. Ironically, drawing philanthropic resources together to address social issues is perceived by most funders as among their highest priority and most important social function because no one institution has the resources to solve societal problems on its own. Exhibit 6.2 illustrates the location and isolation problem.

The combination of these two industry characteristics—the disparity of resources available for research and the lack of research distribution—traps knowledge resources for philanthropy at the top of the industry pyramid, isolating the bulk of philanthropic partners from information and knowledge that could help all donors do their work and fulfill their social mission.

It is important to recognize two things about philanthropic knowledge resources. First, many of them exist entirely outside of the philanthropic pyramid. In fact, in some way or another the community expertise outside of philanthropy informs and feeds into all useful information and knowledge inside of philanthropy. In Exhibit 6.2, this is represented by the floating "i" off to the side of the pyramid. Second, while the institutions at the top of the pyramid are the most likely sources of packaged, independent, credible knowledge and research for distribution, the philanthropists and

EXHIBIT 6.2   INFORMATION AND RESEARCH RESOURCES IN PHILANTHROPY

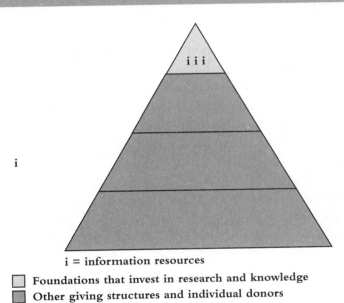

i = information resources

☐ Foundations that invest in research and knowledge
■ Other giving structures and individual donors

institutions at the base of the pyramid are not operating in vacuums. They tend to be very informed about their issues or their communities. This knowledge is not insignificant, it is simply largely unavailable for transfer to other organizations. One of the great possibilities of building systems to share knowledge across the pyramid is the chance to connect external sources, local sources, and top-tier sources in robust, meaningful, and cost-effective ways.

Reaping a Return on the Knowledge Investment

In the best-case scenario, the isolation problem pictured in Exhibit 6.2 allows a foundation to receive a return on its research investment equal to its own funding commitment to an issue. In other words, a foundation that spends $100,000 on research and then changes its own $1 million grant-making priorities to act on the research findings has achieved a 10-fold return on its research investment. Imagine if the same foundation saw that $100,000 research cost as a means to influence not only its own budget but also the budget of its peers.

This might require an additional investment of $25,000 in network meetings, publications, one-on-one exchanges, and all of the other costs of sharing information. The return, however, could mean a $150,000 investment that influences the grant budgets of 10 foundations, each with $1 million programs—or a 660 percent return on the research costs. Imagining this possibility, the isolation problem in Exhibit 6.3 shifts slightly as the peer institutions at the top begin to build connections.

If we focus on the knowledge assets, several of the challenges now besieging philanthropy become opportunities. For example, the connecting tissue between institutions and individuals is most likely to take the form of information and relationships. The same is true for the difficulties facing institutional collaboration: Information and knowledge are more easily exchanged than financial assets. Information and knowledge are also critical to defining the public benefits that groups of funders can jointly pursue. Finally, knowledge exchange is critical to linking local and global philanthropy.

Several examples of knowledge networks shed early light on the power and potential of knowledge as a philanthropic resource. Several of these use technology as a key providing system, but their power comes from the content, not the technological innovation. For example, Eureka Fellows, a

EXHIBIT 6.3   CONNECTING KNOWLEDGE SOURCES AT THE TOP

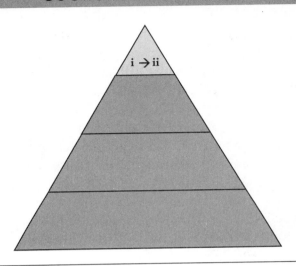

well-regarded fellowship program for nonprofit executives, has catalogued and put online the best evaluation resources identified by these leaders. This knowledge resource keeps fellows in touch with each other, helps them connect with others, and allows other philanthropists and nonprofits to benefit from the intelligence of this selective group.[10]

A different approach to leveraging knowledge is embedded in the Merrill Lynch Community Foundation Partnership, which is built around both asset management tools and knowledge. The financial advisers of Merrill Lynch will help identify philanthropic clients, who then benefit from access to the local expertise of community foundation staff people around the country. The assets are held by the community foundations and managed by Merrill Lynch. The foundations' local knowledge—significantly less fungible than the financial assets—form the distinguishing feature of this arrangement.

Knowledge resources are also being developed to focus on social entrepreneurship (*www.Gexsi.org*), communities of practice, (*www.SocialEdge.org*), and global development (*www.changemakers.net*; *www.globalgiving.org*), and within issue areas such as education (*www.edfunders.org*) or affordable housing (*www.knowledgeplex.org*). Once again, however, we see knowledge connections primarily being built by and for peer groups; deliberate efforts to connect individuals and institutions are still few and far between. We are at the cusp of change in this regard as several issue-based affinity groups are seeking ways to reach out to and serve individual philanthropists. The leaders in this arena so far appear to be the identity-based affinity groups such as Hispanics in Philanthropy (HIP) and Asian Americans Pacific Islanders in Philanthropy (AAPIP). Not only do these groups welcome both institutional and individual members, they are very cognizant of the various forms philanthropy takes across cultures and national boundaries. They also are actively reaching out to include commercial purveyors of charitable products, examining partnerships with issue-based groups or Social Venture Partners, and have long collaborated with other identity-based groups through the Joint Affinity Group.

The existing knowledge exchanges in philanthropy also tend to operate within existing philanthropic circles. The key to building truly powerful philanthropic revenue streams will be connecting the various institutions and individuals within the system. Institutions that invest in research need to involve and listen to the individual funders who will maintain programs over time, the program designers and managers, and researchers and policy experts on those issues. Current operational cultures still foster a closed-door attitude by funders. Foundations may invite expert opinion, but they rarely seek to partner with the experts, the programs, or the downstream funders over time. This change will make the standing networks within philanthropy truly powerful.

If information and research were used as the currency of these networks, the isolation problem identified in Exhibit 6.4 would cease to exist and information flows would look like those pictured, with information crossing boundaries and facilitating the clustering of like-minded philanthropists, regardless of their own ability to invest in the research.

This kind of exchange, wherein research, information, and knowledge are the organizing currency, and financial resources follow, is the first step in building stronger networks and more effective individual organizations. They require several changes in the mindsets of existing organizations. For example, standing behind one's research and seeking partners to implement the findings is one part of what I call *endorsement philanthropy*. It depends on the commissioning funder to be confident enough in the validity, applicability, and research basis of its work to stand behind it and seek partners.

The same principles apply to foundations endorsing the organizations with which they partner. It is one thing to publish a list of the organizations a foundation funds or even the research it commissions. It is another thing entirely to promote the work of partner organizations, to attest to the value of the research that underlies those decisions, and to call for others to join in.

Knowledge in the Marketplace

This kind of behavior would have several important effects on philanthropy as a whole. If the foundations that invested in staff and research made their research and background materials available, other funders would be able to assess that work directly. High-quality work would attract other funders, and unsubstantiated decisions or sloppy research would be ignored. The marketplace would come to judge the information and help allocate financial resources. Foundations or donors that could not or would not invest in high-quality research themselves would have access to that conducted by others. By virtue of this access, they could choose the lowest administrative cost options to manage their financial assets because the

EXHIBIT 6.4   MOVING KNOWLEDGE ACROSS THE INDUSTRY

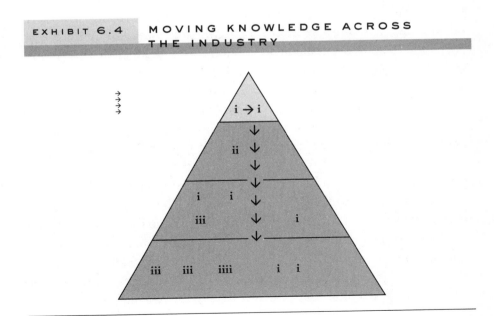

costs of professional information would be effectively spread among them. These practices would spur the openness and transparency to foundation decision making that so many have called for because the quality of the information and the reasoning behind decisions would be visible to others.

Just as in other industries such as academia, media, music, or health care, the opinions of others would come to matter in philanthropy. Markets assess the quality of information and service all the time in these other industries, either through publicized reports on the best colleges, doctors, hospitals, or movies or through more sophisticated mechanisms such as citation counts for professorial tenure or the number of major prize winners on a faculty or staff. Of the two major philanthropic products, the market has already proven itself a powerful force when it comes to asset management tools. It can be equally discriminating and informative when it comes to quality research, strategy, grant making, and evaluation—if the information were put into the marketplace.

A market for philanthropic information would also spur independent research and knowledge sources. These are emerging now and mostly taking the form of either comparative indices of nonprofit activity or competitive products from various consulting firms. In the index category, we can point to Charity Navigator, the analyst reports on GuideStar, and the promises of Philanthropix Partners as new entrants into the field. Modeling themselves on Morningstar's ratings of mutual funds, these services aim to provide independent analysis of certain giving options. They are focused on the nonprofits themselves, not on the giving vehicles, but the next step is clear.

The competition among consulting firms can be seen in the many types of articles and presentations they now produce. Just as in management consulting and commercial work, the prominence, credibility, and awareness of a consulting firm is seen as related to the quality of its publications. Using the same kinds of tactics as those who consult to gas companies or food wholesalers employ, foundation consultants seek new business through publications, speeches, conferences, and seminars. The trade publications in philanthropy are few and far between, but those that exist receive many submissions from consulting firms or actively seek big-name consultants and researchers as contributors. These forces are all in favor of building a market for philanthropic research and information, and the value of such a market will be better informed philanthropy at all places in the revenue stream.

Regulating Knowledge

As seen earlier, the other force at work to change philanthropy is the regulatory structure in which it operates. To date, regulations have focused primarily on asset management tools and have had little to say about information and knowledge assets. Indirectly, the requirements on qualifying distributions affect the industry's creation and use of knowledge or professional staff. In the 2003 debate over changing foundation distribution requirements, the Council on Foundations advocated (and encouraged its members to do so also) on behalf of retaining administrative expenses within these payout limits. The reasoning? Those expenses are often used for professional staff, technical services to nonprofits, and research—all characteristics of better-quality philanthropy, argued the Council.[11]

Regulators have made one major advance regarding philanthropic information, and that was the requirement in 1969 that basic financial information on these organizations needed to be publicly available. Like their nonprofit brethren, both public and private foundations must file returns with the Internal Revenue Service that show their financial activity year to year, identify board and management, and reveal the recipients of their grants. The degree to which these requirements are outdated can be seen simply in the requirement for published grant information. In an era when most large foundations are regularly posting this information on the Internet, they also must dedicate resources to print publications each year.

Regulating information is significantly more challenging than regulating asset management tools and should not be entered into lightly, if at all. It is much more likely that market forces will push valuable information into the public eye and the move toward independent and credible measures will continue than it is likely that fair and appropriate regulations could be developed that would meet the industry's needs. Given this, what role is there for regulation?[12] Certainly, the basic financial information now required from institutional philanthropy should continue to be required, although the technological advances since 1969 might invite a revisiting of the format questions. Governance disclosures, accuracy in reporting financial activities, and clear efforts to avoid conflicts of interest are also important. Beyond that, I do not believe that the regulatory stick is the right one to wield where philanthropic information is concerned; however, it is worth considering whether the regulatory structures can provide a carrot to encourage release of information and research.

For example, foundations that invest in research, professional staff, or technical assistance are clearly investing in activities above and beyond the bare basics of grant making. How do they account for the results of these investments? Counting them as part of the qualifying distribution does nothing to ensure that the expenditures produce any community good, but doing away with the qualification for these expenditures would surely reduce them. By marrying the regulatory provisions that encourage these investments with the power of the market to determine quality, philanthropy could take major strides towards greater effectiveness, cost savings, and aggregated action.

Imagine a regulatory structure that rewarded knowledge contributions to a philanthropic marketplace. It could reduce excise taxes in return for supporting knowledge exchanges, publications to the field, or by contributions to a citation index. Those foundations that make no investments in knowledge would be regulated solely according to their asset qualifications. Those charitable vehicles that invest financial resources in knowledge assets would be regulated on two fronts—one structured to encourage the other. A foundation with professional staff that provided due diligence and research support for other foundations with like interests could be given greater range for its overall administrative ratio. Those that publish research that is widely cited or employed in the field could receive similarly flexible monitoring. The market will be the more important and reliable determinant of quality, but regulation that rewards problem solving, knowledge exchange, and resource alignment should be incentive-based rather than punitive.

There is one exception to this scenario. The lack of regulations or credentials for philanthropic advisors is a scandal waiting to happen. We have seen them in the asset management product line and will no doubt soon see a violation wherein a consulting firm, advisory service, or independent ratings groups was in fact funneling philanthropic resources to its own purposes or providing a front for some kind of criminal activity. Market forces will play a significant role in weeding out ne'er-do-wells and inept service providers, but the market is too big and the providers so small that it may take a long time for a scam to rise to the necessary level of attention for the market to stop it. What should philanthropic program advisors need to know? How do program advisors relate to accountants, investment managers, and lawyers—all of whom serve this market and are (at least to some degree) regulated by professional standards and monitoring bodies? In the likely evolution of this service industry, self-defined standards and credentials may appear first and serve more as a signal of quality than as a preventive measure against scandal; however, the trajectory is inevitably toward more professionalism, accountability, and visibility.

Knowledge Resources

Share your knowledge. It's a way to achieve immortality.

—Attributed to the Dalai Lama, e-mail chain letter, 2003

The Dalai Lama's view of perpetuity, not surprisingly, portends rather different strategies for endowed foundations than the current focus on investment strategies and payout rates. The inexact science that is the current status of philanthropic assessment set the stage for a burst of interest in learning communities, knowledge management, and communities of practice. New technologies suddenly make data plentiful and readily accessible, and the trick seems only to learn how to interpret, share, and use the information to improve work practices, enhance grantee relations, and lead to greater outcomes. Once again, the rise of these practices in corporations and government, the flow-over of consulting firms that serve the private sector and now work in philanthropy, and the pervasiveness of certain press outlets in institutional philanthropy helps move these practices through the sector.

A good example of the deliberate distribution of knowledge can be seen in the Hewlett Foundation's recent experience in children and youth grant making. Sparked by the Foundation's rapid growth in assets that ensued after Mr. Hewlett passed away, the board voted to add a program area focused on children and youth to their portfolio of interests. High level experts from academia and the public sector were brought in to run the program, and they spent a year or so collecting data, analyzing research studies, working with expert advisors, and involving leading nonprofits to advise the direction of the program. By the time this was done, the stock market had crashed, the foundation's endowment was significantly less than once envisioned, and the board chose to focus on the original programs and not invest any more in children and youth. But what to do with the research? How to get some return on the enormous investment in time and money that had already been made, and the effort and energy of the researchers, nonprofits, and expert advisors? Rather than simply publishing papers or uploading data to the Web, the Foundation instead invested in an active program of research distribution—sharing white papers, hosting meetings, sending staff on road shows to other funders, and actively seeking to inspire others to use their work and take it further.

Efforts like this are rare. Using information technology well and staffing organizations in ways that people can effectively use knowledge is itself quite a trick. Nothing has shone a brighter light on the challenges of philanthropic organizational cultures quite like the recent experience of using technology well and trying to use foundation knowledge as a resource. Both goals are achievable and both hold promise for improving philanthropy. A startup effort by Grantmakers for Effective Organizations (GEO) to connect foundation knowledge managers is underway. Several industry conferences have featured sessions on knowledge and knowledge management, and the major trade publications have written about it. The believers and the skeptics have met head to head on several panels and debated the merits and fallacies of knowledge in philanthropy and philanthropy in a knowledge economy.

Just as it has taken more than 20 years to establish a common set of tools for evaluation (and even that set is by no means universally adopted or well-deployed), it will take years for knowledge practices to become meaningful parts of philanthropic activity on a scale of any importance. What foundations have learned by virtue of their efforts to change is as important as the lofty goals of change themselves. The need for leverage points and organizational leadership, the role that networks and associations can (and cannot) play in promoting change, the costs of change, the resistance to it and the need to identify incentives, and the unclear connections for so many foundations among resources, operations, and results are some of these lessons.

Ideas and strategies such as learning or knowledge management seem to move through philanthropy in a fairly predictable pattern. Aided by industry associations, publications, and peer networks—as well as consulting firms, advertising, competition, ego, and the Internet—I believe there is a fairly common trajectory of ideas to action in philanthropy that involves big ideas, early adopters, revisionists, networks, publications, consultants, researchers, critics, and adaptation.

The trajectory includes two inevitable periods, one of Evangelism and one of Dismissal. Some ideas become jargon du jour, whereas others go back underground, where they are implemented at some organizations, experience some success, and may reignite on the industry idea list a few years later, better tested and adapted to a variety of philanthropic environments. These become a "soft standard" of the field.

An example of this is the theory of social change explained so well by Malcolm Gladwell in *The Tipping Point*. Gladwell's contribution was simplicity and eloquence; the ideas and theories were already out in the academic literature, but he made them interesting, relevant, and understandable. The year or so after his book was published, foundations hosted a frenzy of readings and promotions of his work. That energy has died down, but three years later we find the book in the new staff orientation materials of several foundations, it is still being swapped around among peers, and a common vernacular exists in which foundation staffs speak to each other of collectors, mavens, and salesmen.[13]

Toward a Knowledge Foundation

Imagine an organization that routinely gathers data, systematically derives new learning from it, makes decisions based on those lessons, and invests both dollars and the expertise that is gathered from the organizations it supports, and you have a new institution: the knowledge foundation. Such an organization relies on a revaluing of foundation assets to include not only their financial resources, but also their information technologies, knowledge bases, and organizational learning systems.

One caveat about knowledge as a resource: Valuing foundation knowledge neither subtracts from the importance of financial resources nor is it meant to distract foundations from thinking strategically about those resources. Rather, knowledge assets add to the foundation's resources, as they become strategic guides in deploying financial resources, as well as one of the desired returns on those investments.

The development of new ways of using and sharing knowledge will improve the ability of individual foundations to accomplish their missions. It will also improve the ability of the industry as a whole to calculate the overall contributions it makes to society in return for the public trust it holds. Foundations that can manage knowledge and apply it strategically will leverage other private and public funds to their issues and initiatives and manage more effective partnerships. They should also be able to measure improvements in their internal efficiency and the effectiveness of their staff and board decisions.

A *knowledge foundation* is a philanthropic institution that views knowledge as a distinct asset and strategically develops, captures, uses, and shares knowledge to achieve its mission.[14] The foundation recognizes that it relies on both external and internal knowledge and develops strategies that are appropriate to both sources. Several strategies are currently being tried to connect knowledge capture and use with mission accomplishment.

IMAGINE THIS

The K Foundation is committed to helping children learn and develop into healthy adults. It funds after-school programs as part of this mission. In addition to research and advocacy, it funds several local programs. In each of these proposals, it notices a budget item for transportation.

After several years, the foundation staff realizes that they have been spending tens of thousands of dollars every year on bus insurance. They know from research on after-school programs that transportation is a key to success. They also know from informal conversations that their peer foundations are effectively funding the bus and insurance companies as well. They also know that the local city government spends millions on public transportation. They decide to see if there isn't a more efficient and effective approach.

The K Foundation's evaluation staff reviews five years worth of grant proposals and develops a standard means of calculating transportation expenditures. A graduate student researcher is hired to gather the same data from as many of their local foundation peers as possible, and they assemble historical data from 20 foundations, totaling several million dollars annually. The K Foundation convenes its peer foundations and the nonprofit organizations that were being funded by most of the foundations to run these programs. They share the data analysis and ask the group, "Isn't there a better way?"

After several discussions, the group decides to jointly investigate pooled transportation opportunities. It also proposes several ideas for working with the city to better use public transportation facilities. One of the foundations has its research staff analyze the local public transportation system and budget on behalf of the group, while another foundation's reference librarian identifies model transportation partnerships. The researcher contacts the local newspaper's transportation and city desk reporters for data and past analysis and to let them know the work is happening. A report is developed, and the foundations and nonprofits invite several department heads from the city and school district to review the study and help them develop alternative, cost-effective solutions for transporting the city's children to after-school programs.

The joint group of foundations, nonprofits, and city leaders identifies numerous short- and long-term options. They include a private bus pool, safety monitors on public bus lines so parents will allow children to ride by themselves, new public bus routes, reduced bus rates for program staff so they will ride with the children, a public awareness campaign, parent information workshops, and coordinated schedules and locations for after-school programs. Some of the short-term solutions are implemented, work begins on the longer-term strategies, the media covers the story, and other cities begin to seek out the lead nonprofit, foundation, and department heads for advice.

Over the years, the individual foundations see a decrease in expenditures for transportation and bus insurance. The programs track improved attendance rates, and the city sees an increased use of its public transit system without an increase in safety violations. The foundations share their analyses of the joint work with the nonprofits and the public, and new opportunities for helping young people learn and develop are identified.

The simplicity of this example is intentional. Many foundations executives will read this and say, "Of course, we are already doing this." But the subtleties are important. How often do foundations actually conduct the syntheses and analyses of grant reports and share that information with a group of nonprofits? How often do they work with community agencies to identify the next round of community education goals to pursue? How often do they tap journalists as data resources? How often do they work to publicly demonstrate how what they are learning is informing their next round of decision making or actively seek ways to help nonprofit partners demonstrate the same thing?

Acting the way the example describes would require new types of behavior by most foundations. It would involve a level of participation in the problem-definition stage that few foundations open up to the nonprofits. They would have to, as the Schwab Foundation seeks to do, co-create strategies with the partners who will carry them out. It would require a willingness to reveal what sources and research are being used to inform strategy development. It also would involve foundation staff (or board) members sitting at the table, learning from and with nonprofits, local government, and journalists; doing some of the heavy lifting (synthesis and analysis), while acknowledging that the nonprofits themselves are the source of the data, the information and much of the knowledge about what families need to access high-quality after-school programs. In this example, the foundation is developing, using, and sharing this knowledge.

These changes essentially require foundations to see themselves within an industry of others and to build themselves accordingly. As one expert on corporate structures has noted:

> Knowledge does not directly convert to utility or living standards. If each of us specializes in a single branch of knowledge but attempt to use this knowledge without relying on others, the standard of living achievable would be less than if everyone had become a jack-of-all-trades. Although knowledge can be learned more effectively in specialized fashion, its use to achieve high living standards requires that a specialist somehow use the knowledge of other specialists. . . . This difference between the economic of acquiring and using knowledge has profound implications for social organization. . . . Firms and industries must form a pattern of economic organization that takes account of the need for acquiring knowledge in a more specialized fashion than the manner in which it will be used.[15]

Such changes require new staff structures and responsibilities. They need new definitions of communications and evaluation. They call for a different role and emphasis in the work of program staff. Many foundations are, in fact, moving on some of these tracks and hundreds have expressed interest in working together to solve these problems,[16] but the example of the K Foundation shows the careful dance that must be done between organizational change and industry movement. Experience shows that to in-

fluence the industry, real changes must be made simultaneously and strategically within each organization. As Demsetz, the organizational expert,
notes, "Economic organization, including the firm, must reflect the fact
that knowledge is costly to produce, maintain and use. In all these respects
there are economies to be achieved through specialization." To justify
these costs, each foundation then needs to develop "this knowledge into
products or services that can be transferred between firms cheaply."[17]

While the impact of the philanthropic endeavor will be felt at the industry level, individuals guide the organizations that serve as key nodes in
the network. It is counterintuitive to suggest that one can ease the burden
of such a load by thinking beyond the boundaries of the single organization to clusters or networks of other organizations and resources. But doing
so is critical if duplicative effort is to be minimized, creative and practical
management ideas widely deployed, and organizational goals attained.

PROMOTING HYBRID ORGANIZATIONS AND STRATEGIES

The nonprofit sector is rife with commercial ventures, and much is known
about how to work with Unrelated Business Income and manage different
revenue streams to achieve a social mission. The hybrids that are playing a
role in philanthropy are something different. They are at once more present and more invisible. They include commercial consulting firms with
nonprofit arms or subsidiaries (e.g., Foundation Strategy Group and the
Center on Effective Philanthropy; Bain and Company and The Bridge-
Span Group) where the resources of the commercial entity (financial and intellectual) are designed to support the nonprofit venture. We can also find
examples of nonprofit philanthropic associations and community foundations providing commercial consulting services as a new revenue source.

Philanthropy is also being pushed to change by the rapid evolution of
hybrid service providers, vendors, policy groups, and philanthropic institutions. These organizations are proliferating and range from subindustry
research and development organizations such as Community Foundations
of America (CFA) to nonphilanthropic networks with new philanthropic
interests (World Economic Forum) to commercial conference providers
that dedicate all revenue to grant-making foundations (the TED Conference and The Sapling Foundation).

The importance of these hybrids is not so much their commercial/non-profit structures but their product and service mix. As we try to imagine the directions in which philanthropy is moving, it is necessary to constantly remind ourselves of the new ways in which asset management and advisory services are being packaged and delivered. These hybrids raise real challenges to the philanthropic structures with which we are familiar. If we continue to see philanthropy as a mix of independent, community, corporate, and operating foundations, and individual donors as something else altogether, we miss the true nature of the industry. That static vision relegates all other entities in the industry—research centers, associations, vendors, consulting firms, and the trade press—to a tangential status that misses their growing importance.

More important, it makes it nearly impossible to see what role these entities play when they start to provide new services or products or align in new ways. For example, when a community foundation underwrites a tax attorney to write planned gifts for any donor and any nonprofit, what does that do to our common assessment of community foundations as managers of a pool of endowed assets?

Or what about when these entities engage in new product development with commercial vendors to address long-standing challenges for nonprofit grant makers. For example, the nonprofit CFA has partnered with the commercial firms B2P Commerce and Microsoft to produce Impact Manager, an evaluation tool for nonprofit community foundations. We see commercial asset managers being matched with nonprofit advisors (Calvert Giving Folios) and private foundation presidents leading efforts to attract donors to certain issues. We can find examples of philanthropic gifts being used to develop drugs deemed not commercially viable and then distributed by public health systems and major pharmaceutical companies.[18] We also see efforts such as the creation of affordable water pumps that will stimulate sustainable and commercial farming in sub-Saharan Africa and other drought-stricken areas of the world, all made possible by initial philanthropic investments.[19]

If we hold onto the old definitions of organizational structure and roles, these examples look incidental. If, however, we adjust our vision to focus on the two primary products in philanthropy—asset management and advisory services—we suddenly start to see that these aberrational hybrids are everywhere. And evolutionary theory tells us that the resilient mutants among these hybrids are likely to succeed.

REDESIGNING THE INDUSTRY INFRASTRUCTURE

As the industry changes, it is clear that new means of supporting it, speaking on its behalf, and attracting new participants to it is necessary. Despite the allusion to an engineered system, the philanthropic infrastructure is more aptly described as a set of organizations developed in opportunistic fashion over several decades than as a system of support that provides essential services to all components of the industry.

In recent years, awareness of the infrastructure has increased. This is partly the result of specific efforts by members of that infrastructure, such as regional associations, and partly the result of a sense that the support organizations that constitute the infrastructure were proliferating faster than was sustainable. Although some close analysis has been performed to identify infrastructure organizations and occasional efforts have been made to present a coherent framework for thinking about the infrastructure, these efforts have had little impact.[20] Part of the reason for that limited impact is the nature of those conducting the research: Most of it has been done by the organizations that constitute the infrastructure. Their reach is already limited, either by their deliberate exclusion of individuals as members (and therefore their lack of relevance to 80 percent of philanthropy) or by the fact that the current membership organizations for institutional philanthropy collectively involve fewer than 10 percent of their target market.[21]

Given the lack of collective vision about the shape and role of the philanthropic industry, the limited view of the infrastructure is not surprising. Even as individual organizations work collaboratively to map the infrastructure, they do so from the assumption that they are important to the well-being of the whole industry. This results in a set of mutually exclusive Ptolemaic visions of the infrastructure, with each organization presenting a map of the universe with itself at the center.

Although joint gap analysis is important, and serious discussion has ensued about how to collaboratively meet the needs identified in Exhibit 2.1, the planning has taken place without a shared sense of direction or even a common agreement about who is to be served. It has involved the existing core players in a way that results in accretive reform, rather than crafting a new vision for a new industry. This kind of visioning is difficult, but it can truly benefit from thinking about philanthropy as it compares to other industries, be it the recording industry, financial services, movie making, or health care.

These other industries provide fodder for our imagination as we consider the necessary components of a philanthropic infrastructure. We can look outside of philanthropy to see the role of membership associations, state and federal regulators, credentialing bodies, the media, independent ratings groups, lobbyists, and promotional organizations. We can compare those possibilities with philanthropy as we understand it. And then we begin to imagine an infrastructure not patched together from existing parts, although surely many existing organizations will continue to play key roles, but one that is derived anew from a sense of the future.

In other words, we must look at the industry as it is now and not as it once was. The current infrastructure is organized primarily around types of organization and then qualified according to geographic location, issue, or identity. Thus we have a Council on Foundations, regional associations, and affinity groups (identity or issue-based). We have several research organizations (Association for Research on Nonprofit and Voluntary Action, Aspen Institute, university centers), policy organizations (National Center for Responsive Philanthropy, Independent Sector), and a patchwork of executive education programs, training opportunities, standard setters, lobbying firms, regulators, and vendors of everything from advice to specialized software.

Some of these organizations are critically important, but few of them easily align with the industry's six key components. A robust infrastructure for the industry would provide support for each of these pieces to flourish, for collective work to occur, and for standards of excellence to be promoted while rooting out fraud. Moreover, a visionary infrastructure would capture, organize, package, and distribute relevant market and industry research, share useful program knowledge, strengthen and certify the professional qualifications of those doing the work, and lay the groundwork for organizing philanthropic resources into a viable revenue market. Its distinct pieces would be self-sustaining, providing those products and services that the industry participants were willing to pay for. The infrastructure should serve all who participate in the industry as they need it, and pricing and fees should reflect both the industry-wide nature of the support and the pay-as-you-go nature of certain services.

Framed in this way, the infrastructure begins to revolve not around organizational type, but around services and supports. The key elements of those services and supports are presented in Exhibit 6.5, as they relate to each of the six components of the industry.

The picture presented in Exhibit 6.5 is an astonishing view of the philanthropic infrastructure. For the most part, the usual suspects do not appear as the existing providers. In fact, several of the entities identified as providers would not see themselves as part of the infrastructure, whereas organizations that consider themselves cornerstones of that structure are notably missing. This table reinforces the commonly held sense that yesterday's infrastructure is out of alignment with today's philanthropic industry.

POTENTIAL LEVERAGE POINTS

What we begin to see in comparing this view of the infrastructure with the industry's potential is the opportunity to reconfigure the infrastructure to advance the industry. Two of the biggest opportunities can be found in product and services innovation and alliance building.

Product Alliances

The first opportunity covers two characteristics: product innovation and alliances. Currently, financial product innovation is the purview of the commercial entities in the philanthropic industry. These firms have expertise and experience in banking regulations, tax code review, product pricing and marketing, and retirement laws, whereas few community foundations have the staff to research and pilot test new financial products. They lack the in-house expertise on donor motivation, effective giving protocols, family dynamics, and community indicators that the nonprofit vendors provide. Both ends of the industry could capitalize on the distribution access of the other. A research and development product incubator supported by both commercial and nonprofit vendors would efficiently marry the sets of expertise and serve the marketing needs of both.

This idea reflects the product and service nature of today's philanthropy and uses the incubator concept to go deeper than just replicating traditional organization structures (such as foundations) to design products and

EXHIBIT 6.5	SERVICES NEEDED TO SUPPORT THE PHILANTHROPIC INDUSTRY	
Industry Component	**What Needs to be Done**	**Current Providers (examples)**
Capital for investment	*Financial capital* Marketing to emerging philanthropists to keep the capital coming	*Financial capital* ➤ Professional advisers ➤ Community Foundations
	Human capital Human capital core competencies and standards	*Human capital* ➤ Small-scale training programs. No industry standard or required certification
Firms, markets, and customers	*Industry-wide* research on who is participating and where growth opportunities might be	Proprietary research done by commercial firms and community funds. No single industry source
Products and services	Innovation to capitalize on changing regulations and new markets. Knowledge resources to centralize, capture, repackage, and qualify useful information	Commercial financial service firms
Competition/Alliances	Efficiency-building tools to streamline costs of alliances and remove barriers to partnerships	Community Foundations of America
Regulation/public policy	Maintain relationships with regulators and provide proactive proposals to enhance, strengthen, and diversify philanthropic products and participants	➤ Council on Foundations ➤ Regional Associations ➤ GEO ➤ Private lobbying firms
	Industry metrics that allow for comparative analysis or sector-specific investment assessments	➤ Foundation Center tracks limited data
Media attention/ public awareness	Build awareness of the options and accomplishments and how to effectively participate	➤ National and local newspapers ➤ Trade press

services for the entire industry. Such a research and development effort would allow the industry as a whole to quickly build and distribute the donor-advised fund of tomorrow. Ironically, such an effort would not be a diversion from the past relationships but a continuation of them, banks having given rise to community foundations, which gave rise to donor-advised funds, which were promoted so heavily by financial firms that they became seemingly indispensable products for community foundations.

Alliances for Efficiencies

Similarly, certain subsectors of the industry are concentrating hard on building efficiencies that will allow them to serve the local and global interests of philanthropists. Merrill Lynch and several community foundations have launched a joint asset management and advising service that brings the global reach of the brokerage firm along with the local knowledge of the community foundation. Similarly, the CFA has started work on a multimillion-dollar technology initiative that will give community foundations a common back office to lower the costs of donor transactions across geographic boundaries. A joint programmatic initiative is also being discussed, a model for which community foundations need look no further than the local Rotary Club. In 1985, Rotary International, a global network of local volunteer organizations, launched PolioPlus to help eradicate polio. Eighteen years and hundreds of millions of dollars later, polio is now found in only six countries around the world, and Rotary Clubs continue their local fundraising efforts for this global partnership work.

What differentiates both the proposed financial research and development effort and the work of the CFA from so many of the existing networks and alliances is the focus on a specific objective. Most of the philanthropic associations that now exist expect and depend on members to join year after year and participate in the ongoing activities of the association. The alliances described are modeled after a movie production company, which comes together to make a movie and then the partners disband to work on other projects, occasionally reassembling as a whole. This strategy is much more applicable to today's philanthropic industry than the good citizenship model that underlies so many of the existing structure organizations.

Such alliances could efficiently and effectively meet many of the service needs identified in Exhibit 6.5. In addition to new financial product development, several other products could be built by temporal industry alliances, hybrid partnerships of existing players, or new commercial entrants. Here are a few such ideas:

- An efficient knowledge resource that would decrease duplicative investments in evaluation or situation analyses
- Subscription program and due diligence services
- Mechanisms for new philanthropists to find peers with similar interests
- Sector analysis of philanthropic investment in the arts or community development
- Distance learning programs on issues or grant making
- Independent ratings systems of philanthropic investments

Once again we can look to other industries to see the potential and the risk of these strategies. One of the most important recent developments to track will be the independent research structure imposed on brokerage firms by the recent settlement with the New York Attorney General's office. This well-publicized $1.4 billion agreement requires the major investment banks to separate analyst pay from investment banking revenues, to contract for research from a set of independent providers, and to clearly acknowledge the sources of information and conflicts of interest. Only one of the banks involved, Citigroup, is attempting to spin off a new business unit to perform these functions. In its newly reconstructed Smith Barney subsidiary, Citigroup will try to produce and sell research that is independent, credible, and valuable enough to be purchased first by its own retail brokers and eventually by Citigroup's other divisions, namely private banks, asset managers, institutional traders, and investment banks.[22]

Although the conflicts of interest that roiled investment banking and led to this new structure do not have direct counterparts in philanthropy, the parallels between the research and due diligence functions and the asset management functions in the two industries is striking. The opportunity for philanthropy is to consider if a similar independent and credible approach might provide a higher-quality, lower-cost research product that would facilitate philanthropic grant making for many customers at once.

Networks as Key Delivery Mechanisms

The greatest opportunity for a new infrastructure is to connect the discrete ends of the nonprofit revenue stream. Currently, individual donors and institutional philanthropists are connected programmatically through the nonprofits they support. So an individual contributor to an organization may read the donors' list and note the foundation supporters, or staff from a foundation may meet individual donors at certain fundraising events or other functions. Even when the individual is also connected to a foundation directly (e.g., as a board or family member), there are few strong mechanisms for helping that person wear both hats simultaneously.

One such mechanism that has accomplished this is the giving circle, although this result was unintentional. For example, in Seattle the 1998 launch of Social Venture Partners (SVP) focused on bringing individuals together to think and act philanthropically as a community. The focus of the work was on easing new donors into philanthropy and helping them connect with nonprofits in the community. After several years, it became apparent that the individuals who participated in these partnerships were also in charge of several other charitable or philanthropic opportunities and were able to quickly transfer the SVP resources—research, staff, community connections, due diligence tools—to the giving they did as part of a separate foundation, through their company, or with their family.[23]

In other words, unintentionally, donors who participated in SVP used what they learned in their SVP giving and in their other philanthropy. The SVP resources were a central hub of skill development, contacts and networking, community research, and idea generation. For these donors, their SVP participation served the role of an advisory service, influencing their decisions on asset allocation from several other pots of money than just those they had committed to SVP.

The power of a network is seen in the influence it has not just on its direct participants but also on the more tangential nodes. In the SVP example, we can track the immediate funds brought to bear through SVP's asset management tools and see that the advisory and learning elements of the network reached and influenced other non-SVP resources as well. It is not only the local impact that matters. Through its burgeoning international

network, SVP International now counts more than 1,200 individual partners and more than US$14 million in grants made.[24]

Networks have a power that cannot be matched by any single organization or individual. They allow for pooled resources, joint idea and knowledge generation, connections to other networks, and an amplification of the
resources of each participant. Institutional philanthropists have known this
for years, and the hundreds of different associations and networks for foundations alone testify to this understanding. A 2002 scan of philanthropic networks found more than 200 operating at local or regional levels. Another
hundred or so can be identified at the national and international level,[25] but
very few of these associations work deliberately to connect institutional and
individual members; they tend to be formed around issues, identity, or geography and then broken down by structural type (institution or individual).
In the last year, a major national association and several regional associations
of giving institutions have reached out to include individuals, but those efforts are so new as to have barely registered on the landscape.[26]

Networks that can connect individuals and institutions are the beginning
of a new revenue flow within philanthropy. It is easy to see how foundations
could share their research within these groups and help encourage or identify additional individual investors to those areas of interest. Similarly, the individuals who might participate are likely to have insights into organizations
or communities that professional foundation staff may not ever access.

In addition to connecting the early- and later-stage funding of institutions and individuals, strong networks allow us to imagine entirely new
ways of organizing and moving information. If a network on funding
strategies to end homelessness included staffed foundations, foundations
with no staff, donor advisors, charitable gift fund purveyors, individual
donors, researchers, and community organizations, it could significantly
streamline the research and due diligence conducted by each organization
and spare the individuals the costs of conducting such analysis themselves.
The professional advisors in the group (program staff, knowledge officers)
could conduct the same amount of work they normally would for their
own organization but have a means of sharing it with several other entities.
Such an opportunity allows for greater return on the analysis investment,
lower costs of philanthropic operations, and potentially lower costs for the
nonprofit agencies.

These kinds of networks would unleash the intellectual assets of a single institution and allow access to it by all types of financial assets. By bringing greater financial resources to bear, the network might also invest in a greater level of independent research on sectors, trends, and opportunities, knowing that more organizations and donors would have access to the information. Not only do the networks provide an opportunity for strong idea exchanges and bring in national or global perspectives, but they also offer a way of underwriting operational costs by several partners.

In essence, the network idea is a description of the most valuable work of community foundations. Community foundations sit at the intersection of the key players—community organizations, individual donors, institutional philanthropists, professional staff, and relevant research. Some community foundations recognize their prime location at that intersection and operate in ways that are specifically designed to share the expertise gained from that location. For example, the Minneapolis Foundation offers consulting services to individuals, foundations, and corporate grant makers that allow those clients to use the professional staff and expertise of the community foundation.

The Minneapolis model is close, but it has not yet evolved as far as it might. The foundation is still trying to operate as a central hub, with the services offered as one of many spokes into communities of nonprofits and donors. The network model, however, is more fluid, with nodes or participants but not necessarily hubs and spokes. The value of the network model is that the intellectual assets would be held in common, although the financial assets need not be. This simple inversion actually reveals the greatest possible challenge to our current models of philanthropy, almost all of which center around financial assets under management. While intellectual assets must be held in common, financial assets need not be. To build truly powerful networks of philanthropists—individuals, institutions, and all of the combinations thereof—a new center is needed.

Endorsement Philanthropy

Finally, in addition to the four emerging elements described in the previous section, a subtle shift can be detected—still on the margins—that holds great promise for deliberate industry action. I call this the emergence of *endorsement philanthropy.*[27] Endorsement philanthropy involves an attitudinal and cultural shift, as well as a set of practices.

It is an ingrained practice in philanthropy—both individual and institutional—to look at the names of the supporters for an issue or an organization as one factor in making a giving decision. Reviewing board lists, donor lists, advisory committees—these are all part of telling potential new supporters who is already involved in the work. And most foundations are aware that their grant to an organization can be a door opener to other foundations, an imprimatur of credibility. At its most basic level, the thinking underneath this practice is that "If so and so supports it, or if X Foundation funds it, the organization must meet a certain standard of functioning and effectiveness." From the nonprofit side of the equation, publishing those lists is partly a means of conveying this message of approval as new supporters are being courted.

Yet, most foundations are remarkably uninterested in capitalizing on the value of their imprimatur or helping the nonprofits benefit from the work the foundation staff has done to assess the organization's viability. They want the foundation listed in reports and even displayed prominently in some cases, but the promotional burden is placed on the nonprofit. Foundations know that the organizations they support need other people's money as well; in fact, many foundations require that support as a condition of funding. But few foundations are going to help the nonprofit find other financing, and even fewer see such resource development as a critical asset they can bring to achieving their own goals.

But there are changes to be seen in this set of behaviors. Foundations that use professional staff to conduct extensive research into an issue, develop goals and objectives with nonprofits, draft complicated grant agreements, and monitor the progress of that work are beginning to see that sharing the results of that effort with other funders is one way to earn a greater return on the foundation's investment. Some of these foundations, from Roberts Enterprise Development Fund in San Francisco to the Sisters of Charity of St. Augustine Health System and its four foundations in Ohio and South Carolina, carefully track the financial resources their grants help attract. They use this information as one of many performance measures for their own staff. The foundations that take this approach also actively share the tools and reviews they have developed with other potential funders. The idea is "write once, raise many" where due diligence, program and operational review, and case statements regarding an organization's work is concerned.

These approaches save the foundations' funding partners time and administrative resources. If looked at in the aggregate, one would see the work of a single program professional being shared by many funders, thus lowering the cost to funders and the nonprofit of the review process. It also amounts to more money to support the work of the nonprofit. In a time of tremendous pressure on foundation administrative budgets, directing more funds at a lower overall administrative cost should be an attractive prospect.

Endorsement philanthropy can be seen in other ways as well. For organizations such as The Tides Foundation, a collection of donor-advised funds focused on progressive social issues, the potential message of their endorsement is to assure new donors that the groups being supported are viable, legitimate, and effective. Tides can make the point that working with their staff a donor will receive professional program review services and be able to find the small grassroots network that a lone donor might never find or have the time to assess. Although this approach is particularly valuable given the challenging work that some Tides' donors stand behind, the same principle applies for community foundations working with their donors.

Another form of endorsement philanthropy can be found in TouchDC, an online portal hosted by Network for Good that allows Washington-area nonprofits to make themselves known to individual donors. At first blush, this approach looks like little more than an easily accessible database of area organizations, all with Donate Now buttons prominently displayed on their links. What distinguishes TouchDC, however, is the set of partners behind it, led by the regional association of grant makers, several private foundations, public funding agencies, technology-driven industry resources such as GuideStar and VolunteerMatch, local media outlets, the community foundation, and federated funds.[28]

In this regard, TouchDC is an example of institutional funders helping nonprofits reach individual donors. The site shows the funders' recognition of their influence and is built on the trust that their support engenders for individual donors. A similar strategy is embodied in the Massachusetts Catalogue for Philanthropy, an initiative of the Ellis L. Phillips Foundation.[29] The purpose of the Catalogue, created in 1997, is "to increase and improve charitable giving," a goal it measures through increases in the Generosity

Index, average size and rates of giving noted on income tax reports, and direct attribution of gifts.[30]

Ranging from the immediate personal accountability seen in performance measures for foundation staff to broad, regional efforts such as TouchDC, endorsement philanthropy comes in many variations. Some see it as a threat, a characteristic that would only make foundation giving all the more a matter of who you know. But the efforts described move far beyond that and are focused on foundations trying to share *what* they do know with those they do not know. The expense of this foundation knowledge alone justifies sharing it broadly. These approaches not only help foundations earn a greater return on their review costs, but they also meet individual donors' needs for credible, reliable insight into charitable organizations that goes beyond financial data while also expanding a non-profit's marketing and development reach.

THE DIRECTION OF EVOLUTION

Improving the philanthropic industry is an enormous task. The stimuli of market forces and regulatory revision will catalyze significant change for the industry; however, deliberate action is required to ensure that these changes amount to progress. The baseline shift—from organizational structures to expanding, mixable suites of products and services—has already occurred; the opportunity is to capture those tools to grow and diversify philanthropy.

The other attributes described—knowledge as a philanthropic resource, the roles of hybrid organizations and strategies, a new industry infrastructure, and the attitudinal and practical shifts evident in endorsement philanthropy—are all potential contributors to a more robust philanthropy. Those in a position to lead the further development of these approaches include the leaders of major philanthropic institutions, leaders of the hybrid organizations, and all those with a vested interest in the industry structures, both the familiar and the emergent. An inclusive vision of the industry brings all of these components in from the edges and significantly alters our understanding of what philanthropy is and where it can go. That same degree of inclusiveness is necessary to take philanthropy forward.

CHAPTER 7

New Nodes on the Network

Always design a thing by considering it in its next larger context—a chair in a room, a room in a house, a house in an environment, an environment in a city plan.[1]

—Eliel Saarinen, architect

The pressures and strains on the larger system that may bring about the types of changes described in Chapter 6 come both from within and from outside of organized philanthropy. An equally important question to consider is what existing philanthropic organizations can do to strengthen the philanthropic system.

Cynics who read this will react with disbelief. Why would I even imagine that those who inhabit these lofty perches might seek to significantly alter them? Such a question is not totally off the mark. From the vantage point of the well-paid foundation professional, there is not much incentive to change the system. And it is likely that many of the existing staffed foundations will be among the last to change. As Waldemar Nielsen noted in another context:

> The first and fundamental fact about foundations is that they do not start with a concept or an organization chart or a strategic plan. A foundation starts with a person, the donor. That human being, by his or her major charitable act, is the fountainhead from which all else—good, bad, or indifferent—flows.[2]

This is true not only for foundations, but also for all philanthropic entities, as we have seen in the Giving Portfolio representation of philanthropy. While Nielsen presented this truism as a reminder of the
inconsistency of philanthropy, I believe its fingering of the individual decision maker may be a harbinger of positive change for philanthropic institutions yet to be created.

However, many philanthropic entities, including foundations, are already
deliberately mutating themselves—seeking operations that make more impact, finding meaningful ways to work with peers and downstream funders,
and building off the knowledge assets of their community partners. As important, the philanthropic system is changing around these extant organizations. Although the real laws of evolution may not apply—it is unlikely that
"change or die" will ever come to rest in philanthropy unless regulations requiring universal spend-down policies are implemented—it is possible that
the odd, punctuated movements of ideas and practices will move through
the same competitive channels as noted earlier.

Chapter 4 presented the power of several types of joint action. These
examples showed several different ways that donors and foundations work
together across organizational boundaries. Equally important, and perhaps
a more realistic model for others to follow, are the instances of individual
organizations drastically reconsidering and realigning their services. For
foundations, this essentially means the careful and deliberate assessment of
all of the organization's resources and the deployment of them in ways that
reinforce each other and advance the foundation's mission.

One example is the organization of services at The Tides Family of Organizations. Known to most people as either the Tides Foundation or the
Tides Center, the Tides Family actually includes both of those entities, as
well as the Tsunami Fund, Groundspring.org, and the Community Clinics Initiative. Each of these entities emerged independently over the last 25
years, and the managers are working hard to build on naturally occurring
reinforcing elements, design ways for the entities to strengthen each other
and reduce overall costs, and work in complementary fashions to advance
the overall goal of progressive social change. To that end, the Foundation
serves donors and makes grants, the Center provides facilities and services
to progressive nonprofits, Groundspring.org is dedicated to helping grassroots groups use the Internet to raise funds, and the Tsunami Fund raises
funds and advocates for social change.

The Community Clinics Initiative is currently positioned as the test case for receiving the services of the others. The Initiative is a multi-million dollar regranting program funded by The California Endowment to strengthen health clinics. Its staff is located in the Tides Center; managers have worked for the Tides Foundation for years and are searching for ways to include Foundation donors and programs in the Initiative. Clinics participating in the Initiative have access to the expertise and products of Groundspring.org. Given the opportunistic nature of each of these entities, the efforts to connect the resources of the Tides Family Organizations are highly ambitious. In the current market, however, the leaders of the different entities know that they have no choice.

Another example of strategy alignment is seen in the Schwab Foundation's application of its knowledge, staff, grant making, convening, and partners. All of these activities must be tied together in logical ways, they are all measured for impact, and the Board routinely holds management and staff accountable for the added value of any one of these activities.

For example, the Foundation's work to prevent homelessness started with a comprehensive research scan and data collection effort. The program officer in charge, who spent two decades heading a major shelter network, took leadership positions on several local and national commissions to assist the Foundation in identifying funding, program, and research partners. The research report was presented to funders in a "road show" across the country to make clear that there were viable strategies to reduce homelessness, to reveal the drop in foundation funding, and to build a network of funders on the issue. The Foundation worked with local service providers to identify the key elements of a comprehensive strategy. The funding priorities range from data management to help programs track their work better, preventive measures, and housing initiatives that can provide both shelter and supportive services to break the cycle of homelessness. The program staff at the Foundation works with the research and communications staff to send weekly updates on the issues to an email list of hundreds of partners. The staff is held accountable for specific quantifiable outcomes as well as the amount of additional funding their efforts help bring to the issue.

In a similar example from the Foundation's substance abuse program, an intensive research effort by staff uncovered a single program that had found a way to access hundreds of thousands of dollars from the federal government. The staff convened all other programs in the state, had the director of the first program show the others how to qualify for these funds and mentored them through the process. Through research and convening, the Foundation helped the programs raise more public financing than ever before—and it had not yet spent a dollar on grants!

As is often the case, the funding community is learning to align its resources in reaction to the work of its nonprofit partners. As nonprofits have become smarter and more strategic about the relationships between direct services, policy making, advocacy, and revenue sources, they are showing foundations the importance of alignment and communication. The CompuMentor Project in San Francisco exemplifies this. Once a local provider of technology mentors, CompuMentor has grown into an international provider of discounted technology products, sector-specific technology advice, and direct consulting services. The organization has developed a "pyramid of services" model to explain to other nonprofits and funders how these services interact and mutually reinforce each other. Managing those interactions is key to CompuMentor's growth and its emerging leadership role among nonprofit technology providers.

The Enterprise Foundation embodies similar efforts to align its work as it searches for ways to connect several grant making, fellowship, research, and investment programs. The core of the Foundation's efforts is developing ways to share information across its multiple departments and find activity-specific indicators of progress toward shared goals. Another example can be seen in the reorganization of Social Venture Partners Seattle, which took the results of an independent evaluation to redesign the complementary links between its grant making, donor education, and peer networking functions.

ORGANIZATIONAL IMPLICATIONS

The changes in the philanthropic system will have multiple meanings for foundations. This section presents an overview of the operational choices now present for all foundations, and then looks at the options specific to community foundations and independent foundations. The choices for foundations are exactly that—choices. Although the regulatory structure for philanthropy may require new reporting or administrative practices, it is highly unlikely that any other external force will demand industry-wide operational changes for foundations in the near term. Over time, the proliferation of newer philanthropic forms, the pressures to perform, and the market/regulatory demands discussed earlier will influence the practices of extant foundations, but the motivation to improve results, to reduce operating costs, and to have an impact will all come from within the existing organizations.

Foundations should act differently from commercial corporations. Even as foundations focus on their individual operations and strategies, they should do so in ways that align with their unique bottom lines—mission accomplishment. In general, foundations do not compete for market share and their success does not depend on beating the competition. In fact, achieving stated missions actually might require active collusion. As noncompetitive structures, for which market share makes little sense as a prime motivator, foundations have the chance to develop deliberate alliances in the new philanthropic economy, to work together to deliberately promote social change.

This opportunity is particularly ripe now because the numbers and types of philanthropic institutions are increasing rapidly. As the numbers increase, new regions of intense philanthropic density are emerging. This density eases the way for funders to capitalize on the skills and resources of their peers. The tools of information technology that have played such a role in changing corporate behavior can be used by foundations to share information, conduct joint research and grant making, and pool skills and resources.

The changing tools of philanthropy give donors more options in structuring their giving. Today's philanthropists are consciously choosing multiple giving tools: private foundations, venture networks, issue-oriented public charities, and donor-advised funds. In doing so, they are trying to derive the greatest value from each philanthropic structure to maximize the reach of their giving. This presents a new challenge for philanthropic institutions to emphasize their strengths and clarify their unique value given the expanding industry and choices.

What might this mean for foundations? What do foundations provide that donors cannot accomplish through private bank advisors, charitable gift funds, corporate philanthropy, or pooled funds? These questions have had little relevance for foundations in the past. Even now, established foundations may feel little pressure to prove their unique value; after all, their endowments ensure their existence. For individual institutions the option will always remain to do as they have always done. For philanthropy as a whole, however, foundations have the opportunity to lead the field and help answer the question "wither philanthropy?" in a way that none of the other philanthropic institutions can. Foundations can actually focus the question on the impact of giving on social change, and not on the tax benefits and management fees differences that the market-driven options are likely to emphasize.

Foundations are both independent and interdependent organizations. They are still products of individuals, families, or corporations that wish to stand recognized for their unique contributions. As Waldemar Nielsen noted almost a decade ago:

> Private foundations are now a distinctive national phenomenon, both numerous and rich. They are elitist institutions left remarkably free by a democratic, egalitarian society to involve themselves in almost any field—education, science, medicine, religion, the arts, and international affairs, among others. Not bound by voters, shareholders, or customers—and with only feather-light oversight by government—they couldn't possibly be allowed to exist with such power and utter freedom in a democratic society. But they do.[3]

Foundations still manage their portfolios separately, hire individual staffs, perform their own (often repetitive and redundant) due diligence on grants, and publish their own reports on the impact of their work. Yet they increasingly operate within loose associations, the growing density of like organizations has not been lost on them, and there is frequent talk of networks of funders and partnerships with grantees.

The key operational choices for all foundations align with the components of improved philanthropy that were introduced earlier. These five attributes—diverse, aggregated, integrated, well-timed, and committed—lend themselves naturally to operational imperatives for all philanthropic institutions that include the following:

- Organizational structures, staff skills, and priorities that center on partnerships

- Access to, use of, and contributions to bodies of independent, credible issue-specific knowledge

- An assessment strategy that rewards identifiable contributions to meaningful, achievable results

These broad choices have different implications for the structures with which we are familiar. For community foundations, federated funds, donor-advised fund purveyors, and public grant-making charities, making these choices will require:

- Earning revenue from core products and services
- Aligning revenue structure to reward alliances

For independent foundations, the options will require:

- Organizing as a knowledge node on a larger network
- Building systems and incentives to partner and leverage others' funds

The next section discusses the overarching implications of these strategies, and then identifies specific opportunities for community foundations, independent foundations, and corporate philanthropy.

PARTNERSHIP BUILDING

Partnership building is something that foundations speak of frequently, attempt often, and fail at most of the time. There are many reasons for this. Some of them are purely structural. Currently, philanthropic institutions are organized in such a way that the only things that really matter are the assets, strategies, and outcomes of the specific institutions. Philanthropic entities that are designed to be successful in this broader industry will not fall prey to the same operational limitations as their predecessors. If they build themselves to be part of the broader philanthropic economy, they will need to build structures that emphasize and facilitate partnerships, aggregation, and integration.

Remember Batman and Robin? Mansion-dwelling, thief-catching, nerds-by-day, superheroes by night? Sometimes it feels as if the professional staff of foundations would do well to learn a few superhero tricks. Faced with declining assets, mounting public deficits, and seemingly insurmountable social needs, philanthropic foundations and their staffs have experienced a whiplash awakening from good times to bad. Batman and Robin succeeded against formidable forces of evil through prudent uses of technology and other resources, long-term planning, and joint action—they were a team of two that could always call on Batgirl and other friends if things got really ugly.

And things are pretty ugly for American foundations today. Although staffed foundations are one of the nation's oldest structures of institutional philanthropy, they are by no means a dominant form within the philanthropic system. Institutional philanthropy typically provides less than 20 percent of annual giving in the United States, a percentage that has held steady for decades. The median drop in endowment size in 2001 was 10 percent for reporting foundations. Nine of the country's 10 largest foundations lost a combined $8.3 billion in the first half of 2002 alone. The year saw a decline in overall giving of 2.3 percent, and the 6 percent annual creation rate for new foundations is expected to slip back to the more typical 2 to 3 percent.[4]

Where is the silver lining in this picture? Well, it is difficult to find one. The asset transfers of individual small foundations to funds at community foundations offers one glimmer of hope because it lowers overall administrative costs and facilitates resource pooling.[5] The underlying assumptions behind large transfers of wealth, the aging of baby boomers, and the known cyclical nature of the economy are other positives.[6] The significant marketing and advertising that commercial firms have committed to underwriting philanthropy is yet another. Years of metaphors about the philanthropic ecosystem also come to mind, leaving us with the hope that the diversity and dispersion of philanthropic resources will lead to healthier and more resistant structures.

As philanthropic entities—institutional and individual—multiply and morph, the role of staffed foundations in the system becomes even more precious. The nonfinancial resources that they bring to philanthropy distinguish them from all the other entities. Their professional staff, research capacity, facilities, partnering capacity, institutional memories, and reputation, are valuable and unique resources. Their value depends on how they are deployed in the larger system. Individual foundations that have seen their endowments drop should not be asking the question, "What do we do now that we are only the 35th largest arts funder in (our nonfiction) Gotham City?" The question for this down-cycle, the next up-cycle, and the foreseeable future in philanthropy should be, "Who else is on our team of superheroes and how are we going to jointly succeed?"

The questions and possibilities of partnerships are not new to foundations. And they are not easy. In tight times, sharing resources has been the key to survival and success for species, communities, nations, and industries. In evolutionary terms, the strongest of a species are those that flourish, but in becoming the strongest they must be able to change. It is the resilient mutants in every species that survive.[7] New "strains" have developed in almost all aspects of philanthropy in the last decade, and like "mutants" in natural systems, they evolve to fit particular niches.[8] Now is the time to see which organisms will mutate resiliently and which will become increasingly irrelevant.

But as an industry unbounded by the typical financial returns or electoral results to account for performance, the philanthropic industry operates with an unusual opportunity for networks, alliances, and joint ventures. Whereas the recent expansion of the field provides an increasing base of experience for evaluation and understanding, the very extent of the enterprise threatens to isolate foundations from the accumulated learning, knowledge, and innovation of their peers. New foundations often find themselves reinventing the wheel, while established institutions may fail to capitalize on the fresh ideas of inventive newcomers. If philanthropy as an industry is to maximize its impact, it will need to develop new strategies and structures for knowledge sharing, communication, and cooperation.

Models such as university research and the high-growth years of Silicon Valley provide useful precedents for thinking about how this might happen. Tenure-track professors at universities, insulated from economic competition for their positions (much as foundations are built to last in perpetuity by their endowments), compete to advance ideas and theories, building their names and reputations not on proprietary development but on their contributions to the field. This commitment to the advancement of knowledge fosters a system wherein the exchange of ideas within and between institutions and the development of collaborative networks are the key to promoting a collective innovation that goes beyond the capacity of any single constituent institution.

Similarly, industrial researchers credit a shared commitment to networks and collective progress as a key factor in the success of Silicon Valley. When compared to other regions of high-tech development, Silicon Valley companies have engaged much more frequently in forming joint ventures, cross-licensing patents, and developing formal and informal networks between firms and employees. This collaboration ensures that technical advances spread rapidly and that whole industries grew as a predicate to the success of individual firms.

These two models show the power of sharing research, forming joint ventures, and licensing ideas across institutions. The solutions to complex scientific problems often require the resources from many academic institutions, just as the creation of viable new markets for silicon chips takes the product development assets of several companies.

Foundations should take heed of this example. Many foundations are driven by missions to address complex social problems that their own financial resources, while often large, are never enough to solve. Unfettered by the profit motive, foundations have the opportunity to develop a new model for cooperating around these issues that will leverage their individual financial investments. Foundations can distinguish and differentiate themselves not just by how much money they give, but also by how the knowledge they develop and share contributes to achieving common social goals. Doing so will increase the collective impact of the industry on pressing societal issues and help define niches, track added value, develop individual foundation identities, and increase accountability within the industry.

THE ROLE OF MONEY

Money matters to philanthropy. What partnership-oriented foundations would do is address the classic "now or later" conundrum regarding resource stewardship in a way that looks to both external partners and to internal goals. When philanthropists make decisions about endowment structure, they do so most often with an eye toward family issues, legacies, and asset size. The true guiding questions for choosing between a perpetual or spend-down structure should be the availability of other resources to address the issue and the time sensitivity of the issue itself.

Unfortunately, this is rarely the case, either in choosing the initial structure or in setting investment policies and program budgets once the structure is set. If the organization is to exist in perpetuity, assets must be maintained for the future. If the choice instead is to focus on immediate issues, an aggressive spending policy that will distribute the corpus of the endowment is more appropriate. The "now or later" question is not usually as black and white as these two examples—how much for now and how much for later might be better phrasing of the real question. The issue emerges in debates about payout rates, spend-down policies, and grant-making reserves. The 5 percent payout rate that applies to private foundations and influences the rate of excise tax they must pay has become a de facto industry standard, although it was created to apply to only one type of foundation and to serve as a floor, not a ceiling.[9]

CHARTING PHILANTHROPIC CYCLES

In addition to the influence of regulation, foundation executives must also attend to market forces and gyrations as they steward the financial resources of their organizations. The booms and busts of philanthropy follow those of the larger economy. But we do not really know how closely after a recession or market collapse a giving drop will appear. Because of the manner in which foundation grants budgets are generally calculated, the effect of a market drop on any individual institution may not be immediate. The effects on organized philanthropy as a whole also take time.

It is important that the industry knows how the different components of philanthropic giving respond to changes in the larger economy. Leo Arnoult, who chairs the AAFRC Trust for Philanthropy, notes that:

> Research shows that giving is closely tied to the economy. Not surprisingly, giving in 2001 fits the pattern that we have seen during previous recessions. . . . In six of the eight recession years since 1971, giving dropped by 1 to 5 percent when adjusted for inflation. Despite fears last fall that giving might decline precipitously, in fact, the change in giving in 2001 falls within the normal range for a recession year.[10]

Exhibit 7.1 above shows the nearly constant growth in foundation giving in the United States from 1975 to 1999. With the exception of a few flat spots, the trend line is basically straight up. The giving in recession years often flattened, but it rarely shows a drop. The growth is particularly dramatic between 1980 and 2000, a time in which the number of foundations increased by 156 percent, their assets rose by 909 percent, and their giving by 712 percent.[11] The only declines that show up in year-over-year comparisons are in 1983 and 1994. Three years, 1981, 1989, and 1991, show increases of less than 2 percent over the prior year.[12]

A cursory comparison of the timing relationship between recessions and drops in foundation giving shows a lag time between the onset of the economic slump and the flattening of grant budgets. This is caused by the trailing 60-month average that most foundations use to set their grant budgets.

EXHIBIT 7.1   FOUNDATION GIVING AND INFLATION

Foundation giving grew ahead of inflation during recessions over the last quarter-century*

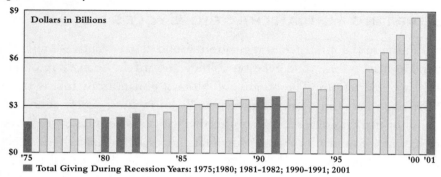

■ Total Giving During Recession Years: 1975;1980; 1981-1982; 1990-1991; 2001

* Figures estimated for 2001. Constant 1975 dollars based on annual average Consumer Price Index, all urban consumers, U.S. Department of Labor, Bureau of Labor Statistics, as of March 2002.

Source: *Foundation Yearbook, 2002*. New York: The Foundation Center, 2002.

In considering this relationship, foundation giving should be noted as only one component of the philanthropic revenue stream. The impact of recessions and economic dips on individual and corporate giving does not necessarily follow the same timing or pattern as foundation giving. Knowing how each of these components of the revenue streams works over time, and investing in a better understanding of the foundation component, will give senior managers of foundations an important planning tool.[13]

If the historically accurate relationship between larger economic indicators and philanthropic giving can be determined, foundation staff would have several quarters to a couple of years in which to plan for declining budgets. Planning for the downside when the upside is upon you is no one's favorite task—witness the $80 billion in state deficits addressed by governors and legislatures in building their 2004 budgets; however, it behooves foundations to face these decisions, not only from the investment manager's or finance office, but from the programmatic perspective as well.

Some foundations do so already. The creation of reserve funds in flush times that can be used to soften the slope of a declining grants budget or mitigate a steep drop has allowed some foundations to maintain high grant-making levels without dipping into the corpus of their endowment.[14] This strategy limits grants budgets on the upside during a period of rising endowments, but a steady source of grant funds over an extended period of time is more easily maintained.

For foundations the alignment of resource management strategies with program strategies is critical. When investment strategies fail, and billions of dollars are lost in a matter of months, program strategies are sure to fail as well unless reserves, pooled funds, or corpus expenditures are to be used.[15] A clear picture of how the different components of the revenue stream for nonprofit organizations respond to economic shifts is important at both the community level and for the industry as a whole.

Calls for increasing the required payout rate are coming from within organized philanthropy (e.g., National Network of Grantmakers), from outside of it (e.g., Senator Bill Bradley, McKinsey & Co.), and from its regulators. Those who are calling for new regulations and those working to avoid such changes disagree on direction.[16] They both understand that an industry-wide change is likely to be the result of regulatory forces. This is particularly unfortunate because the diversity of philanthropic interests calls for a diversity of investment and payout strategies; however, the system as a whole would benefit greatly from an industry-wide standard of setting these policies based on the external reality of the issues at hand, a strategy that would greatly facilitate partnerships with both public and private funders as well.

Mixing Up the Menu

Foundations have grown increasingly savvy about the menu of resources they have at their disposal. Financial resources, convening, access to decision makers, research, and information brokering are all part of their mix. Decisions about how the menu gets used during times of growth and retraction are the next step for strategic grant makers. Foundations from different regions and of varying sizes have found that building strong relationships with public policy makers when times are good will afford them access and a seat at the table when resources are stretched on all sides. Batman and Robin kept an open phone line to the mayor and chief of police at all times, and they knew when to lead and when to follow in those relationships.

Of the various foundation types that exist, corporate funders are particularly skilled in applying various assets to their communities. Dollars are granted, employees volunteer, facilities are made available, marketing and distribution expertise can be applied, managers often serve on boards of directors, and products and services can be provided in kind. These resources all have value, and corporations have found intriguing ways to apply them to communities. As a leader in the application of various resources, corporate funders are a critical part of the overall industry network.

Affinity groups and regional associations seem to be well aware of these roles and provide members (and potentially others) with the mechanisms to convene thought leaders and decision makers or distribute research and white papers that can be used as deliberate strategies by foundations. This happens now, albeit inconsistently and not necessarily in sync with a foundation's planning cycle. The best of these support organizations are regarded by foundations as resources that help them achieve their organizational goals, not just as trade groups. Needless to say, foundation members are in the position to shape these associations to their needs, but have instead often seen them as "good neighbor memberships" and not tools for leveraging their own resources.

Cross-foundation gatherings allow for joint planning or idea sharing among peers. Although most foundations set their grant budgets as a matter of internal policy, working with peer organizations and tracking the overall revenue flows to certain issues or regions is valuable input to that process.

Here is an example of how failing to look externally can lead to unfortunate internal decisions. A major economic downturn in the economy led three major foundations in one area to reduce their anticipated grant budgets for the next two years. All three organizations had supported environmental issues over their lengthy histories. All decided—independently—to end their environmental funding. A leader in the local environmental community estimated the effect to be an immediate 25 percent reduction in philanthropic resources for environmental work. The cumulative effect of their independent decisions meant a quick and ugly demise to several programs and organizations that had long received their support. Some joint planning, asset mapping, or revenue projections by the three foundations could have been enough to reduce the cumulative size of the funding drop or, at least, spread its impact over time.

Understanding change in philanthropy requires a long view and a steady eye. Like language, philanthropy is made up of innate, individual human qualities and it reflects broad cultural tensions. It changes by accretion and excision, deliberately and unknowingly, and constantly but inconsistently.

NEW ASSESSMENT STRATEGIES

What is the relationship between resources, operations, and results for foundations? Although much has been made of the need for nonprofits to align their structures with their missions (think strategic restructuring, mergers, or the omnipresent sense that nonprofit organizations are duplicative), there is no such pressure on foundations as a whole. Many argue that allowing operational expenses to count against the payout calculation is, in fact, a deterrent to efficient operations. As a whole, though, looking again at the small percentage of foundations that employ staff, one could assume a general predisposition among donors to keep operational costs to a minimum.[17]

At some level, each donor makes a decision about the relationship between resources, operations, and results. Each of the choices in the Giving Portfolio presents a different mix of costs, structures, and—presumably—results. For every option in the Giving Portfolio there is some presumed relationship between resources and structure and results.

For each structure that involves staff, space, consultants, evaluation, and other operational expenses above the minimum requirement to distribute grant dollars, we might even say that somewhere, in every organization, is its own implicitly held formula for:

Resources + Operations = Results[18]

What is left to be defined by each organization is how the components of this equation depend on each other. Are operations a dependent variable of resources? Of results? What do you need to change first to maintain a balanced equation?

There is no universal answer to this question. As managers consider laying off staff, adding new expertise, partnering with other foundations, and other choices, they must do so with an eye toward the implications for their missions and objectives. In some cases, layoffs have followed an across-the-board statement of reduced resources, operations, and results. The message in this case is that the foundation is simply no longer pursuing certain interests, regardless of progress, outcomes, or need.

Other foundations may find such a direct reduction to be unacceptable and are looking for another variable in the equation. These decision makers choose the following equation:

(Resources + Operations) $f\,X$ = Results

The mathematical symbol f indicates that resources plus operations would work as a function of X, where X can represent many options. For example, X may represent the use of another foundation's staff or expertise, a change in process so that fewer people can do well the same work of more people, or a partnership with intermediaries or nonprofits or the public sector that puts no weight on the foundation but can still contribute to their work. Obviously, X is part operations and part strategies. Sharing success stories about how to find X for an organization under resource pressure would benefit the sector enormously.

BUY OR RENT?

These operational choices represent a textbook business school "buy or rent" proposition. Businesses typically answer this question by backing up and assessing their purposes, their profit margins, their skill sets, and their long-term plans. What expertise or execution steps does the foundation need to own (have on staff)? What can it outsource? What can it borrow from peers or ally with others to create in a joint venture? If philanthropy really addressed its work in this way, I believe we would see very different organizations from those with which we are familiar. The redundancy in tasks across foundations, the impositions they make on nonprofits to meet the requirements of their boards, and the "hoops" they set for staff in terms of grant deadlines, docket preparation, and grantee reporting are legend. Much of this gets talked about, internally and externally, but little changes. Common application forms are about as close as the industry has come to really streamlining the processes.

The irony, as is well known, is that the people who have to carry out these operational practices have the ability to change them. Boards who seek to reduce costs should be interested in measures that would streamline staff workloads, allow them to use their hard-earned professional expertise, and devote their energy to catalyzing efforts to achieve organizational goals, instead of preparing the same analysis as their peer down the street, requiring reports that must go unread, meeting false deadlines, and managing consultants.

Short of overhauling all operations, making buy or rent decisions still needs to be done and should be informed by a well-understood, organizationally valid set of criteria about what the foundation needs to do and what it can outsource. Using contractors, setting term limits, and advancing the professional careers of foundation staff are all part of this picture. They all come down to a clear answer to the question "what is the work?" The work may be done in different ways in different times, but those differences should hinge more on external changes in needs, opportunities, or resources and not on internal ambivalence about what matters.

RESULTS

Results are what you expect, and consequences are what you get.

—*The Ladies Home Journal*, 1942

Results matter in philanthropy, even though they tend to be nebulous, hard to find, difficult to claim, and limited in scope. Born from a move in the public sector toward performance measures, accelerated by the corporate world's interest in investment returns, and brought home to nonprofits by virtue of a nationwide change in United Way strategies in the mid-1990s, the emphasis on results is no longer simply rhetorical. A significant amount of good work has been done on developing quantifiable measures of impact. From the Harvard Family Research Project to the KidsCount Data and United Way's community indicators, philanthropy has worked alone and in partnership to create meaningful assessment tools and benchmarks.[19]

The growth of philanthropic resources in health care has also contributed to the emphasis on quantifiable results and indicators. The last two decades of the twentieth century saw a sharp increase in health philanthropy, and health resources more than doubled between 1995 and 2000 alone.[20] The creation of new health foundations and the interest in health by several of the world's largest foundations drove the growth in resources. The nature of health issues and medical reporting seemed to drive the interest in quantifiable, measurable results in health philanthropy. Medicine and public health are further along than many other human service, education, or arts fields in using data for making decisions. Although evidence-based medicine is an emerging field of practice, in general, health is a results-driven, scientifically oriented, hard numbers field. Not surprisingly, health funders tend to be focused on results, have been pioneers in data-sharing efforts across foundations, and have helped push the envelope on the use of data and outcomes as real tools for philanthropic strategic planning and assessment.[21]

A new contributor to the role of outcomes in philanthropy will be the follow-up analysis of grant-making responses to the September 11th tragedy. In what seems like record time, at least three reports have already been widely published analyzing the philanthropic response to this single event.[22]

Despite all this, the evaluation and outcome-measures and results can hardly be pointed to as a strong suit of institutional philanthropy. Some have argued that the focus is misplaced, and foundations and philanthropists should trust their instinct, not faulty social science.[23] This argument is not too surprising, given the independent nature of foundations and the rather youthful state of the field as an industry. Even medicine, from which most of the emphasis on data and accountability stems, does not universally embrace systematic performance improvement approaches. Other very different industries (e.g., aviation and hospitality) are noted for using far more rigorous systems for evaluating results and improving performance than those used by hospitals.[24]

What we do know is that philanthropy uses several common tools and indicator sets; logic mapping, asset mapping, community indicators, portfolio assessments, and cluster evaluations have all become increasingly common tools for those foundations that take the time, thought, and money to evaluate their work or support their grantees in doing so.[25] The late 1990s also saw a rapid increase in philanthropic interest in organizational effectiveness, a field said by some to have been born at the David and Lucile Packard Foundation and catalyzed by the results-oriented emphasis of the late-1990s philanthropic boom. By 2001, more than 500 organizations and individuals were members of Grantmakers for Effective Organizations (GEO), an affinity group that was only five years old at the time.

Certainly, this recent work provides philanthropists who are interested in tracking the results of their work with many new tools to do so. Yet, there remain no industry standards; there are few points of leverage for organizational outsiders to push for greater results or improved reporting; and the explicit (and implicit) connections between inputs, operations, and outcomes are difficult for most foundation personnel to map.

Moreover, most experienced foundation professionals recognize that a critical factor in seeing grants and strategies achieve desired results is time.

Time horizons are beginning to expand at large foundations—several seven- to ten-year strategies and initiatives can be found. The challenge has become finding ways to stay a course, report on meaningful progress, weather economic downturns midstream, maintain the focus of board and staff members, and remain responsive and flexible. Oddly enough, despite this understanding of how long results take, foundations that are endowed in perpetuity have generally employed only historical methods and analysis for institutional recordkeeping.

Perhaps what is needed is a balance between real-time reporting and progress measures, and a broad-based, analytically substantiated framework for how philanthropic resources interact with and influence social life, public good, and public systems over time. As the size of philanthropy grows, and organizational assessments of their projects increase in number, the potential increases for being able to look back and say with some credibility, "These types of philanthropic strategies work or fail on these kinds of issues in these kinds of circumstances." Such analyses would be helpful to both established and emerging philanthropists. As Thucydides wrote on his own work as an historian, it was intended for those "who desire an exact knowledge of the past as an aid to the interpretation of the future."[26]

Some foundations are trying to balance these tensions by employing different strategies, timelines, and assessment expectations for different parts of their work. The level of evaluation analysis desired (as compared to that which can be effectively conducted) has shifted from individual grants to program areas or portfolios to entire organizations. The "executive dashboard" that allows a corporate CEO to know the stock price, profit/loss, productivity, defect rate, and other key statistics about every company division at any given time is very difficult to create for foundations that operate distinct programs in the arts, education, health, and environmental justice.

THE SUM OF THE PARTS

Foundations that focused on partnerships would use external criteria to develop their investment policies, grant strategies, and staff skills. Those foundations that are committed to knowledge sharing would recognize the need to interact quite differently with community partners, researchers, consultants, and peers—all of whom would be seen as critical resources to the success of the foundation. And these organizations would assess their results in a new fashion. Having built themselves deliberately to work and learn with others, the meaningful metrics for each institution would be an assessment of contribution toward overall progress, not a need to quantify specific outcomes.

These practices may appear small or large to different readers. They were drawn from observations and assessments of actual practice, and so for some foundation executives the sense will be that they are already on this path. Other foundations continue to see themselves as independent, self-contained entities, and the scope of change—in vision and in practice—represented by these operations choices is all-encompassing. Were these choices to be made across all of institutional philanthropy, the cumulative change would be enormous.

Community Foundations

Although every foundation has its own choices to make, community foundations are the most immediately responsive to industry competition. In the last decade, they have proven to be rapid innovators, able to market their core strengths, and strong advocates for a policy framework that promotes philanthropy in many forms. The organizational form has solidified, with more than 650 community foundations in the United States, 125 in Canada, 50 in Germany (with 80 in formation), 20 in Mexico, and 15 in Russia. The last global count put the number of community foundations worldwide at close to 1,100.[27]

But even as the organizational structure has become relatively common, the changes in the industry place significant new pressures on community foundations. The changing nature of philanthropy, specifically the rapid diversification of products and services, calls into question the organizational structure of community foundations. The typical mix of community board members, endowed funds with few restrictions, and a mix of additional philanthropic options to attract donors has reached a troublesome balance.

Emmett Carson, CEO of The Minneapolis Foundation, has articulated the mission-related tensions inherent in the current product mix at most community foundations. Carson sums up the tension as one of community-centered versus donor-centered community foundations, and identifies the competition for donors as the source of tension.[28] Carson is correct in his analysis of the tensions, but the implications of them are not only mission-related but speak to the very nature of the community foundation business. Is their product mix sustainable? Can community foundations compete?

The core value of most community foundations is perpetuity. They were started as a way of building endowments for geographic communities and have morphed over the years to focus on a variety of identity-based communities. They have diversified their product lines and become much more sophisticated in their marketing approaches.

But even as they have changed their names, their marketing, their advisory boards, their product mix, and their geographic reach, community foundations have remained focused on a revenue source that fundamentally limits their ability to function in today's industry. Almost regardless of the product, community foundations derive their operating budgets from asset management fees levied on the funds donors entrust to their care. The competition of the 1990s led to a typical industry situation in which price wars drove down the fees, even as new services were added to make the community foundation products more compelling than those sold by their competitors. A 2003 study by the Community Foundation for Greater Atlanta concluded that the foundation—one of the nation's largest—was losing approximately $475 on each donor-advised fund it managed.[29] Whereas large foundations with hundreds of millions in assets will earn enough from their other fees to subsidize these losses, smaller community foundations will slowly sell themselves out of business with such a revenue model.[30]

How can community foundations survive in this market? The key is for them to assess their core products and services and to bring their revenue structure into alignment with that assessment. Unlike the opportunity for community foundations that existed in 1914 when the first one was created, the product and service assessment in 2003 needs to be done in the context of the entire philanthropic industry. The Giving Portfolio (see Exhibit 3.3) is helpful here. As these foundations assess the product mix they can offer to continue to provide flexible endowed resources for their communities, they should be looking for ways to build alliances and partnerships across this portfolio.

Several community foundations across the country have begun to reorganize themselves in direct response to the industry components and changes discussed. The next section describes several of those changes, organized according to the industry components.

Products and Services

Community foundations have long offered an array of financial products to their donor customers, including donor-advised funds, field of interest funds, unrestricted pools, supporting organizations, and even chartered family foundations. In addition, many offer donors various investment options to match their comfort with risk or reflect their social values. In the last decade, community foundations have branched out to offer estate planning services for any individual (community foundation donor or not), and thereby shore up their position as local promoter of philanthropy. This has endeared them to their community nonprofits that cannot afford planned giving officers, strengthened their relationships with local wealth and estate advisers, and provided them with a unique set of products to offer.[31] Community foundations also took advantage of the boom in giving circles that marked the late 1990s, and offered their services to several Social Venture Partner groups (and started some of their own). All of these innovations represent a diversification and broadening of the philanthropic asset management products offered by community foundations. As estate tax laws and retirement planning options change, we should expect community foundations to be active in developing new types of philanthropic asset management products as well.

In addition to these asset management products, community foundations have been in a constant state of refining their advisory services since the rise of commercial donor-advised funds. The most common point of differentiation between community foundations and commercial funds is the community knowledge, local expertise, or community connections the foundations lay claim to. It is not coincidental that the issue of knowledge management in philanthropy came to the forefront concurrently with the rise of commercial funds because for all foundations the advent of these no-frills, low-cost charitable services begged the question of value from other structures. Over the last decade the community foundations' need to deliver on a promise of community knowledge has led to innovations in services for donors, new Web site functionality, donor education services, evaluation, community meeting facilities, partnerships with nonprofits and other community foundations, as well as more coordinated marketing strategies.

Some community foundations are experimenting with shared back offices, research and knowledge products for donors and potential donors, contract consultants for major donors, evaluation workshops for donors, and various other expressions of community expertise.[32] In all of these actions they are seeking to develop viable, affordable commodities out of their experience and community connections.

National Alliances, Community Knowledge

As community foundations get better at developing commodities out of their community knowledge, the niche and alliances that make sense in community philanthropy begin to change. Although the financial service firms were once viewed by some community foundations—but by no means all—as outlandish competitors, productive alliances have been made between community foundations and financial services firms for years.[33] One might reasonably date the start of financial service firms and community foundation alliances back to the very beginning, in Cleveland, when the first community foundation was created out of a local bank.[34] More recently, the arrangements have developed on local scales, with community bank presidents often serving on foundation boards, trust officers working with foundation program officers, and foundations keeping some portion of their assets at the local bank.

As commercial banking has moved toward ever-greater consolidation, the community foundations have sought to build meaningful relationships with the "super regionals" and national bank chains that now dominate commercial banking. These relationships have proven somewhat more difficult to manage because the larger banks have many more levels of decision making to contend with and are seeking partners who can serve their customers in all markets, not simply in one community. The direct result of the changes in commercial banking since the late 1990s repeal of the Glass–Steagall Act has been the creation of "national back-offices" to allow these alliances with the big banks. This pressure increased as the walls between commercial banks, brokerage houses, and interstate bank laws came tumbling down. Community foundations are now actively developing national partnerships with brokerage firms such as Merrill Lynch and Company, managing relationships with the super-regional bank in their market, and many still rely on relationships with local community banks.

The challenges in these relationships include both scale and products. For community foundations, identifying, packaging, using, and selling their knowledge of the community in ways that are attractive to national partners is a whole new business. To help with this, several dozen community foundations have joined to form the Community Foundations of America, which helps negotiate with national partners and develops common marketing, technology, and evaluation tools so that the individual community foundations can provide a common backbone.

The easier part of this relationship is building out that infrastructure. Community knowledge and culture varies profoundly, and foundations have few common mechanisms for sharing meaningful information. Of course, it is precisely their close-to-the-ground know-how about their community that is valuable to donors. So in many cases, the result is a shared infrastructure to facilitate the transactions of philanthropy, with an emphasis on personal relationships still providing the cornerstone of the knowledge services.

Each of these relationships relies on a different role for financial assets and knowledge assets. The three most common relationships between donors, community foundations, and financial firms are noted in Exhibit 7.2, with the management of the financial and knowledge assets noted in italics. These models are by no means mutually exclusive; to the contrary, more and more community foundations and financial firms are managing all of them at once.

For each of the first, second, and third donors in Models A, B, and C, the community foundation needs to provide a different level of service. They may need to develop different tiers of knowledge products for each donor as well. For example, personal meetings and customized memoranda of recommendations are possible for Donor One in each model. Not only are they possible, but they are probably an important distinguishing level of service for the types of donors who now provide the bulk of community foundation gifts. Donor Two needs very little in terms of service.

Donor Three and her accompanying financial advisor provide the newest challenge to community foundations. Community foundations are just now developing the cost-effective level of service for these donors, plus a useful but cost-efficient niche of knowledge products (e.g., newsletters, database access, group meetings, educational seminars). This product development is a new type of work in and of itself. More important is the still-unanswered question of return on investment for the community foundation. The foundations also need to contract for new sets of skills or bring them in house, and they will need a new set of distribution channels

EXHIBIT 7.2   COMMUNITY FOUNDATIONS
AND KNOWLEDGE

Model A

Donor 1 → Community Foundation → (Financial firm)
(Financial assets are property of CF, managed with aid of financial firm)
Donor 1 ← Community Foundation
(Community knowledge assets)

Model B

Donor 1 → Community Foundation → (Financial firm)
(Financial assets are property of CF, managed with aid of financial firm)
Donor 1 ← Community Foundation
(Community knowledge assets)

Donor 2 → Financial firm
(Financial assets)
No community knowledge

Model C

Donor 1 → Community Foundation → (Financial firm)
(Financial assets are property of CF, managed with aid of financial firm)
Donor 1 ← Community Foundation
(Community knowledge assets)

Donor 2 → Financial firm
(Financial assets)
No community knowledge

Donor 3 & Financial Advisor → Financial firm/community foundation Partnership
(Financial assets owned by CF, managed by financial firm)
Donor 3 & Financial Advisor ← Community Foundation
(Community knowledge assets)

Note: For all relationships shown here, there may be a professional advisor (attorney, CPA, investment manager) who introduces the donor to the community foundation initially.

for these knowledge products because their typical one-to-one relationships with donors will never scale to the necessary level.

Structural and Operational Choices

All of which leads directly to the operational ramifications for community foundations trying to build and maintain these new alliances or to use their community knowledge as their distinguishing factor. For years, community foundations have been selling donor-advised funds to donors as an attractive means of working with the community foundation. These donors and their gifts now account for almost one-quarter of all assets at community foundations.[35] The most laggard community foundations, however, have tried to graft the new services for these donors onto their preexisting staff structure.

What is really needed is a rethinking of the staff roles and skills. Program officers are only just beginning to be recognized and organized to serve donors, while donor service staffs are just beginning to provide direct links to program information to the potential donors. Until community foundations structure themselves to "put their staff where their money is," their claims of providing higher levels of service to donors than financial firms will ring fairly hollow.

The implications for this need in practice are enormous. Every element of the community foundation should be examined for its contribution to meeting community needs, informing donors, and partnering with financial service partners. In addition, the technological underpinnings of community foundation service need to keep pace with those provided by banks and brokerages. Up-to-date information—available around the clock—on fund accounts, gifts, investment returns, and community indicators will soon be a minimum standard for community foundations. After all, this is no better level of service than a donor now expects from his bank, broker, grocer, and utility company.

Staff that can manage the technological underpinnings—either proprietary systems or nodes on a national community foundation technology platform—are in high demand. Amortizing the costs of this expertise over several community foundations is key because most of the 560 community foundations in the country have very small operating budgets. Technological expertise is not the only new skill set needed. Communications experience, evaluation support, and access to policy analysis or regulatory review are increasingly more common needs for community foundations (and independent foundations as well).

What is by now apparent is the need to reconsider the common staff structures (and board compositions of foundations) and to ask the "buy or rent" question for each of these resources. In many cases, the option of contracting for communications, evaluation, research, or regulatory expertise makes much more sense for foundations than having those resources on the payroll. This demand for service changes the market for the infrastructure organizations that serve these foundations because they are (or should be) prominent competitors to provide these services to their members and potential members. The evolution of Community Foundations of America, founded to address the common technology infrastructure needs, shows both the opportunity and potential for success of these shared resources.

As community foundations advance their work around community knowledge assets, the opportunities for customizing and mass-producing packages of information, and developing common indicators of success, increase. The opportunity now in front of the industry is to imagine whole new content provider/distribution channel/asset management relationships that allow each organization to best serve the market, while partnering for the expertise that is available elsewhere. This shift—from sole source philanthropic provider to allied product and service delivery—will have profound implications for the industry. New fee structures and products will emerge. It also will require significant cultural shifts among the mass of foundations, and will no doubt be led by a small group of large functioning foundations to start.

Marketing and Measuring

The reconsideration of the structures and networks that underlie community philanthropy will require the adoption of new positioning, marketing, and vision statements. Marketing messages that convey the many facets of donor giving, the alliances that can serve those needs over time, and the defined complementary value of the asset management, community knowledge, and national networks/local expertise components will succeed. The emphasis must be on the donor and the community and how these networks best serve both groups. In addition, the opportunity to build an infrastructure of philanthropic services that can actively expand the philanthropic market is very much upon us. Efforts to date have been fairly unimpressive because the giving by individuals has stayed within a fairly narrow range for decades. A measure of success of a new philanthropic system would be to significantly expand the average percentage of income given and to be able to track those figures through the complicated web of resources that now serves donors.

A community foundation that recognizes its place in the Giving Portfolio will quickly determine that it is only one vendor selling asset management tools to its donors. The foundation must begin to learn about its donors and their uses of the other products. How might their current donors find the community foundation helpful with regard to these other products? What about advisory services? Are there ways for the community foundation to provide its community expertise to donors regardless of where their assets are managed? If they are going to do this, the very first step community foundations must take is unbundling their fees from their assets.

This seemingly small suggestion is actually one of the biggest changes looming on the philanthropic horizon. For all vendors in the philanthropic industry, asset management fees are a barrier to partnership building and cross-selling services to donors. As long as the independent business models of the various vendors in the industry depend on asset management fees, each of the other vendors is a competitor, not a partner. The corollary observation is that the vendor that develops an alternative revenue source will be in a position to partner and cross-sell services with all of the other vendors in the industry. This is the opportunity that awaits community foundations. Unbundling their services and products so they can continue to directly serve their own donors while also informing other philanthropists is the key to building community resources for the future.

INDEPENDENT FOUNDATIONS

Unlike community foundations, independent foundations do not face the same challenges where fees are concerned. They face a different challenge, one of managing their work within a set of restrictions on operating costs. These parameters are defined by board members and increasingly by legislation. The opportunity for these foundations is to restructure themselves so they can partner with others, aggregate and integrate their resources, and commit to strategies over time without incurring additional operating expenses.

The positive news is that structures that are built as deliberate nodes on a network can be less costly than those that are built to stand alone. One of the toughest challenges for today's independent foundations is the "buy or rent" question discussed earlier. If several foundations were to invest in shared resources—be they staff, consultants, research databanks, or even investment managers—the overall costs and the costs per organization would diminish. Some small examples of this principle can already be seen. For example, the few national foundations that are interested in learning disabilities spent several years sharing staff, research, board members, and pooling their grant funds in order to reduce the overall operating costs and to facilitate learning across organizations. In other cases, new large foundations facing payout pressures have experimented with outsourcing certain program work to peer foundations, simply adding their funds to those of the existing foundation but using the first foundation's staff, grant systems, and connections to make sure the funds are spent wisely. An even more familiar situation is a partnership between a private foundation and community foundations, where there is a long history of using the financial resources of the former and the knowledge of the latter to achieve common goals.

Independent foundations are in the best position to align their structures, operating principles, staff skills, grant mechanisms, resource strategies, and knowledge sources with the rest of the network. As the previous examples show, there are small examples involving two, three, or four foundations at a time that are doing exactly this; however, the overarching challenge will be to build the industry tools and systems that make this network more quickly accessible to new entities, so they can experience the cost savings of being connected sooner than they can now.

This is the potential of the changing infrastructure, the hybrid organizations, and the small clusters of true partnerships that now dot the industry. They may all push together to tip the industry toward a system that functions around and rewards its own diversity, aggregation, and integrated components. Independent foundations, which constitute the bulk of the institutional universe—and are currently the most isolated—are key agents in bringing on these changes.

CHANGING ONE TO CHANGE MANY

The organizational level is the one at which change is most immediately effected, although not necessarily the one at which change has the greatest impact. But starting at this level will prove fruitful to the industry as a whole, as long as it is done with an eye toward strengthening that broader system. Some of the strategies recommended cannot be done alone. For example, sharing staff resources, pooling private foundation funds to be directed by one set of experts, or partnering with the public sector to identify aggregated and integrated program strategies inherently depend on multiple organizations.

Other choices have implications first on the organizational level, but ultimately rest on working as part of a network. For example, a philanthropic entity that deliberately appoints community leaders to sit on the board or advise the fund inherently demonstrates a different commitment to knowledge and partnership than an entity that is advised entirely by heirs or colleagues. It is not enough to simply name community advisors to an organization, however. A community-guided philanthropic fund needs to use the expertise that such advisors bring. Public board members can help find other partners, identify government agencies and actions, represent the concerns of residents with backgrounds distinct from those of the philanthropic founders, and provide access to new and varied networks.

Staffing decisions present another opportunity to make choices for a single organization that will expand or limit its success as part of the network. Organizations that intend to work in partnership with others need people with expansive networks, who are successful in teams, who can work collaboratively over an extended period, and who are eager to learn and share with others. They then need to be placed in jobs that reward these behaviors and not others that might be more single-minded or isolationist.

The systems that support a foundation's staff decisions will also make or break the success of a partnership strategy. The use of other people's research, rewards and incentives for contributing knowledge and information, and helping to influence funds beyond the foundation's are all parts of an internal system that functions as one node on a network.

Ultimately, of course, the test of a network's success lies outside the success of each of its parts. If many independent organizations choose the new staff skills or system requirements, they must still work together and assess their impact collectively. The research and funding they make available must be part of a broader community timeline, integrated with public and commercial funds. Their goals must be aspirational, and real success must be shared. This work cannot be tangential or marginal within the purpose of each entity, but it must be central. Their connections to each other must come from their torsos, not their extremities.

The qualities of networks and communities of interest hold the greatest promise for foundations to lead the way in developing a new philanthropy. The current operational practices of foundations quite possibly stand in the way of capitalizing on the full power of the philanthropic assets under management, the talents and skills of foundation executives, and the vast

"Oh, __that__ three billion dollars."

knowledge of social change that foundations have accrued individually over the years. Such individualistic actions run contrary to what we have now seen to be some of the truly transformational elements of the economy—valuing and applying information, networking communities of interest, and leveraging financial assets.

CHAPTER 8

Building New Systems for Social Good

The future is just as much a condition of the present as is the past.

—Friedrich Nietzsche[1]

American philanthropy is at a critical point in its history. Strong forces are pulling on each leg—markets, regulations, and public good—of the three-legged stool that frames the industry. The combination of tensions will be felt to different degrees by different players in the industry, and it may take some years for the full impact of the pressures to be felt. As the markets continue to fragment, new products come on line, and regulatory debate shifts to action, all of the pieces are in place for striking changes in the industry.

We have seen how philanthropy has morphed into a two-product system (asset management tools and advisory services) before our very eyes. The examples of collaborating foundations, networks, alliances, partnerships, and portfolio advising offer a mere snapshot of the ways foundations and individuals are beginning to use knowledge as a currency of engagement. And we have identified the possibilities that can be pursued if like-minded philanthropists—regardless of institutional affiliation—can find each other, aggregate their resources, and drive toward common goals. This is the potential for new philanthropic capital markets.

As we try to predict the future, it would be most helpful if the tea leaves of the present could be read to tell the exact story of what is to come.

Although that is not possible, we can project several options based on the current mix of change drivers and the experiences of other industries.

Changes in the regulatory structure are most difficult to predict. New tax laws at the federal level, property tax assessments at the local level, new rules about foundation payout rates, and tax incentives to encourage individual giving are all in place. Given the interest in change on the part of federal legislators and the budget pressures on state and local officials, the likelihood of significant revision (beyond the repeal of the Estate Tax) is still high. If philanthropy responds to new regulations the way the motion picture industry did in 1948, the brokerage industry did in 1975, or the recording industry did in 2000 we can expect to see new alliances that strengthen the presence of some large institutions but subsume the rest.[2] Rapid innovation and new product development—led by the commercial sector—will follow from new tax or banking regulations. Tighter regulations regarding information disclosure and governance will result from media-revealed scandals, as was the case with Enron, Andersen Consulting, and the passage of the Sarbanes-Oxley Act in 2002.

If philanthropy faces a prolonged decrease in the availability of capital, we might see something akin to the oil or steel industries' typical response to inventory challenges, which is to say protectionist regulation pushed by the major industry leaders. We would then be likely to see a blossoming of alternative approaches and eventually a bleeding over of new products and old vendors, as we now see in the solar consulting and household power systems being sold by old oil industry stalwarts Shell Oil and British Petroleum.

If philanthropy responds to technological innovation in the manner of the music industry, we will see lawsuits, efforts to maintain market dominance, and a backlash by donors. If, instead, it embraces new technologies, we might see the philanthropic equivalent of Napster, with peer-to-peer knowledge exchange replacing membership associations. We might see the development of independent firms of philanthropic analysts providing research and recommendations on a subscription basis to asset management vendors of all stripes. In this case, program officers would cease to exist, at least in the manner in which they now serve only one organization.

If opportunity continues to catalyze new vendors to the philanthropic market, we will see rapid product innovation, massive marketing campaigns, and the rise and fall of philanthropic media akin to the boom days of *The Industry Standard, Business 2.0, Red Herring,* and *C/Net* TV. We might see a consortium of community foundations take over the donor-advised funds of major financial service firms and a consolidation of back-office vendors with private-labeled products for managing philanthropic assets.

If public budgets continue to shrink and decision making devolves to the county or municipal level, we will see new political alliances and public–private partnerships with new power dynamics. The common good will be defined by neighbors and communities, some of which will have all of the necessary resources, whereas others will be bereft of public and private financial assets. Co-production of basic services—from neighborhood watches to recycling to health care and elderly support—will become commonplace. New regulations on giving to individuals or organizations without 501(c)(3) status will be necessary, and social services may be provided entirely by commercial vendors. Such a scenario bodes poorly for global giving because communities may be forced to focus on themselves. At the same time, it may bode well for maintaining community resources, and the global geographic displacement between natural resources and wealth may diminish.

There are obviously many factors involved in shaping the industry over which we have little control. No amount of philanthropic action is going to change demographic trends, although these changes will have dramatic impact on philanthropy. But by focusing on a vision of a new philanthropic market, one that is diverse, aggregated, integrated, well-timed, and committed, we can begin to choose the levers we do need to shift, identify the forces over which we do have influence, and shape an industry that is more effective, efficient, and robust.

THE FUTURES WE CHOOSE

There are many possible futures, and the real picture will no doubt encompass some of what we are familiar with today, some of the scenarios drawn earlier, and some elements that are not visible on today's horizon. It is important to recognize the forces at work and their likely effects on the philanthropic industry, but it is equally important to ascertain who can guide these forces, how they might be used to portend a chosen future, and what might be best avoided.

There are three fundamental components of a positive future for the industry. These components are the building blocks of a new philanthropic capital market. They include new revenue systems, industry leadership, and a deliberate, practiced emphasis on diversity. Each of these three characteristics—and its relation to a positive common future for the industry—is discussed in the following sections.

New Revenue Systems

The changes in the marketplace of philanthropy have shed light on an age-old challenge to nonprofit success. One of the important offshoots of the debate about venture philanthropy that filled so much intellectual space in the late 1990s was its focus on the inconsistent and ultimately damaging mechanisms for financing nonprofits. As they struggle year after year to repackage success and tout their ability to innovate, nonprofits are consistently undercapitalized and consumed by the need to raise funds rather than focused on service or product delivery. As Jed Emerson and others have made clear, the financial tools in the nonprofit market are too few and too simplistic to accomplish the organizations' goals. Emerson and others have presented several strategies for bringing a greater mix of resources to bear, from endowment investments to sophisticated financial products.

Underlying the problems of the financial tools available to nonprofits and their perennial lack of capital is a fundamentally confused and irrational set of relationships among the different revenue sources. The revenue stream for nonprofit activity consists of individual contributions, government contracts, fees for services, and institutional philanthropic support. These sources of revenue to nonprofits are unaligned, uncoordinated, duplicative, and unreliable.

This is not a new problem, nor is it any kind of revelation to nonprofits; however, funders, both institutional and individual, are newly interested in considering the system of financing as a whole. Such a change will be a critical component of a chosen future. Sustainability of success is important to almost all actors in the industry. It is time to recognize that the individual actors in the philanthropic exchange can work together to revise the capital market in ways that will benefit all parties. Several online exchanges have been developed to facilitate direct connections between individual investors and nonprofits. Some of these, the Global Exchange for

Social Investment, Virtual Foundation, and GlobalGiving, are underwritten by foundation and corporate support. Operating within the distinct spheres of social entrepreneurism and international aid, these are two early-stage efforts to change the dynamics of nonprofit financing.

There are many examples of different types of institutional funding partners coming together. The Calvert Giving Folios model a new type of partnership between a mutual fund financial services firm and several non-profits and grant makers. The Humboldt Area Foundation and the Seventh Generation Fund are working together to address Native American issues in four northern California counties. Giving circles, funding collaboratives, and some philanthropic associations offer other vehicles for funders to partner. Several large foundations have attempted to incorporate ongoing funding strategies into their work from the beginning. The Gates Foundation has achieved some success in reshaping the ways pharmaceuticals are sold abroad, and the Packard Foundation's California Conservation Initiative sparked significant additional philanthropic investment as well as the passing of state bond measures for land conservation.

What is really needed, however, is a wholesale reexamination of how the system works. Assumptions by the philanthropic sector that the public coffers will continue to fund their successful experiments have not borne themselves out since the 1960s. Yet even as this model has finally begun to die in the collective mentality of foundations, no clear alternative has emerged to replace it. Public decision making and funding will continue to devolve to states and municipalities, and public sector budgets in the next decade are likely to be marked by red ink. The need to rethink the financial markets and systems for philanthropic financing of innovative new approaches and essential basic services is critical. Which players in the financing stream are best at which roles? Who should specialize in research and development? Who carries startups to a level of stability? Who carries small programs to scale? As the players in the philanthropic landscape move to examine these questions, the possibility for real change across the industry grows.

INDUSTRY LEADERSHIP

Imagine this: You are the leader of a multi-billion dollar industry that has experienced several years of unprecedented growth. Over the course of the last two years, however, the media has taken every opportunity to expose scandal in your ranks, the pace of growth has slowed significantly, regulators and legislators are panting at the chance to enact real change in how the industry works, and new competitors are popping up on all sides. While the newcomers are much smaller than the current industry leaders, many of them are financed by huge established institutions with lots of R & D capacity and deep pockets.

Sound like high tech or the music industry? Try again. This is philanthropy today. The only thing about this picture that should surprise anyone who has been paying attention over the last few years is how meek the industry's reactions to these changes have been. And, anything that has been done, has been done as a reaction. There has been remarkably little leadership across organizational types and almost no proactive proposals to foster the ethical, credible, and valuable application of billions of dollars. There are no coalitions to present alternative solutions or lead industry efforts at self-regulation, media support, or proposed regulatory changes to boost investment in the industry.

A very large challenge to the industry is to identify its leaders—who are they? Who should they be? And why—after all these years— are these questions so hard to answer?

Most of the players in philanthropy are small; it is a big industry of mostly mom-and-pop shops. It is difficult for them to find one another in a crowded landscape and to work together. This is true of individual donors and of most foundations. The individual approaches of foundations and the competitive aspect of the changing market exacerbate the fragmentation in the industry. Just as the time to come together and build alliances and joint ventures is so clearly upon us, the forces at work in industry growth are pulling institutions apart.

The prominent foundations—those recognized most often for the size of their endowments—are extremely privileged players in this industry that rarely act on its behalf. In the current landscape, these organizations benefit not only from their permanence, but also from their experience, stability, professional expertise, and unique view of the rest of the industry. Unlike the few other industry participants that pay attention to trends, market research, and industry-wide challenges and opportunities, these large endowed foundations are not seeking to profit from the market; rather, they genuinely profess to care about the industry's well-being.

These foundations face two issues in exerting leadership. First, they have little experience with actually working together and speaking on behalf of the industry. This is exemplified in the last-minute hiring of a lobbyist to make their case against provisions of the CARE Act in 2003. Whereas other industries retain such assistance and are ready to mobilize on a moment's notice, organized philanthropy moved so slowly to this cause that it was national news when they finally hired a former Congressman to make their case.[3]

Second, foundations have spent most of their efforts attempting to differentiate themselves from the other players in the industry even as the importance of those differences decreases. The lines between public, private, and independent sector are blurred now in ways perhaps not seen since the American colonies first formed. Generations X, Y, and beyond are used to commercial operators of public schools, church-based ecumenical soup kitchens, employer-provided nonprofit health benefits and public hospitals that depend on private insurers, and alcohol companies underwriting everything from athletic events to art exhibitions. These generations are unfazed by federal agents, local police, and private contractors working together to screen bags at airports. In these contexts of shifting roles and expectations for government and business, the unique role of nonprofits and philanthropists is even harder to articulate. And the industry's pattern of trying to focus on the uniqueness of the sector, rather than its contributions in partnership with the others, raises more questions than it answers.

Not only does the new century bring a new focus on the capital issues within philanthropy, but the larger marketplace is also forcing a redefinition of the activities of the whole industry. As one observer noted about the potential extent of blurring lines between commercial, independent, and government activity, "In capitalism, that which can be privatized, will." What this means for public service and what it means for philanthropic endeavor remain to be seen.

Nonprofits and philanthropy must define their value in relation to shifting commercial and government sectors. Private firms have moved into education, child care, and other social services. Health care and the arts have long been the purview of all three sectors: commercial, public, and independent. The federal government continues to devolve policy and budgetary decisions to the states. There is concern that the private sector will "cream" the easiest to serve while the government will continue to contract for service rather than serve, leaving the independent sector ever more responsible for the most disenfranchised and disadvantaged sectors of society. This is a problem because even as philanthropic assets have grown, the percentage dedicated to social justice has not kept pace. The ability and willingness of the philanthropic sector to replace public services is as doubtful a proposition today as ever.

Moreover, nonprofits and philanthropy are rightfully concerned about being seen as too close to government, especially as they are increasingly responsible for providing what were once public services. Given the low level of public faith in government, most nonprofits are not interested in co-opting its reputation. Furthermore, many foundations and nonprofits see their work as falling on either end of the political spectrum and in direct contrast to the activities of a more centrist government.

In this context, it is ever more critical to develop clear strategies for how philanthropic funds and knowledge interact with and add to the private and public spheres of American life. To do so, philanthropy needs to stand on and communicate its values. The rise of endorsement philanthropy is one positive indicator of this change. Standing in partnership with the public sector and commercial entities should not overshadow philanthropy's willingness to advocate for change, push for reform, promote alternative visions, or try new strategies.

As efforts to evaluate their work proliferate, and new donors bring business-oriented metrics to the work of social change, many fear that the heart and soul of philanthropic endeavor is being lost. On the contrary, what has been lost is the independent voice of philanthropy, its willingness to express its commitments, and its confidence in itself. As a growing and diversifying industry, the goal must not be to reduce all action to the lowest common denominator. Rather, the industry must encourage debate, recognize its obvious fractures, and be explicit about what it stands for and where it stands together or apart. If managed well, the different motivations, political aspirations, social theories, and commercial structures of the industry will thrive and provide a robust system of solutions to donors and communities. If managed poorly and glossed over in the name of unanimity, these fissures will rend the whole helpless, and only those factions that can negotiate markets and regulation will survive.

Philanthropy also needs to actively promote itself as an industry. To the public, this amounts to marketing campaigns such as those conducted by industries as diverse as avocados, milk, or even the State of New York.[4] To the public overseers, this means working to integrate funding and sharing success to maintaining consistent relationships with regulators in all 50 states and at the national level. The industry is likely to experience tighter regulatory oversight in the near and long term. Just as the confluence of Enron, Andersen, and Tyco scandals led to new governance structures for American corporations, the scandals over online donation processors, the misuse of dedicated funds, and the proliferation of negative media stories about charitable oversight have set the stage for continued regulatory revision regarding philanthropy.

Several industry watchers have been saying for years that "all it will take is one good scandal and the other shoe will drop" on philanthropy. In June 2003, with the announcement that PipeVine Inc., a nonprofit spin-off from the United Way of the Bay Area, had used charitable donations to cover its own operating expenses, that shoe seemed to drop. This case is still unfolding, but it is important to note how the tone of scandal has changed, even from 2001 when similar charges about misuse of funds were levied at the Red Cross. At that time, the accused organization first defended its actions, claiming that it had never committed to using funds raised in the wake of September 11 only for relief from that tragedy. Public outcry ensued, the Director of the Red Cross was fired, and public apologies were offered only after the damage was out of control. In the PipeVine case, the organization at issue called for auditors on its own behalf, turned over all materials to the Attorney General immediately, and the public statements were immediately remorseful and focused on making good on the lost funds.[5] It is too early to know what mistakes or crimes were committed, but the difference in public tone is notable.

Whether or not the industry has learned lessons just about working with the media or has truly turned a corner in terms of interactions with regulators remains to be seen. The PipeVine case may be the other shoe dropping for philanthropic credibility. It also might be a turning point for the industry, the inevitable collapse of a single bad apple that pushes the rest of the innovators in the right direction.

Some of the subgroups within philanthropy may be more inclined to use regulation to their benefit than others. Small foundations and rural foundations (especially rural community foundations) are in fairly close contact with local and state representatives. The Association of Small Foundations reports that a majority of its members know their congressional representatives. The association encourages its members to get to know their local government officials. Rural community foundation executives also reported high engagement with local and state government officials—"everyone knows everyone out here." These groups and others, such as the Council on Michigan Foundations, which has a program to introduce foundation executives to state and local representatives, believe such relationships are important for communicating the value of philanthropy and in gaining access to regulatory decision makers.

For the most part, however, foundations retain their distance from public policy makers until there is an industry crisis. While the national trade associations and membership groups such as the Council on Foundations and Independent Sector may be able to track policy changes, communicate them to members, and galvanize responses, the infrastructure at the state level is significantly more varied and less ready to address policy. Currently, only ten of fifty states have professional associations located in state capitols and with regulatory review and public policy as part of their mandate.[6]

There is an opportunity for philanthropy to come together as an industry and promote a regulatory structure that encourages giving, that facilitates partnerships, and that can support the industry's efforts to grow and diversify. There is also a great likelihood that the competitive pressures within the industry will favor those organizations that understand the power of a proactive regulatory approach and have the connections to promote one.

Finally, as we seek to improve the philanthropic system, we must always do so in pursuit of a greater common good. High-functioning philanthropy for its own sake is of limited interest and limited use. Philanthropy must be encouraged, diversified, aggregated, integrated, and monitored because of its relationships to the larger whole. That whole is not just the independent sector, but also the precarious balancing act it shares with those in elected office and with our commercial resources. We know from history that neither the public sector nor the private sector can represent all viewpoints, carry forth all visions, support all political beliefs, or nurture beauty, or ensure justice for all by themselves. Philanthropy and the independent sector are responsible for encouraging alternative and minority views, testing unprofitable ideas, pushing the boundaries of knowledge, and advocating on behalf of those in need. This larger common good is why philanthropy matters. These enormous responsibilities fall to philanthropy and the independent sector and are why it is important to constantly pursue improvement.

DELIBERATE DIVERSITY

One of the great myths among contemporary American foundations is the "great battle between community foundations and financial service firms." The story is premised largely on the acts of one community foundation, albeit a very large one, The California Community Foundation. The core of the myth is that the advent of commercial donor-advised funds in the 1990s was met with immediate and universal distrust and animosity from all community foundations. The story would have us believe that all of the community foundations in the United States came together and lobbied hard to have the commercial funds declared illegal. As the decade passed and community foundations started to partner with various financial firms—first in small regional ways and ultimately through national alliances with Merrill Lynch—the story is used to show the error of the earlier ways.

The problem is that the earlier way never happened. Community foundations in 1992 were in no position to organize and fight Fidelity Investments or anyone else. Several community foundations did seek legal advice and did call for review by the Internal Revenue Service of the proposed funds. But these foundations were neither representative of community foundations as a whole nor speaking on behalf of the industry.

The real lesson of the nonexistent great battle is the power of the industry when it does act in concert. Since 1992 community foundations have galvanized under the umbrella of the existing industry association by developing a Community Foundations Leadership Team at the Council on Foundations. They have also created an independent trade group focused on research and development for the field, Community Foundations of America. In addition, community foundations in several states and some smaller regions now meet in formal leagues and informal associations, they develop products and marketing campaigns together, and—as represented by the Merrill Lynch Partnership—they form formal business alliances together.

The advent of the commercial gift funds had profound effects on community foundations and all of philanthropy. They represent the first, large-scale, stand-alone product innovation in philanthropy in several years.

Since 1992, philanthropic vendors have launched and marketed private-labeled foundation administrative products, supporting organizations, chartered family foundations, and turnkey private foundations.

Vendors in philanthropy—both commercial and nonprofit—have worked harder and harder to define their added value, their unique niche, and their core contributions. Price wars have raged across vendors, and the demand for results has led to the development of new measurements, new monitoring tools, and new associations focused on evaluation and effectiveness. And the once-clear boundaries between commercial and nonprofit vendors have become progressively blurrier as hybrid organizations and strategies for everything from asset management to outcome measurement test the waters.

Rather than being the end of philanthropy as we know it, the introduction of commercial gift funds in 1992 precipitated one of the most innovative, dynamic, and high-energy periods in philanthropic history. The new diversity in philanthropic products drew new participants into the market and spurred product and service creation among more staid institutions. The wide new range of giving options puts increased pressure on those already in the market to demonstrate their value and to build alliances. Comparisons to the importance of biodiversity in ecosystems or product innovation in marketplaces are both apt. Diversity in philanthropic giving strengthens the individual giving options, the communities involved, and the industry as a whole.

Even as the product lines diversify, philanthropy as an industry has a long way to go in pursuing deliberate diversity. Everything from the racial composition of most foundation boards to the types and mechanisms of philanthropic activity that the industry tracks needs to be broadened. Foundations cannot adequately serve America's communities if they remain closed to racial and ethnic diversity. The products and services sold need to advance culturally diverse traditions of philanthropy. These range from self-help in a Muslim community where debt is forbidden to the system of transnational remittance in Mexican families, which at more than $300 million annually is larger than formal American investments in our southern neighbor's economy.[7] The industry needs to track donor-advised funds in the same way it counts foundations; it needs to encourage industry initiatives in research and development; and it needs to actively promote and encourage innovation and diversity.

LOOKING BACK FROM THE FUTURE

The present moment in philanthropic history will not be fully understood for another quarter or half century. No matter how pressed for time we become or how rapid change seems, the perspective gained from time passing will always be a valuable analytic tool. So let us imagine we could look back on American philanthropy at the turn of the twenty-first century from the year 2050. Based on the recommendations made in this book and the application of lessons learned from other industries, we may be able to actively create an industry that fits the following description:

- Is strengthened by the diversity and complexity of financial products used to make resources available and to manage philanthropic assets. At the same time, managers of these assets invest in and rely on common, credible metrics to define problems, assess progress, and measure success.

- Takes advantage of the many cultural traditions for philanthropy, and counts all such activities as part of the industry. Philanthropic entities thrive in all communities and philanthropic resources can be easily identified, informed, and aggregated regardless of whether they are held in a private foundation, a donor-advised fund, or a religiously-affiliated trust.

- Philanthropically-funded research findings and knowledge are available to any and all who want access to them and foundations invest heavily in the use and application of the industry's research findings. Contributions to and use of this knowledge base is a more widely cited ranking of foundation and philanthropic individuals than simply the size of their gifts or their investment portfolio.

- Public problem solving is the coin of the realm, and all who have something at stake are invited to help advise the distribution of resources. Philanthropists involve community members and affected residents in the design and implementation of proposed initiatives.

- A public trust exists where the technical skills of philanthropic decision making can be accessed, so that issue experts and experienced decision makers can help guide the philanthropic resources of many individuals and institutions rather than one at a time.

- Philanthropic assets are regularly aggregated by issue and informed by common goals. The professional challenge in philanthropy is seen as

attracting other people's money to an issue and applying the joint resources of many to make change happen.

- The regulatory structure guiding philanthropy is informed by active
  participation of experienced philanthropists working in partnership
  with the monitoring bodies at the state and federal level. The purpose
  of regulation is to encourage giving and support the use of knowledge
  and research in conducting philanthropic business.

- An internationally based and accessible clearinghouse of successful
  philanthropic strategies is maintained by public and private investment. It serves as a research and development infrastructure to philanthropists and the public sector.

This is a philanthropic industry that embodies diversity, aggregation, integration, timing, and commitment. It continues to grow, and its influence
and importance is well understood by the general public and regulators.
New entrants and outsiders know where to find industry research, resources, and tools if and as they need them. The diversity of the forms and
explicit links between them allow the industry as a whole to thrive, even
as the inevitable scandals rock prominent organizations or new regulations
and public budget challenges open the door to new products and services.

American philanthropy has changed drastically since the founding of
the colonies or the creation of its first great institutions. It changes in a
rhythm marked by demographic shifts, market punctuations, and regulatory revision. It moves in concert with changing expectations about the
role of the public sector or attitudes about corporate citizenship. It is a
growing industry because of the adaptability of its different components.
This characteristic must not be allowed to wither because the demise of the
industry's variation will be the demise of philanthropy. The future of philanthropy is in building deliberate connections between the many disparate
pieces and recognizing the power of many over the influence of a few.

Copyright Information

Several sections of this book have been drawn from previously published articles and papers by the author. In addition, several of the speeches delivered to grant-maker conferences or meetings by the author have informed this work. Copies of those presentations are available by contacting Blueprint Research & Design, Inc., at *www.blueprintrd.com*. Previously published papers and articles include the following:

Collective Wisdom: Regional Associations in the 21st Century. Washington, DC: Forum of Regional Associations of Grantmakers, 2001.

Critical Junctures: Philanthropic Associations as Policy Actors. Los Angeles: University of Southern California, Center on Philanthropy and Public Policy, May 2002.

"The Deliberate Evolution." Washington, DC: *Foundation News and Commentary*, May/June 2002.

Foundations for the Future: Emerging Trends in Foundation Philanthropy. Los Angeles: University of Southern California, Center on Philanthropy and Public Policy, 1999.

Full-Service Foundations. Washington, DC: Foundation News and Commentary, April 1998.

Future Impact: Considering foundation philanthropy in California. Los Angeles: The J. P. Getty Foundation and Lilly Endowment, conference abstract, August 1999.

"The Future of Philanthropy History: Suggestions for Research and Practice." In Ellen Condliffe Lagemann, *Philanthropic Foundations: New Scholarship, New Possibilities*. Indianapolis: Indiana University Press, 1999.

Health Care Conversions and Philanthropy: Important Issues for Practice and Research. Washington, DC: The Aspen Institute Nonprofit Sector Research Fund, conference report, 1999.

The Industry of Philanthropy: Highlights from Key Industry Analyses. Highlights from Blueprint's publications, 1999–2002, July 2002.

Managing Up in Down Times. Baltimore, MD: The Annie E. Casey Foundation, January 2003.

New Giving Partners. Baltimore, MD: The Annie E. Casey Foundation, July 2001.

Philanthropic Comparison Shopping. Washington, DC: The Council on Foundations, October 2001.

"Spending Smarter: Knowledge as a Philanthropic Resource." In Frank Ellsworth and Joe Lumarda (eds.), *From Grantmaker to Leader: Emerging Strategies for Twenty-First Century Foundations*. New York: John Wiley & Sons, 2002.

Bernholz, Lucy and Gabriel Kasper. *The Currency of Change*. San Francisco, CA: Blueprint Research & Design, Inc., 2001.

Bernholz, Lucy and Kendall Guthrie. "Knowledge is an Asset, Too." Washington, DC: *Foundation News and Commentary*, May/June 2000.

———. *Philanthropic Connections: Mapping the Landscape of U.S. Funder Networks*. Washington, DC: Forum of Regional Associations of Grantmakers, 2003.

Bibliography

California Foundations: A Snapshot. Los Angeles: University of California, Center on Philanthropy and Public Policy, 2000.

"Charitable Gift Funds Ranked by Assets under Management." *InvestmentNews Databook 2002*, December 23, 2002, p. 14.

Giving USA 2002. Washington, DC: AAFRC Trust for Philanthropy, 2002.

"The Graying of the Globe." *New York Times* Editorial, April 12, 2002.

"Great Expectations." *American Demographics*, May 2003.

"Help in the Right Places." *The Economist*, March 15, 2002, pp. 73–74.

"High Tech Hopes Meet Reality." *Chronicle of Philanthropy*, June 14, 2001, pp. 1, 8–23.

Indicators of Effectiveness. Boston: Center for Effective Philanthropy, 2002.

"The Knowledge Bank." *Knowledge Management*, June 2001, pp. 24–26.

Mission Possible: 200 Ways to Strengthen the Nonprofit Sector's Infrastructure. Washington, DC: Union Institute, 1996.

Philanthropy Measures Up. World Economic Forum, Global Leaders Tomorrow, 2003, www.salesforcefoundation.org.

The Nonprofit Almanac: Dimensions of the Independent Sector. San Francisco: Jossey Bass, 1996.

"The Real State of the Union." *The Atlantic Monthly*, January/February 2003.

2003 Community Foundation Global Status Report. Worldwide Initiative for Grantmaker Support—Community Foundations, www.wings-cf.org/global_report. Accessed on May 23, 2003.

Abramson, Alan, and Rachel McCarthy. "Infrastructure Organizations." In Lester A. Salamon, *The State of The Nonprofit Sector.* Washington, DC: Brookings Institute Press, 2002.

Bakal, Carl. *Charity USA: An Investigation into the Multi-billion Dollar Charity Industry.* New York: Times Books, 1979.

Bank, David. "The Man Who Would Mend the World." *Wall Street Journal*, March 14, 2002.

Barabasi, Albert-László. *Linked: The New Science of Networks*. New York: Perseus Publishing, 2002.

Barman, Emily A. "Asserting Difference: The Strategic Response of Nonprofit Organizations to Competition." *Social Forces*, June 2002, 80(4): 1191–1222.

Bell, Daniel. *The Coming of the Post-Industrial Society: A venture in social forecasting*. New York: Basic Books, 1973.

Billitteri, Thomas A. "A Run for the Money." *Chronicle of Philanthropy*, April 20, 2002.

Blau, Andrew. *More Than Bit Players: How Information Technology Will Change the Ways Nonprofits and Foundations Work and Thrive in the Information Age*. A report to the Surdna Foundation, May 2001, *www.surdnar.org*.

Boisture, Robert A., and Lloyd H. Mayer. "Weighing the Alternatives to Private Foundations." *Journal of Taxation of Exempt Organizations*, May/June 2000, 11(6): 257–263.

Bradley, Bill, and Paul Jansen. "Faster Charity." *New York Times*, May 15, 2002.

Brilliant, Eleanor L. *Private Charity and Public Inquiry: A History of the Filer and Peterson Commissions*. Bloomington: Indiana University Press, 2000.

Brown, John Seely, and Paul Duguid. *The Social Life of Information*. Boston: Harvard Business School Press, 2000.

Bruck, Connie. "The Monopolist." *The New Yorker*, April 21/28, 2003, pp. 136–155.

Bukowitz, Wendi R., and Ruth L. Williams. *The Knowledge Management Fieldbook*. Edinburgh: Pearson Education Limited, 1999.

Carson, Emmett. "Community Foundations Facing Crossroads." *Chronicle of Philanthropy*, May 16, 2002.

Celente, Gerald. *Trends 2000*. New York: Warner Books, 1997.

Chernow, Ron. *Titan: The Life of John D. Rockefeller, Sr*. New York: Random House, 1998.

Choi, William, and Ingrid Mittermaier. "The Tax Exempt Status of Commercially Sponsored Donor Advised Funds." *The Exempt Organization Tax Review*, July 1997. In Joe Lumarda, "Philanthropy, Self-Fulfillment and the Leadership of Community Foundations," *From Grantmaker to Leader*. New York: John Wiley & Sons, 2002.

Cohen, Adam. "Too Old to Work." *New York Times Magazine*, March 2, 2003.

Cortada, James W. *Best Practices in Information Technology*. Englewood Cliffs, NJ: Prentice-Hall, 1998.

Cortese, Amy. "The New Accountability: Tracking the Social Costs." *New York Times*, March 24, 2002, p. C4.

Crane, Dwight B. *The Effects of Banking Deregulation*. Washington, DC: Association of Reserve City Bankers, 1983.

Davenport, Thomas, and Laurence Prusak. *Working Knowledge: How Organizations Manage What they Know*. Boston: Harvard Business School Press, 1998.

De Bono, Edward. *Future Positive*. London: Maurice Temple Smith, 1979.

Demko, Paul. "Something for the Little People." *CityPages* [Minneapolis], May 28, 2003, p 1.

Demsetz, Harold. "The Theory of the Firm Revisited," in Oliver E. Williamson and Sidney G. Winter (eds.), *The Nature of the Firm: Origins, Evolution, and Development*. New York: Oxford University Press, 1991, pp. 159–178.

Drucker, Peter. "The Next Society." Letter to the Editor. *The Economist*, November 3, 2001.

Drucker, Peter F. *Managing the Nonprofit Organization: Principles and Practices*. New York: Harper Collins, 1990.

Drucker, Peter. *Landmarks of Tomorrow*. New York: Harper Brothers, 1957.

Dugery, Jacqueline, and Caroline Hammer. *Coming of Age in the Information Age*. Richmond, VA: The Pew Partnership for Civic Change, The University of Richmond, 2000.

Frey, William H., and Bill Abresch. "New State Demographic Divisions." *Spectrum: The Journal of State Government*, Summer 2002, 75(3): 18–22.

Friedman, Lawrence J., and Mark D. McGarvie. *Charity, Philanthropy and Civility in American History*. New York: Cambridge University Press, 2003.

Foundation Growth and Giving Estimates. 2002 Preview. New York: The Foundation Center, 2003.

Fox Keller, Evelyn. A Feeling for the Organism: The Life and Work of Barbara McClintock. San Francisco: Freeman, 1983.

Frumkin, Peter. *On Being Nonprofit: A Conceptual and Policy Primer*, Cambridge, MA: Harvard University Press, 2002.

Fuchus, Marek. "The Economic Hard Times Beneath the Steeple." *New York Times*, March 29, 2003, p. A10.

Fulton, Katherine and Andrew Blau. *Trends in 21st Century Philanthropy*. Working Paper. Emeryville, CA: Global Business Network, June 2003.

Gaddis, John Lewis. *The Landscape of History: How Historians Map the Past*. Oxford: Oxford University Press, 2002.

Gadeish, Orit, and Scott Olivet, "Designing for Implementability," in Frances Hesselbein, Marshall Goldsmith, and Richard Beckhard (eds.), *The Organization of the Future*. New York: The Peter F. Drucker Foundation for Nonprofit Management, 1997, pp. 53–64.

Garvin, David A. *Learning in Action: A Guide to Putting the Learning Organization to Work*. Boston: Harvard Business School Press, 2000.

Geisler, Eliezer. "Harnessing the Value of Experience in the Knowledge-Driven Firm." *Business Horizon*, May–June 1999, pp. 18–25.

Geisst, Charles R. *Wall Street: A History*. New York: Oxford University Press, 1997.

German, Kent. "Charity Beat: Newspapers are devoting more attention to covering philanthropies." *American Journalism Review*, September 2000, *www.ajr.newslink.org/ajrkentsept00.html*.

Gladwell, Malcolm. *The Tipping Point: How Little Things Can Make a Big Difference*. New York: Little Brown and Co., 2000.

Golembe, Carter H. *Commercial Banking and the Glass-Steagall Act*. Washington, DC: American Bankers Association, 1982.

Gould, Stephen Jay. *Triumph and Tragedy in Mudville*. New York: W.W. Norton, 2003.

Graham, Carol. *Private Markets for Public Goods: Raising the Stakes in Economic Reform*. Washington, DC: Brookings Institute Press, 1998.

Greenhouse, Linda. "Supreme Court Rules Charity may be Charged with Fraud." *New York Times*, March 6, 2003, p A1.

Hall, Peter Dobkin. *Inventing the Nonprofit Sector and Other Essays on Philanthropy, Voluntarism, and Nonprofit Organizations*, Baltimore: Johns Hopkins University Press, 1992.

Halstead, Ted, and Michael Lind. *The Radical Center: The Future of American Politics*. New York: Doubleday, 2001.

Hammond, Allen. *Which World? Scenarios for the 21st Century*. Washington, DC: Island Press, 1998.

Hansen, Morten T., Nitin Nohria, and Thomas Tierney. "What's Your Strategy for Managing Knowledge?" *Harvard Business Review*, March–April 1999, pp. 106–116.

Hanvey, Chris, and Terry Philpot. *Sweet Charity: The Role and Workings of Voluntary Organisations*. London: Routledge, 1997.

Harreld, J. Bruce. "Building Smarter, Faster Organizations," in Don Tapscott, *Blueprint to the Digital Economy: Creating Wealth in the Era of New Business*. New York: McGraw-Hill, 1998, pp. 60–76.

Havens, John J., Paul G. Schervish, and Mary A. O'Herlihy. *2003 Survey of Planned Giving Vehicles*. Boston, MA: Boston College Social Welfare Research Institute. June 2003.

Havens, John J., and Paul G. Schervish. "Why the $41 Trillion Wealth Transfer Estimate is Still Valid: A Review of Challenges and Questions." Boston: Boston College, Social Welfare Research Institute, January 6, 2003.

Hayes, Samuel L. III (ed.). *Wall Street and Regulation*. Cambridge, MA: Harvard Business School Press, 1987.

Hesselbein, Frances, Marshall Goldsmith, and Richard Beckhard (eds.). *The Organization of the Future*. New York: The Peter F. Drucker Foundation for Nonprofit Management, 1997.

Huang, Kuan-Tsae, Yang W. Lee, and Richard Y Wang. *Quality Information and Knowledge*. Englewood Cliffs, NJ: Prentice-Hall, 1999.

Ingo, Walter (ed.). *Commercial Banks' Increasing Presence in the Investment Banking Business: Repeal of the Glass-Steagall Law: The Debate and Current Chronicle*. New York: New York University. Occasional Papers in Business and Finance, Salomon Brothers Center, Number 9, 1989.

Jarboe, Kenan P. *Knowledge Management as an Economic Development Strategy*. Washington, DC: U.S. Economic Development Alliance, 2001. Available at *www.athenaalliance.org*.

Jansen, Paul. and David Katz. "For Nonprofits, Time is Money." *The McKinsey Quarterly*. Number 1, 2002.

Johnson, Steven. *Emergence: The Connected Lives of Ants, Brains, Cities, and Software*. New York: Scribner, 2001.

Kador, John. *Charles Schwab. How On241 e Company Beat Wall Street and Reinvented the Brokerage Industry*. New York: John Wiley & Sons, 2002.

Kaplan, Robert D. "The World in 2005." *Atlantic Monthly*, March 2002, pp. 76–118.

Kemp, Roger L. "Cities in the 21st Century: The Forces of Change." *Spectrum: The Journal of State Government*. Summer 2001, 74(3): 21–25.

King, Willford Isbell. *Trends in Philanthropy: A Study in a Typical American City*. NewYork: National Bureau of Economic Research, 1928.

Larose, Marni D., and Brad Wolverton. "Donor-Advised Funds Experience Drop in Contributions, Survey Finds." *Chronicle of Philanthropy*, May 15, 2003, p. 7.

Lester, Toby. "Oh, Gods!" *Atlantic Monthly*, February 2002, pp. 30–38.

Levitt, Theodore. "Marketing Myopia." *Harvard Business Review*, 38(4): July–August 1960.

Litman, Jessica. *Digital Copyright*. Amherst, NY: Prometheus Books, 2001.

Lloyd, Tom. *The Charity Business: The New Philanthropists*. London: John Murray Ltd., 1993.

Luck, James I., and Suzanne L. Feurt. "A Growing and Flexible Service to Donors: Donor Advised Funds in Community Foundations." Washington, DC: Council on Foundations, 2002.

McDonough, William, and Michael Braungart. *Cradle to Cradle: Remaking the Way We Make Things*. New York: North Point Press, 2002.

McMillan, John. *Reinventing the Bazaar: A Natural History of Markets*. New York: W.W. Norton, 2002.

McWhorter, John. *The Power of Babel*. New York: HarperCollins, 2001.

Meadows, Donella. *Leverage Points: Places to Intervene in a System*. Hartland, VT: The Sustainability Institute, 1999.

Naisbitt, John, and Patricia Aburdene. *Megatrends 2000: Ten New Directions for the 1990s*. New York: William Morrow & Co., 1990.

Nalder, Eric. "CEO Rewards at Nonprofit." *San Jose Mercury News*, April 27, 2003, p. A1.

Nielsen, Waldemar A. *The Golden Donors: A New Anatomy of the Great Foundations*. New York: E.P. Dutton Books, 1985.

Nielsen, Waldemar A. *Inside American Philanthropy: The Dramas of Donorship*. Norman, OK: University of Oklahoma Press, 1996.

O'Dell, Carla, and C. Jackson Grayson, Jr. *If Only We Knew What We Know*. New York: The Free Press, 1998.

O'Neill, Gerald K. *2081: A Hopeful View of the Human Future*. New York: Simon & Schuster, 1981.

Orme, William. "World's Population Aging Fast, Study Says." *San Francisco Chronicle*, March 1, 2002, p. A16.

Owens, Marcus S. Memo for the Council on Foundations. "History and Analysis of the Laws Governing Qualifying Distributions of Private Foundations." Washington, DC: Caplin & Drysdale, November 30, 2001.

Pfeffer, Jeffrey. "Will the Organization of the Future Make the Mistakes of the Past?" in Frances Hesselbein, Marshall Goldsmith, and Richard Beckhard (eds.), *The Organization of the Future*. New York: The Peter F. Drucker Foundation for Nonprofit Management, 1997, pp. 43–51.

Phillips, Kevin. *Wealth and Democracy: A Political History of the American Rich*. New York: Broadway Books, 2002.

Pink, Daniel. *Free Agent Nation: How America's New Independent Workers Are Transforming the Way We Live*. New York: Warner Books, 2001.

Porter, Michael, and Mark Kramer. "Philanthropy's New Agenda: Creating Value." *Harvard Business Review*, November 1999.

Porter, Michael. *Competitive Strategy*. New York: The Free Press, 1980.

Powell, Walter W. *The Nonprofit Sector: A Research Handbook*. New Haven, CT: Yale University Press, 1987.

Prahalad, C.K., and Venkatram Ramaswamy. "Co-opting customer competence." *Harvard Business Review*, January–February 2000, pp. 79–87.

Rand, Ayn. *The New Intellectual.* New York: Random House, 1961.

Reinhardt, Erika. "Halting and Beginning to Reverse the Incidence of Malaria . . . and Other Major Diseases." *UN Chronicle,* December 2002–February 2003, 39(4): 42–44.

Riche, Martha Farnsworth,. "Implications of the Census 2000 Results for the Environment." Paper prepared for the Surdna Foundation. June 2001. Available at *www.surdna.org.*

Rynecki, David. "Can Sallie Save Citi, Restore Sandy's Reputation, and Earn her $30 Million Paycheck?" *Fortune,* June 9, 2003, pp. 68–78.

Schambra, William A. "The Evaluation Wars." *Philanthropy,* May/June 2003.

Scott, Jason. *Building a philanthropic marketplace: Obstacles and opportunities, www.allavida.org.*

Smith, Jared. *Guns, Germs and Steel: The Fates of Human Societies,* New York: W.W. Norton & Co., 1999.

Stauber, Karl. "Mission-driven Philanthropy: What do we want to accomplish and how do we do it?" *Nonprofit and Voluntary Sector Quarterly,* 30(2): June 2001, 393–399.

Strom, Stephanie. "California Charity Firm Folds, Leaving Some Clients at a Loss." *New York Times,* June 4, 2003, p. A22.

Strom, Stephanie. "Charity Collector Says Audit Showed Shortfall in Revenue." *New York Times,* June 5, 2003, p. A27.

Strom, Stephanie. "Donors Add Watchdog Role to Relations with Charities." *New York Times,* March 29, 2003, p. A8.

Strom, Stephanie. "New Philanthropists Find Drudgery." *New York Times,* January 12, 2003, p. A17.

Tapscott, Don. *Blueprint to the Digital Economy: Creating Wealth in the Era of New Business.* New York: McGraw-Hill, 1998.

Teece, David J. "Capturing Value from Knowledge Assets: The New Economy, Markets for Know-How, and Intangible Assets." *California Management Review,* Spring 1998, pp. 55–79.

Tittle, Diane. *Rebuilding Cleveland: The Cleveland Foundation and its Evolving Urban Strategy.* Columbus: Ohio State University Press, 1992.

Toffler, Alvin. *Future Shock.* New York: Random House, 1970.

Victor, Richard H.K. "Regulation-Defines Financial Markets: Fragmentation and Integration in Financial Services," in Samuel L. Hayes III (ed.), *Wall Street and Regulation.* Cambridge, MA: Harvard Business School Press, 1987, pp. 7–62.

Wagner, Etienne, and William Snyder. "Communities of Practice: The Organizational Frontier." *Harvard Business Review,* January–February 2000, pp. 139–145.

Walleck, Todd. "Charitable Funding Mystery." *San Francisco Chronicle,* June 4, 2003, p. A1.

Walleck, Todd. "Nonprofit admits spending charities' money." *San Francisco Chronicle,* June 5, 2003, p. A1.

Wattenberg, Ben. "It Will be a Small World After All." *New York Times,* March 8, 2003, p. A29.

Williamson, Oliver E., and Sidney G. Winter. *The Nature of the Firm: Origins, Evolution, and Development,* New York: Oxford University Press, 1993.

Notes

Introduction

1. Stephen Jay Gould explaining the development of his lifelong love of baseball. *Triumph and Tragedy in Mudville*, New York: W. W. Norton, 2003, pp. 28–29.
2. See, in particular, Lester A. Salamon, (ed.), *The State of Nonprofit America*, Washington, DC: Brookings Institution Press, 2002; Walter W. Powell, *The Nonprofit Sector: A Research Handbook*, New Haven, CT: Yale University Press, 1987; and *The Nonprofit Almanac: Dimensions of the Independent Sector*, San Francisco: Jossey Bass, 1996.
3. For the best new exception to this, see Lawrence A. Friedman and Mark D. McGarvie, *Charity, Philanthropy and Civility in American History*, New York: Cambridge University Press, 2003.
4. With acknowledgements to William McDonough and Michael Braungart, *Cradle to Cradle: Remaking the Way We Make Things*, New York: North Point Press, 2002.
5. This estimate only counts direct contributions. The industry also includes millions of volunteer hours, in-kind donations, and thousands of community groups and informal networks that contribute to their communities but whose resources are not counted in the aggregate. For a compelling discussion of what constitutes the nonprofit and voluntary sector, see Peter Frumkin, *On Being Nonprofit: A Conceptual and Policy Primer*, Cambridge, MA: Harvard University Press, 2002.

Chapter 1

1. Belarius in William Shakespeare's *Cymbeline*, Act III, Scene VI.
2. See Frumkin, *On Being Nonprofit*, pp. 10–16 for a quick overview of the naming of the sector.
3. Michael Porter, *Competitive Strategy*, New York: The Free Press, 1980.
4. *Giving USA 2002* reported $212 billion in charitable giving in the United States in 2001. This includes individuals, foundations, corporations, and bequests. *Giving USA 2002*, Washington, DC: AAFRC Trust for Philanthropy, 2002.
5. Ibid.
6. Lucy Bernholz, *Philanthropic Comparison Shopping*, Washington, DC: The Council on Foundations, 2001.
7. March 2003 saw the national launch of the Merrill Lynch Community Foundation Partnership, a broad-based alliance with ambitious goals of managing and advising $1 billion in assets by mid-2004. The field is also rich with local and regional alliances between community foundations and smaller banks or investment firms.
8. See William A. Schambra, "The Evaluation Wars," *Philanthropy*, May/June 2003.

9. Kevin Phillips, Wealth and Democracy: A Political History of the American Rich, New York: Broadway Books, 2002, p. 214.

10. Ibid, p. 129.

11. The San Francisco Foundation ran a billboard campaign in the Municipal Railway stations in San Francisco for several months. Community foundations often place ads in local and regional papers and magazines; see The Minneapolis Foundation and California Community Foundation for examples.

12. John J. Havens, Paul G. Schervish, and Mary A. O'Herlihy, 2003 Survey of Planned Giving Vehicles, Boston: Boston College Social Welfare Research Institute, June 2003.

13. Foundation Growth and Giving Estimates, 2002 Preview, New York: The Foundation Center, 2003.

14. Giving USA 2002, Washington, DC: AAFRC Trust for Philanthropy, 2003.

15. Marni D. LaRose and Brad Wolverton, "Donor Advised Funds Experience Drop in Contributions, Survey Finds," Washington, DC: The Chronicle of Philanthropy, May 15, 2003.

16. Katherine Fulton and Andrew Blau, "Trends in 21st Century Philanthropy," Working Paper, Emeryville, CA: Global Business Network, June 2003, p.4.

17. Ayn Rand, The New Intellectual, New York: Random House, 1961.

18. See Evelyn Fox Keller, A Feeling for the Organism: The Life and Work of Barbara Mc-Clintock, San Francisco: Freeman, 1983 for a fascinating illustration of how scientific knowledge emerges, moves forward, is discounted, and reborn.

19. Stephen Jay Gould calls this process of sporadic change punctuated equilibrium.

20. Cliff A. Joslyn, writing for the Prinicipia Cybernetica Project, http://pespmc1.vub.ac.be/SYSTHEOR.html, as of March 26, 2003.

21. See Donella Meadows, Leverage Points: Places to Intervene in a System, Hartland, VT: The Sustainability Institute, 1999, www.sustainer.org. See also Steven Johnson, Emergence: The Connected Lives of Ants, Brains, Cities, and Software, New York: Scribner, 2001; and Albert-László Barabasi, Linked: The New Science of Networks, New York: Perseus Publishing, 2002.

22. Meadows cites work by J. W. Forrester, a leading MIT scholar and systems analyst. His groundbreaking work includes Urban Dynamics, Portland, OR: Productivity Press, 1969; and World Dynamics, Portland, OR: Productivity Press, 1971.

23. Lucy Bernholz, Collective Wisdom: Regional Associations in the 21st Century, Washington, DC: Forum of Regional Associations of Grantmakers. 2001.

24. Indicators of Effectiveness, Boston: Center for Effective Philanthropy, 2002; Philanthropy Measures Up, World Economic Forum, Global Leaders Tomorrow, January 2003, www.salesforcefoundation.org; and Jason Scott, Building a Philanthropic Marketplace: Obstacles and Opportunities, www.allavida.org.

25. John McMillan, Reinventing the Bazaar: A Natural History of Markets, New York: W. W. Norton, 2002, pp. 160–161.

26. The term public benefit sector is more and more widely used by organizations that are uneasy with defining themselves by what they are not—nonprofit. The term came to light in Great Britain in the early 1990s, where it was used by England's Chief Charity Commissioner Robin Guthrie. See Tom Lloyd, The Charity Business: The New Philanthropists, London: John Murray Ltd., 1993, p. 201.

27. McMillan, Reinventing the Bazaar, p. 182.

28. Roger L. Kemp, "Cities in the 21st Century: The Forces of Change," Spectrum: The Journal of State Government, Summer 2001, 74(3): 25.

29. Lloyd, The Charity Business, pp. 188–192.

Chapter 2

1. The example is fictitious. The data on the scope of diseases and the size of the markets comes from Erika Reinhardt, "Halting and Beginning to Reverse the Incidence of Malaria. . . and Other Major Diseases," UN Chronicle, December 2002–February 2003, 39(4): 42–44.

2. Tom Lloyd, *The Charity Business: The New Philanthropists*. London: John Murray Ltd., 1993, p. 4.
3. Ibid, p. 116.
4. Op. Cit., pp. 177–178.
5. *Indicators of Effectiveness*, Boston: Center for Effective Philanthropy, 2002.
6. Lucy Bernholz, *Collective Wisdom: Regional Associations in the 21st Century*, Washington, DC: Forum of Regional Associations of Grantmakers, 2001.
7. Ibid.
8. Exhibition Brochure, "Me, Myself and Infrastructure: Private Lives and Public Works in America," American Society of Civil Engineers, The Concourse at One Market, San Francisco, CA, February 28–April 11, 2003.
9. The influences of market and regulatory structures on philanthropy have tended to overwhelm individual players in the industry. Left unchecked, these two forces will, I believe, force change on individual philanthropic institutions and the infrastructure.
10. This is due to an increase in the numbers of lawsuits against nonprofits that directly challenge their handling of a donor's gift. The nonprofits involved range in type from community foundations to universities; the donors include living individuals and trustees of bequests; and the suits can be found from New York to Texas. See Stephanie Strom, "Donors Add Watchdog Role to Relations with Charities," *New York Times*, March 29, 2003, p. A8.
11. See Strom, "Donors Add Watchdog Role to Relations with Charities"; and Paul Demko, "Something for the Little People," *CityPages*, May 28, 2003. p A1.
12. *Philanthropy Measures Up*. San Francisco, CA: World Economic Forum Global Leaders Tomorrow. Accessed at *www.salesforcefoundation.com*

Chapter 3

1. Gerald Celente, *Trends 2000*, New York: Warner Books, 1997; Edward De Bono, *Future Positive*, London: Maurice Temple Smith, 1979; Peter Drucker, *Landmarks of Tomorrow*, New York: Harper Brothers, 1957; Allen Hammond, *Which World? Scenarios for the 21st Century*, Washington, DC: Island Press, 1998; Gerald K. O'Neill, *2081: A Hopeful View of the Human Future*, New York: Simon & Schuster, 1981; John Naisbitt and Patricia Aburdene, *Megatrends 2000: Ten New Directions for the 1990s*, New York: William Morrow & Co., 1990; Alvin Toffler, *Future Shock*, New York: Random House, 1970.
2. Toffler, *Future Shock*, p. 4.
3. Several investment magazines run an annual feature in which each January they quote several experts on their predictions for the year and even have those experts advise imaginary investment funds. These funds can then be reviewed at the end of each year and the experts called to explain their positive or negative results. The cycle is then repeated for the next year.
4. Lucy Bernholz, *Foundations for the Future*, Los Angeles: University of Southern California, 1999; and Lucy Bernholz, *New Strategies for New Futures*, unpublished paper, The Charles Stewart Mott Foundation, 2002.
5. For the 2002 study, *New Strategies for New Futures*, we examined future research in the arts, biotechnology, health, demography, economy, financial services, the media, technology, and in the general press. We were particularly interested in the timeframe 2000 to 2015. For the purposes of this discussion, a longer timeframe, the 21st century, is implied.
6. "The Geography of Diversity," Population Reference Bureau, *www.prb.org/ameristat*.
7. "Growth of the U.S. Foreign-born Population," Population Reference Bureau, *www.prb.org/ameristat*.
8. Hawaii, New Mexico, and California are less than 50 percent non-Hispanic white. Vermont, Maine, and New Hampshire are more than 95 percent non-Hispanic white.

9. The U.S. Census does not ask questions about religious identity. The largest survey of religious identity in the United States is The National Survey of Religious Identification, conducted in 1990 by the Graduate Center of the City University of New York, followed by the American Religious Identity Survey conducted in 2001, *www.adherents.com* and *www.gc.cuny.edu/studies/aris_index.htm*. It should be noted that religious identity numbers and groupings are as hotly contested as are racial and ethnic counts.
10. Toby Lester, "Oh, Gods!" *Atlantic Monthly*, February 2002, p. 37.
11. "The Next Society," *The Economist*, November 3, 2001, pp. 79–91.
12. Population Reference Bureau, Data Sheet, 2002, *www.prb.org*.
13. Martha Farnsworth Riche, Ph.D. "Implications of the Census 2000 Results for the Environment," paper prepared for the Surdna Foundation, June 2001, *www.surdna.org*.
14. U.S. Census predictions, *www.census.gov/population/predictions*.
15. United Nations forecasts; William Orme, "World's Population Aging Fast, Study Says," *San Francisco Chronicle*, March 1, 2002, p. A16.
16. See Robert D. Kaplan, "The World in 2005," *Atlantic Monthly*, March 2002, pp. 54–56.
17. "The Graying of the Globe," *New York Times* Editorial, April 12, 2002, p. A2.
18. Riche, Implications of the Census 2000 Results for the Environment, pp. 5–6.
19. See "U.S. Immigrant Magnets," *www.prb.org/migration/all reports*.
20. Data from the Population Reference Bureau (*www.prb.org*), the American Association of Retired Persons (*www.aarp.org*), and the U.S. Census (*www.census.gov*).
21. William H. Frey and Bill Abresch, "New State Demographic Divisions," *Spectrum: The Journal of State Government*, Summer 2002, 75(3): 18–22.
22. This section informed by "The Real State of the Union," *Atlantic Monthly*, January/February 2003; pp 76–118; Adam Cohen, "Too Old to Work," *New York Times Magazine*, March 2, 2003, pp. 54–59; and Ben Wattenberg, "It Will Be a Small World After All," *New York Times*, March 8, 2003, p. A30.
23. Cohen, "Too Old to Work," p. 56.
24. Global Business Network, future of the nonprofit sector project, meeting in Emeryville, CA, January 2002.
25. Peter Drucker, "The Next Society," Letter to the Editor, *The Economist*, November 3, 2001.
26. Daniel Pink, Free Agent Nation: How America's New Independent Workers are Transforming the Way We Live, New York: Warner Books, 2001.
27. See the work of the International Forum on Globalization, *www.ifg.org*, and the Benton Foundation's Report on "Youth Activism and Global Engagement," *www.benton.org/OneWorldUS/Aron/aron1.html*.
28. Drucker, *Landmarks of Tomorrow*, pp. 210–229.
29. David Bank, "The Man Who Would Mend the World," *Wall Street Journal*, March 14, 2002, p. B1.
30. Amy Cortese, "The New Accountability: Tracking the Social Costs," *New York Times*, March 24, 2002, p C4.; "Help in the Right Places," *The Economist*, March 15, 2002, pp. 73–74.
31. See "Giving Back the Silicon Valley Way," Community Foundation Silicon Valley, 1998, *www.cfsv.org*; and Riche, "Implications of Census 2000 Results for the Environment," p. 5.
32. De Bono, *Future Positive*, pp. 21–22.
33. These so-called conversion foundations are quite common in health care and are also beginning to develop in education and publishing.
34. *California Foundations: A Snapshot*, Los Angeles: University of California Center on Philanthropy and Public Policy, 2000.
35. New Ventures in Philanthropy has been funded by the Ford, Kellogg, Kauffman, Mott, and Packard Foundations, Atlantic Philanthropies, and Fidelity Investments Charitable Gift Fund. The Annie E. Casey Foundation launched its Place-based Philanthropy Initiative in 2003.

36. The reasons for their departure from funding philanthropy vary, but the David and Lucile Packard Foundation and Atlantic Philanthropic Services had both dropped their programs in support of philanthropy by the end of 2002.

37. Donor Advised Funds Survey 2002, *The Chronicle of Philanthropy*, May 15, 2003, p. 7.

38. "Charitable Gift Funds Ranked by Assets under Management," *InvestmentNews Databook 2002*, December 23, 2002, p. 14.

39. See Ron Chernow, *Titan: The Life of John D. Rockefeller, Sr.*, New York: Random House, 1998.

40. Eleanor Brilliant, Private Charity and Public Inquiry: A History of the Filer and Peterson Commissions, Bloomington, IN: Indiana University Press, 2000.

41. Independent Sector estimates a drop in charitable giving of $1.5 to $5 billion per year based on 1999 levels of bequest giving, *www.independentsector.org/programs/gr/EstatePosition.html*.

42. Stephanie Strom, "Donors Add Watchdog Role to Relations with Charities," *New York Times*, March 29, 2003, p. A8; and Paul Demko, "Something for the Little People," *City-Pages*, May 28, 2003.

43. This information has been discussed and debated with dozens of leaders of community foundations, independent foundations, and philanthropic associations. It is available as a Powerpoint presentation in Lucy Bernholz, *Perpetual Motion: Community Foundations for the Next Hundred Years*, *www.blueprintrd.com*.

44. *Indicators of Effectiveness*, Center for Effective Philanthropy.

45. Lucy Bernholz, *Philanthropic Comparison Shopping*, Washington, DC: The Council on Foundations, October 2001.

46. Based on actual percentage of average giving compared to resources available.

Chapter 4

1. John Kador, *Charles Schwab. How One Company Beat Wall Street and Reinvented the Broker-age Industry*, New York: John Wiley & Sons, 2002; John Cassidy, "The Investigation: How Eliot Spitzer Humbled Wall Street," *New Yorker*, April 7, 2003, pp. 54–73; Neil Weinberg, "Holier than Whom?" *Forbes*, June 23, 2002, regarding the "Lipstick on this Pig" adver-tisement.

2. Kador, Charles Schwab.

3. Riche, Implications of the Census 2000 Results for the Environment, pp. 5–6.

4. Boston College researchers estimate this "intergenerational transfer of wealth" as running between $10 and $41 trillion between 2000–2050. See Havens and Schervish.

5. Robert A. Boisture and Lloyd H. Mayer, "Weighing the Alternatives to Private Founda-tions," *Journal of Taxation of Exempt Organizations*, May/June 2000, (11)6: 257–263.

6. Ibid, p. 260.

7. Op. Cit., pp. 159–160.

8. ———. "Charitable Gift Funds Ranked by Assets under Management," *InvestmentNews Databook 2002*, December 23, 2002, p. 14.

9. The State of Foundation Giving: 2002 Preview, New York, The Foundation Center.

10. See excerpts from William Choi and Ingrid Mittermaier, "The Tax Exempt Status of Commercially Sponsored Donor Advised Funds," *The Exempt Organization Tax Review*, July 1997, pp. 95–96, in Joe Lumarda, "Philanthropy, Self-Fulfillment and the Leadership of Community Foundations," *From Grantmaker to Leader*, New York: John Wiley & Sons, 2002, pp. 75–76.

11. Association of Small Foundations, National Center for Family Philanthropy, Community Foundations of America, Philanthropy Roundtable and National Network of Grant Mak-ers, respectively.

12. See *www.GiftPlan.org*.

13. See, for example, the Princeton Area Community Foundation, *www.pacf.org/Chart.html*, or Giving New England, *www.givingnewengland.org/grid2.html*, or Fidelity Investments *www.charitablegift.org/resource/giving/index.shtml#*.
14. New Visions Philanthropic Research and Development, Donor Education Initiative, 2002, *www.newvisionsprd.org*.
15. Theodore Levitt, "Marketing Myopia," *Harvard Business Review* 38(4), July–August 1960 is the source of the railroad analogy. In a speech to the New England Library Association in 2000, Thomas Mann from the Library of Congress insisted the railroad story is apocryphal. See *www.nelib.org/conf_archOpen.asp?ID=279* for notes from Mann's remarks, "Technical Services: It's More than Just Key Words and Computer Displays."
16. Crystal Hayling, California Healthcare Foundation, April 2003.
17. Vincent Stehle, Surdna Foundation, April 2003.
18. Alexa Cortes Culwell, "Building Stronger Grantee Relationships: How to Increase Impact," Speech to the Donors Forum of Chicago Member Luncheon, January 23, 2003.
19. The Peninsula Community Foundation in San Mateo, California has marketed its "Raising a Reader" program to several community foundations.
20. Ralph Hamilton, in his paper on networks, *Moving Ideas and Money*, proposes a different, more nuanced hierarchy of network structures.
21. Survey of Donor Advised Funds, 2002, *The Chronicle of Philanthropy*, May 15, 2003. Giving U.S. figures for 2002, $212 billion includes gifts to foundations.
22. The Association of Small Foundations has done the industry a service by making it more aware that "large" in assets is not synonymous with "large" in staff. Several foundations with billion-dollar endowments employ fewer than five staff people.
23. Within the operating confines of the public charity test, which these funds have met through repeated inspections. There are boards of directors who must approve the charitable purposes to which the donor-advised funds recommend grants.
24. Eileen Heismann, National Philanthropic Trust
25. In order to register as a donor, a foundation or individual must agree to a disclaimer that recognizes there is no endorsement by GrantPartners.net's original funders. Author interview with founders from the HealthCare Foundation of Orange County, Susan Zapeda; The Health Funders Partnership of Orange County, Ed Kacic; and site designers from Mansfield and Associates, May 12, 2003.
26. Gene Wilson, Comments at the Center on Philanthropy and Public Policy," Forum on "What's New about the New Philanthropy," Los Angeles, California, 2000.
27. *www.schwabfoundation.org*
28. *www.rwjf.org*; *www.eurekalearning.org/resources*; *www.aecf.org*; *www.schwabfoundation.org*
29. Alexa Cortes Culwell, "Letter from the CEO," The Charles and Helen Schwab Foundation Annual Brochure, 2003.
30. Information culled from individual author interviews, the Knowledge Management subgroup of Grantmakers for Effective Organizations, and public Web sites of the foundations mentioned.
31. *www.calvertgiving.com/folios.htm*
32. For more information on the Casey Initiative, see *www.aecf.org/initiatives/pbp*.
33. Author interview, Julie Rogers and e-mail communication, June 3, 2003.

Chapter 5

1. Frederick T. Gates to Rockefeller on the public role of the Foundation and its funds. Quoted in Ron Chernow, *Titan*, p. 563, from Gates, *Chapters in My Life*, New York: The Free Press, 1977, p. 209.
2. Lawrence Friedman, "Philanthropy and America: Historicism and its Discontents," in Lawrence Friedman and Mark D. McGarvie, *Charity, Philanthropy, and Civility in American History*, London: Cambridge University Press, 2002, p. 15.

3. See the talking points for meetings with representatives found on many grant maker association Web sites in late May 2003, as the House Ways and Means Committee prepared to vote on HR 7, The Charitable Giving Act. A sample can be found at *www.indonor.com/charitable_giving_legislation_5_12_03.htm*. For the losses incurred in selling donor-advised funds, see Marni D. Larose and Brad Wolverton, "Donor-Advised Funds Experience Drop in Contributions, Survey Finds," *Chronicle of Philanthropy*, May 15, 2003, pp. 7–12.

4. Sample headlines from newspapers around the country in May 2003: "Some foundations spend lavishly on own board members" *Baltimore Sun*, May 15, 2003; "Billions in Charity Money Could be Saved, Study Says" *New York Times*, May 10, 2003; "Justices Rule Charity May be Charged with Fraud" *New York Times*, May 6, 2003; "Release of Audit Roils Trust Fight at The Barnes" *New York Times*, May 5, 2003; "CEO's Rewards at Nonprofit" *San Jose Mercury News*, April 27, 2003; "IRS Unable to monitor non-profit groups" *San Jose Mercury News*, April 27, 2003; "Donors add watchdog role to relations with charities" *New York Times*, March 29, 2003; "A Withdrawn Aid Offer Leaves Yakima Bruised," *New York Times*, March 6, 2003.

5. Emmett D. Carson, "Current Challenges to Foundation Board Governance: A Worst Case Scenario or The Perfect Storm," Remarks at the Council on Foundations' Board Trustee Dinner, Dallas, Texas, April 27, 2003.

6. In 2003, Community Foundations of America, a nonprofit trade service organization to community foundations, began implementation of a technology platform to link member community foundations.

7. From 1995 to 1999, the assets of foundations grew by 190 percent, while the assets at Fidelity's Charitable Gift Fund grew by more than 500 percent. Thomas A. Billitteri, "A Run for the Money," *Chronicle of Philanthropy*, April 20, 2002. See also "Donor Advised Funds: Assets, Awards and Accounts at a Sampling of Big Providers," *Chronicle of Philanthropy*, May 15, 2003, pp. 11–12.

8. *Trustees of Dartmouth College v. Woodward*. This argument is articulated in its entirety in Mark D. McGarvie, "The Dartmouth College Case and the Legal Design of Civil Society," in Lawrence Friedman and Mark McGarvie, *Charity, Philanthropy, and Civility in American History*, New York: Cambridge University Press, 2003, pp. 91–105.

9. This argument is remarkably resonant today, as public budget deficits once more turn attention to the potential of philanthropy to pick up basic services. The difference in times is best seen in the different dimensions of the two sectors, whereas private resources greatly outweighed public revenues in the early days of the nation, public budgets today dwarf philanthropic resources.

10. McGarvie, Charity, Philanthropy, and Civility, p. 104.

11. Chernow, *Titan*, pp. 564–568.

12. Diane Tittle, Rebuilding Cleveland: The Cleveland Foundation and its Evolving Urban Strategy, Columbus, OH: Ohio State University Press, 1992.

13. The Century Foundation, History of the Federal Income Tax, *www.tcf.org/Publications/Basics/Tax/History.html*.

14. Chernow, *Titan*, pp. 623–624.

15. Ibid, p. 568. See pages 299–300 for descriptions of the public response to Rockefeller's individual giving.

16. *New York Times*, September 14 and September 15, 2001.

17. See Lucy Bernholz, *Perpetual Motion*, a presentation to the Minnesota Council on Foundations for a collection of newspaper headlines from around the country from September 13, 2001–May 2003. Available at *www.blueprintrd.com/publications*.

18. For a broad look at the industries seeking part of the expected wealth transfer, see "Great Expectations," *American Demographics*, May 2003, pp. 26–35. Headlines include those listed in note 4 above.

19. See Eric Nalder, "CEO Rewards at Nonprofit," *San Jose Mercury News*, April 27, 2003, p. A1.

20. Marcus S. Owens, Memo for the Council on Foundations, "History and Analysis of the Laws Governing Qualifying Distributions of Private Foundations," Washington, DC: Caplin & Drysdale, November 30, 2001.
21. Linda Greenhouse, "Supreme Court Rules Charity May be Charged with Fraud," *New York Times*, March 6, 2003, p. A1; *People of Illinois v. Telemarketing Associates Inc.*
22. Stephanie Strom, "Donors Add Watchdog Role to Relations with Charities," *New York Times*, March 29, 2003, p. A8.
23. Ibid.
24. It is important to note that not all foundations choose to deduct these expenses from their distribution requirement—some do pay the 5 percent minimum and take operating expenses, research, and technical support off separately.

Chapter 6

1. Maira Kalman, lecture sponsored by the American Institute of Graphic Arts and Yerba Buena Center for the Arts, San Francisco, CA, May 19, 2003.
2. For a commentary on the lack of professional commonality, see Joel Orosz, "The Grantmaking School: Rationale and Theory of Grantmaker Education," Grand Rapids, MI: Grand Valley State University, 2003.
3. "Exemption Requirements," Internal Revenue Service, *www.irs.gov/charities/article/ 0,,id=96099,00.html*, accessed May 23, 2003. States: "The exempt purposes set forth in IRC Section 501(c)(3) are charitable, religious, educational, scientific, literary, testing for public safety, fostering national or international amateur sports competition, and the prevention of cruelty to children or animals. The term charitable is used in its generally accepted legal sense and includes relief of the poor, the distressed, or the underprivileged; advancement of religion; advancement of education or science; erection or maintenance of public buildings, monuments, or works; lessening the burdens of government; lessening of neighborhood tensions; elimination of prejudice and discrimination; defense of human and civil rights secured by law; and combating community deterioration and juvenile delinquency."
4. Sally Covington, Moving a Public Policy: The Strategic Philanthropy of Conservative Foundations, Washington, DC: National Center for Responsive Philanthropy, 1997. See also David Callahan, $1 Billion for Ideas: Conservative Think Tanks in the 1990s, Washington, DC: National Center for Responsive Philanthropy, 2000.
5. AAFRC Trust for Philanthropy, *Giving USA, 2002*. Figures are for 2001 giving and are rounded to the nearest billion. Total giving in 2001 was $212 billion, with remainder coming from corporations and bequests. For comparison purposes, in 1997 government grants and contracts to nonprofits totaled $249 billion, compared to the $132.1 billion contributed by foundations and individuals. *The New Nonprofit Almanac and Desk Reference*, Washington, DC: Independent Sector, 2002, pp. 96–97, Table 4.2. More recent data are not available, nor does the Independent Sector data break out foundations from individuals in the category of Private Contributions, although on average individuals provide approximately 75 percent of the total each year.
6. In 1997, private payments for service (38%) and government contracts/grants (31%) provided more than two-thirds of revenue (on average) for nonprofit organizations. The variation in revenue sources across nonprofit subsectors (e.g., religion, arts, health, education) is considerable. *The New Nonprofit Almanac and Desk Reference*, Washington, DC: Independent Sector, 2002, p. xxxii.
7. See Robert A. Gross, "Giving in America: From Charity to Philanthropy," in Friedman and McGarvie, pp. 29–48. See also Ellen Condliffe Lagemann, *The Politics of Knowledge: The Carnegie Corporation, Philanthropy, and Public Policy*, Chicago: University of Chicago Press, 1989, on the development of scientific philanthropy.
8. Gross, "Giving in America," pp. 31–32.
9. Ibid, p. 31.

10. *www.eurekalearning.org*
11. Council on Foundations Memo to members on CARE ACT, *www.cof.org*.
12. See Jason Scott, Building a Philanthropic Marketplace: Obstacles and Opportunities, *www.allavida.org*.
13. At least two significant projects are currently underway to better understand how ideas become action in philanthropy. One is being led by the Williams Group for the David and Lucile Packard Foundation and several of its grantees. A second study is being conducted by The BridgeSpan Group to inform its own work on knowledge sharing in the field. The author found the concurrence rather ironic.
14. This definition was developed by Lucy Bernholz and Kendall Guthrie, in "Knowledge is an Asset, Too," *Foundation News and Commentary*, May/June 2000, p. 18–20.
15. Harold Demsetz, "The Theory of the Firm Revisited," in Oliver E. Williamson and Sidney G. Winter (eds.), *The Nature of the Firm: Origins, Evolution, and Development*, New York: Oxford University Press, 1991, pp. 171–172.
16. As seen in the huge response to a survey distributed by Grantmakers for Effective Organizations regarding foundation interest in and commitment to knowledge management. More than 120 of the 500 foundations surveyed responded with great interest.
17. Ibid, p. 173.
18. Institute for One World Health, *www.oneworldhealth.org*.
19. African Development Foundation, *www.adf.gov*, on human-powered water pumps for agricultural use.
20. The Council on Foundations conducted a survey of infrastructure organizations in the late 1980s; the Forum of Regional Associations of Grant Makers produced a map and a study in 2002, and Grantmakers for Effective Organizations is undertaking another such effort in 2003. For frameworks and research on the issue, see Alan Abramson and Rachel McCarthy, "Infrastructure Organizations," in Lester A. Salamon, *The State of The Nonprofit Sector*, Washington, DC: Brookings Institute Press, 2002, pp. 331–354; and *Mission Possible: 200 Ways to Strengthen the Nonprofit Sector's Infrastructure*, Washington, DC: Union Institute, 1996.
21. Calculated on estimates of 58,000 foundations in the United States and the nonduplicative membership of the major associations. Blueprint Research & Design, *Scanning Philanthropy*, Washington, DC: Forum of Regional Associations of Grantmakers, 2002.
22. David Rynecki, "Can Sallie Save Citi, Restore Sandy's Reputation, and Earn her $30 Million Paycheck?" *Fortune*, June 9, 2003, pp. 68–78.
23. Kendall Guthrie and Alan Preston, Transforming Philanthropic Transactions: An Evaluation of SVP Seattle's First Five Years, Seattle, WA: Blueprint Research & Design, 2003.
24. Vincent Robinson, "Giving in the Throes of Change," San Francisco: Social Venture Partners Bay Area, Newsletter, June 2003.
25. Blueprint Research & Design, *Scanning Philanthropy*.
26. For example, both the Council on Foundations and Northern California Grant Makers now invite individuals giving above a certain dollar threshold per year to participate as members.
27. Michael Porter and Mark Kramer also use this term in "Philanthropy's New Agenda: Creating Value," Harvard Business Review, November 1999.
28. For more information, see *www.TouchDC.org*.
29. See *www.catalogueforphilanthropy.org/cfp/about/*.
30. Ibid.

Chapter 7

1. Eliel Saarinen, quoted by his son Eero, in *Time*, June 2, 1977.
2. Waldemar A. Nielsen, *Inside American Philanthropy: The Dramas of Donorship*, Norman, OK: University of Oklahoma Press, 1996, p. 10.

3. Ibid, p. 6.

4. Ian Wilhem, "Foundation Assets Sag," *Chronicle of Philanthropy*, April 4, 2002, p. 8.; Anne Farrell, "The State of Giving," *Seattle Times*, December 31, 2002, p. A30. The percentage drop in giving is adjusted for inflation and includes all giving—individuals and institutions. Foundation giving rose about 2.5 percent (adjusted) during this time. AAFRC Trust for philanthropy, "Charitable Giving Reaches $212 Billion," Press Release, June 20, 2002, *www.aafrc.org/press3.html.*

5. Stephanie Strom, "New Philanthropists Find Drudgery," *New York Times*, January 12, 2003, p. A17.

6. John J. Havens and Paul G. Schervish, "Why the $41 Trillion Wealth Transfer Estimate is Still Valid: A Review of Challenges and Questions," Boston College, Social Welfare Research Institute, January 6, 2003.

7. Jared Smith, *Guns, Germs and Steel: The Fates of Human Societies*, New York: W. W. Norton & Co., 1999.

8. See John McWhorter, *The Power of Babel*, New York: HarperCollins, 2001, pp. 12–13, for the dynamic changes in natural systems.

9. Paul Jansen and David Katz, "For Nonprofits, Time is Money," *The McKinsey Quarterly*, Number 1, 2002.

10. AAFRC Trust for Philanthropy, "Charitable Giving Reaches $212 Billion," Press Release, June 20, 2002, *www.aafrc.org/press3.html.*

11. The Foundation Center, 2001. Number of Foundations: 1980 = 22,088, 2000 = 56,582. Assets: 1980 = $48.2 billion, 2000 = $486.1 billion. Giving: 1980 = $3.4 billion, 2000 = 27.6 billion. All dollars in 2001 dollars.

12. *Foundation Yearbook, 2002.* New York: The Foundation Center, 2002.

13. A complete analysis of the relationship between market and economic indicators and philanthropic giving is beyond the scope of this inquiry. Key indicators include personal income, gross domestic product (GDP), pretax profits, and stock market indices.

14. Stephanie Strom, "MacArthur Foundation Gives $42 Million, Despite Economy," *New York Times*, January 13, 2003, p. A11.

15. New Yorker Collection, no. 52343, July 15, 2002.

16. Bill Bradley and Paul Jansen, "Faster Charity," *New York Times*, May 15, 2002, p. 23; and the CARE ACT, H.R. 7, U.S. House of Representatives, 2003. See also *www.ncrp.org* and The National Network of Grantmaker's "One Percent More for Democracy Campaign," *www.nng.org.*

17. Many argue that this preference lies behind the enormous success of charitable gift funds, which have lower administrative costs than most other philanthropic vehicles. It is significant to note that these gift funds are now being used to manage several $100-million-plus funds, endowments that might have previously been organized as staffed foundations.

18. This is metaphorical. I don't mean to imply that management is formulaic or that answers are simply algebraic.

19. Harvard Family Research Project, Institute of Museum and Library Services analyses; John McKnight, *Building Communities from the Inside Out*, Evanston, IL: Institute for Policy Research, 1993; KidsCount, Annie E. Casey Foundation.

20. The Foundation Center, *Health Funding Update*, 2001.

21. Several health foundations in California have been using a shared data system and exchanging information through an intranet for years now. (This is the healthfunders@work project.) Other health foundations (e.g., Robert Wood Johnson) have led the field in posting evaluation syntheses on their Web sites and making their data and results public.

22. See The Foundation Center's two reports on "Giving in the Aftermath of 9/11,"as well as the National Center on Responsive Philanthropy's report. Several regional associations also published reports, built tracking systems, and have been working with the media and researchers to track the flow and impact of funds expended. The public sector and the media have kept the spotlight on the source, use, and results of the funds as well. A recent report

by the General Accounting Office (GAO) looks at the relationship between public and private disaster-relief efforts. See "More Effective Collaboration Could Enhance Charitable Organizations' Contributions in Disasters," Washington, DC: GAO, December 2002, *www.gao.gov*.

23. William A. Schambra, "The Evaluation Wars," in *Philanthropy*, Washington, DC: The Philanthropy Roundtable, May/June 2003, pp. 29–32.

24. Atul Gawande, *Complications: A Surgeon's Notes on an Imperfect Science*, New York: Henry Holt and Company, 2002, pp. 47–74.

25. We have only a crude estimate of how many foundations support evaluation and how much they invest in it. Using several data proxies, a recent calculation estimated that the 10,000 foundations that report to The Foundation Center spend $145 million per year on research, evaluation, and consultants. Excerpts are available at "Philanthropy 2225," *www.philanthropy.blogspot.com*.

26. Thucydides is quoted in John Lewis Gaddis, *The Landscape of History: How Historians Map the Past*, London: Oxford University Press, 2002, p. 14.

27. *2003 Community Foundation Global Status Report*, Worldwide Initiative for Grantmaker Support—Community Foundations, *www.wings-cf.org/global_report*. Accessed on May 23, 2003.

28. Emmett Carson, "Community Foundations Facing A Crossroads," *Chronicle of Philanthropy*, May 16, 2002, p. 37.

29. Marni D. Larose and Brad Wolverton, "Donor-Advised Funds Experience Drop in Contributions, Survey Finds," *Chronicle of Philanthropy*, May 15, 2003, p. 7.

30. Of the 658 community foundations in the United States, only about 100 have more than $100 million in assets.

31. Rhode Island Community Foundation, Humboldt Area Foundation.

32. Peninsula Community Foundation's Venture Van; New Ventures in Philanthropy.

33. William Choi and Ingrid Mittermaier, "The Tax Exempt Status of Commercially Sponsored Donor Advised Funds," *The Exempt Organization Tax Review*, July 1997; In Joe Lumarda, "Philanthropy, Self-Fulfillment and the Leadership of Community Foundations," *From Grantmaker to Leader*, New York: John Wiley & Sons, 2002.

34. Diane Tittle, Rebuilding Cleveland: The Cleveland Foundation and its Evolving Urban Strategy, Columbus, OH: Ohio State University Press, 1992.

35. James I. Luck and Suzanne L. Feurt, " A Growing and Flexible Service to Donors: Donor Advised Funds in Community Foundations," Washington, DC: Council on Foundations, 2002, p. 2.

Chapter 8

1. An unpublished fragment originally intended to be in Friedrick Nietzcshe, *Thus Spoke Zarathustra: A Book for All and None*, Walter Kaufmann (trans.), New York: Modern Library, 1995.

2. See John Kador, Charles Schwab. How One Company Beat Wall Street and Reinvented the Brokerage Industry. New York: John Wiley & Sons, 2002.

3. Stephanie Strom. "Foundations Hire Ex-Lawmaker to Lobby against a House Bill," *New York Times*, May 28, 2003, p. A19.

4. California Avocado Council; The Milk Council's "Got Milk" campaign; The State of New York's "I Love New York" campaign.

5. Stephanie Strom, "California Charity Firm Folds, Leaving Some Clients at a Loss," *New York Times*, June 4, 2003, p. A22; Stephanie Strom, "Charity Collector Says Audit Showed Shortfall in Revenue," *New York Times*, June 5, 2003, p. A27; Todd Walleck, "Charitable Funding Mystery," *San Francisco Chronicle*, June 4, 2003, p. 1; and Todd Walleck, "Nonprofit Admits Spending Charities' Money," *San Francisco Chronicle*, June 5, 2003, p 1.

6. Lucy Bernholz, Kendall Guthrie, et al., *Philanthropic Connections: Mapping the Landscape of U.S. Funder Networks*, Washington, DC: Forum of Regional Associations of Grantmakers, 2003.

7. Transcript of "The California Report," aired on *Morning Edition*, National Public Radio, June 9, 2003.

Interviews

Alexa Culwell, San Mateo, CA
Crystal Hayling, San Francisco, CA
Ed Kacic, Orange County, CA
Julie Rogers, Washington, DC
Vincent Stehle, New York, NY
Eileen Heismann, Jenkintown, PA
Susan Zapeda, Orange County, CA

Index